THE WORLD'S A ZOO

Other Books by John Perry

OUR WONDERFUL EYES

OUR POLLUTED WORLD

With Jane Greverus Perry

EXPLORING THE FOREST

EXPLORING THE RIVER

EXPLORING THE SEACOAST

FORESTERS AND WHAT THEY DO

VETERINARIANS AND WHAT THEY DO

THE
WORLD'S
A
ZOO

by John Perry

Dodd, Mead & Company, New York

Acknowledgments

The National Zoological Park, of which I am Assistant Director, is a bureau of the Smithsonian Institution. The Smithsonian's Secretary, S. Dillon Ripley, encourages staff members to write and publish with the freedom enjoyed by university faculty members. The manuscript of this book passed through no official review, and the opinions expressed are my own.

In some respects they differ from those of the Zoo Director, Theodore H. Reed, D.V.M. He read the manuscript in draft, called my attention to errors, and made many useful suggestions. He did not ask that I modify any statements of opinion, even those that might seem critical of our zoo.

Dr. Clinton W. Gray, Zoo Veterinarian, and Dr. John F. Eisenberg, Resident Scientist, discussed a number of the chapters with me, and I am grateful for their help.

This is the twelfth book my wife, Jane, and I have worked on together. This time her name does not appear as co-author, since her own commitments kept her from writing with me. She has been involved, nonetheless, in gathering data, criticizing drafts, and editing.

J. P.

Contents

THE WORLD'S A ZOO

1

No Longer Wild

Some of our zoo cages are designed to keep animals out. The National Zoological Park is situated in the heart of Washington, D.C., but it cuts across a continuous belt of parkland extending from the Potomac River far into Maryland. We have a variety of native wild animals at large, living in the shadows of tall apartment buildings, a population far outnumbering the three thousand specimens in our collection.

As I parked my car outside our zoo office building this morning, I flushed a covey of quail. Squirrels scratch at the windowpane if we forget to put out food. Fox sparrows, titmice, chickadees, cardinals, bluejays, and several varieties of woodpeckers come to our feeders. A deer was seen near our offices a few evenings ago. Foxes roam at night. After a light snow, we see many raccoon tracks.

The foxes and raccoons menace our caged pheasants, jungle fowl, and other ground-living birds, and eat their eggs. We try to shut them out by placing metal shields on fence tops or by stringing electrified wires. Our new waterfowl ponds will have islands for safe nesting.

We would like to shut out the wild ducks, if we could find

a way. Last fall a hundred mallards arrived, uninvited, liked our food, and remained. They are so prolific, hungry, and aggressive that our exotic ducks and geese would soon be pushed aside unless we practiced control.

Pigeons are an unmitigated nuisance. At feeding time they swarm into every open pen, blocking our zoo animals from their food by sheer numbers. They consume grass seed almost as rapidly as our gardeners sow it. Pigeons are messy, and they carry disease organisms. We catch a few in live traps. Once we experimented with a mild drug, mixing it with seed which was scattered a safe distance from the exhibits. Soon we had dozens of seemingly drunken pigeons staggering and lurching about, easy to capture. To empty the zoo of pigeons, however, would be as futile as bailing an arm of the sea, for the surrounding city supports a huge population of them.

Like the pigeons, house sparrows are attracted by the free food, and they multiply alarmingly. They build their nests inside every building, as well as in outdoor crevices. Sparrows far outnumber our prized birds in the outdoor flight cages, and they eat a large share of the food provided.

An exterminator is kept busy suppressing rats and mice. Poisons cannot be used where a zoo animal might eat them. Traps check what could become a population explosion. At night, cockroaches pour from their hiding places, especially in the older buildings. The exterminator does his best, but insecticides must also be used with discretion.

Our Reptile House has a fine assortment of venomous snakes, so we take elaborate safety precautions and maintain a quick-response emergency procedure. The only snakebite victim in recent years was a plumber, and the copperhead that bit him was a free citizen, lurking in a drainpipe. The emergency procedure worked, and the plumber was soon back on the job. Happily, zoo visitors have not encountered any of this species.

Most of our uninvited guests are welcome, however. The muskrats living along the creek banks keep to themselves. So do the rabbits and opossums. Buzzards soar overhead. Night herons build their nests on top of the old flight cage, commuting to their feeding grounds along the Potomac. Chipmunks scurry about.

We have no monopoly of urban wildlife. As I drove home through the public park one evening, a great blue heron rose from the creek and flew beside me for a quarter-mile. Moles burrow under well-tended lawns. The annual visit of cedar waxwings announces the coming of spring. An agitated lady called yesterday for advice on ejecting a bat from her attic. Insects are everywhere, of course. Let a city gardener cultivate a single tomato plant and tomato fruitworms will magically appear.

Such urbanized animals have adapted their lives to the presence and the works of man. Some of them find towns and cities more congenial than fields and forests. Others seem equally at home amidst concrete or greenery. Starlings have a vast, unreciprocated affection for the city, returning each evening to congregate in masses above the busiest streets, persisting despite bizarre efforts to drive them away.

The common house sparrow was introduced to the United States in 1850, and spread with unbelievable rapidity. By 1900 it was our most common city bird, roosting in trees and feeding on the grain in horse droppings. As most trees were cut down, the sparrows found other nesting places, one favorite being the crevice below a window air conditioner. Even the disappearance of the horse did not dismay this resourceful bit of fluff. One afternoon in Iowa we watched several sparrows loitering about a gasoline service station. As each car stopped at the pumps, they flew to peck insects caught on its radiator.

Swallows nest under bridges; and there is evidence that one species extended its range as more bridges were built. What did chimney swifts do before there were chimneys? Squirrels nest in trees, but attics are often preferred. Raccoons patrol alleys in search of open garbage cans. Even in the city, a domesticated animal may revert: Thousands of feral cats, wild as tigers, hostile to humans, make their own living in the concrete jungle.

The adaptability of some wild species is awe-inspiring. In their native Africa, cattle egrets follow wild cattle and rhinoceroses, feeding on insects stirred up by grazing. Several years ago these egrets appeared in South America. Some naturalists theorize that they were swept across the ocean by storm winds. Knowing the ways of animal dealers, I suspect that egrets were sold to Brazilian cattlemen who hoped they would eat undesirable insects. Year by year the egrets extended their range, forming symbiotic relationships with dairy cows, Angus steers, and the wild ponies of Assateague Island. I first saw them sitting on the ponies' backs. Now they range as far north as New Jersey, at least. In Florida, cattle egrets have become lawn birds, following power lawnmowers as their ancestors followed rhinoceroses.

Some of our wild neighbors, such as rats and cockroaches, seem determined to live with us despite our most murderous efforts to do away with them. Supermarket shelves display bottles and cans of chemical pesticides with bloodcurdling label legends, but housewives and home gardeners remain on the defensive. Wherever there are food and shelter, some animals will live.

But there are no bison on Capitol Hill, and no wolves prowl outside the city's department stores. Bald eagles have vanished from our urban skies, and only the hardiest fish survive in the malodorous Potomac River, which once ran clear. Some wild species have been eliminated deliberately. More are gone because they could not withstand drastic alterations of their habitats. When a forest is cut down, arboreal creatures depart. If the soil is then plowed and planted, a new group of animals soon occupies the living space.

A natural habitat usually contains a considerable variety of plant species, at various stages of growth and decay; and such a varied food supply supports a diversity of animal forms. Agriculture is highly specialized. If a field is planted in corn, the only primary consumers to invade it will be those that eat parts of the corn plant—which is logical enough, though annoying to the cultivator. Thus the animal community takes on a form unlike its natural one, a few species multiplying to unprecedented numbers.

Some of the farmland outside our sprawling metropolis has been carefully tended. Much has not, and generations of witless exploitation have allowed the soil to wash or blow away, so that boulders now stand like gravestones. Nothing useful to man can be grown here now. Unused, the land invites wild animals to return; but they, like man, depend on the soil's fertility. Grasshoppers whir among the sparse, brown weeds, and blacksnakes sun themselves on the exposed rocks, but the natural complex is impoverished.

In spring and fall, my wife and I enjoy weekend backpacking, often on the Appalachian Trail, which passes through the Shenandoah National Park, ninety minutes from our driveway. The park was assembled in the 1930's from three hundred square miles of mountain land that had been logged, farmed, and grazed almost to exhaustion. It was then politically feasible for the government to acquire it, but not to acquire the fertile valleys on either side of the range. Now the plants and animals of the park are protected. A new forest is growing, and visitors will someday see big trees again. The signs of settlement are vanishing little by little: old logging trails, stone foundations now half-overgrown, an old apple tree that adds a few small fruits to our dinner pot.

The Skyline Drive is a spectacular highway that runs along the ridges. When spring flowers bloom, and when the colors of fall are brightest, traffic is bumper-to-bumper all the way. The foot trails are never crowded. Jane and I may hike all day without encounters. At night, sleeping under the stars, we have the illusion of being in a wilderness.

On our most recent hike we met a bear. The bears were gone when the park was first established. They have returned slowly, moving along the hillsides from the southern Blue Ridge. They are still shy of humans; the bear that saw us fled. Only in the past year or two have a few bears ventured into campgrounds at night. Wild turkeys are seen often now, and an occasional bobcat. White-tailed deer are common. Mountain lions have been reported, but the rangers are officially skeptical.

The national park, like our zoo, is an animal enclosure, an artifact. While no fence surrounds it, the boundaries are confining. A bear or deer venturing beyond them might be shot, but the chief confining influence is ecological. The parkland is slowly reverting to an undisturbed condition. The land outside the boundaries is not. Outside are working farms, highways, towns, resorts. A natural unity has been broken.

"Confinement" is a word to use with caution. Few animal species are affected by wanderlust. Most are territorial, requiring only space sufficient for fulfillment of their needs. A small rodent may find all the food it requires within a few yards; a large carnivore may need a dozen miles or more as the radius of its hunting grounds. An animal may move over a greater distance, of course, if it is displaced from a territory by a rival member of its own species, or if the local food supply fails, or if drought affects its watering place.

The boundaries of a natural habitat are naturally confining, since they limit the area within which the needs of a species can be satisfied. Such a boundary is a joining of woodland and meadow, two natural communities inhabited by different species. An artificial, man-made boundary can be confining in a somewhat different way, however. It may deprive certain species of things they require at certain times of the day or year.

Deer, for example, especially in man-inhabited areas, are likely to remain in cover by day, then come out on the grassy lowlands for evening feeding. Some species are inclined to follow the spring up the mountainsides, then retreat to warmer, more sheltered ground when winter storms whip the ridges. Thus changes outside the park boundary influence natural events within.

The park is lovely, well worth defending against highway building and other development. Some of its most spectacular places are seen by few people, because they can be reached only on foot over steep and difficult trails. This is as it should be, for to make them accessible by automobile would ruin their beauty. Hikers can find a few groves of ancient hemlocks the loggers overlooked. The park is home for many mammals, birds, and reptiles, and more will come; but their lives have been changed. The scent of man is on the pathways, and the sounds of automobiles can be heard in the distance. The park is, indeed, a kind of outdoor zoo, bounded, managed, protected, patrolled.

There is wilder country in the West, where Jane and I have packed deep into regions that are proclaimed wildernesses, far from any roads. Snow-covered peaks rise above the

dark spires of Engelmann spruces, and even in July the roaring streams are fed by melting snow and ice. The wilderness
experience is unique and splendid, a bit frightening for city
people. Wildlife is abundant. We have photographed elk,
moose, pronghorn, beaver, black bear, marmot, pika, coyote,
grouse, trumpeter swan, and many other species.

Yet the wilderness is not so wild as in the days of John
Colter, Jim Bridger, and other early explorers. One sees few
signs of man, other than the trail and campfire ashes; and the
only sound of civilization is the occasional drone of a high-
flying plane. Even a trained ecologist might not recognize
man's influence on the primitive condition. He would see a
patch of light-green aspens on a hillside, and know that
aspens are quick to occupy new openings in the forest. But
was this opening caused by a blowdown, a lightning-set fire,
a tossed cigarette, or the logger's saw?

Even wilderness enthusiasts cannot agree on what should
be done today when lightning shatters a tree and the smolder-
ing stump ignites the dry duff. Prior to our century, the fire
would burn uncontrolled. Aided by summer drought and
high wind, it might crown, sweeping at racehorse speed across
a hundred miles of fine timber, leaving blackened waste behind. Many animals would die. Today the first smoke would
be spotted by a fire watcher and reported by radio. In dry
weather, all of the resources necessary to suppress the fire
would be on stand-by: tanker planes, smoke jumpers, hose-
laying helicopters, bulldozers, hand tools, and manpower. It
is a rare fire now that burns fifty acres before it is stopped.

This is unwarranted interference with nature, some say.
Fire is as much a part of the natural complex as rain and
wind. No tree lives forever, and a mature forest is ready to
die. Spring rains turn blackened acres green. Soon there is

growing brush, aspens, and jackpines. A new cycle has begun, and in time another forest will replace the old.

If fire is suppressed, they say, the natural cycle is disrupted. A mature forest is pleasing to the eye and the lumberman, but it is a low-grade habitat for other than arboreal creatures, since the shade of the tree canopy suppresses growth of understory plants. Brush and young, vigorously growing trees, which follow fire, provide a larger food supply and support more wildlife.

Further, they contend, fire prevention is itself damaging to a wilderness area. A wilderness is supposed to be protected from all forms of human disturbance. Efficient fire control requires fire breaks, fire roads, equipment depots, small reservoirs, and other measures, all intrusive.

In some circumstances, fire prevention increases fire hazard. This has been noted in California's giant sequoia forests. Here, in the past, frequent small fires burned the understory without damage to the big trees. Suppression of these slow fires permitted a buildup of fuel on the forest floor, so that it became more likely that a fire, once ignited, would burn out of control, and that it would kill the giant trees. Further, some foresters are concerned that increased understory growth may subtract from the soil moisture available to the sequoias.

Kirtland's warbler, one of our rarest birds, was pushed to the brink of extinction by fire suppression. It nests only in young stands of jackpine, a species which follows fire. Today the Forest Service is burning selected patches of Michigan forest land to create such young stands, hoping to save the little gray-backed migrant.

"How can we possibly let our wildernesses burn?" ask other conservationists. "We have too few such wild areas. How could we tolerate destruction of a national treasure simply

because nature will restore it in a century or so? Is not burning more destructive than exploitative logging, something we
all oppose?"

Such arguments lead to practical compromises. Wilderness
areas will not be allowed to burn unchecked, in part because
they are usually adjacent to parks and commercial forests. But
construction of fire roads, fire breaks, and other intrusions
will be restrained. All such decisions and compromises affect
animal populations, which were never static because of constant natural changes in their environments.

Only adventurous people see the few remaining wilderness
areas. The vastly larger expanses of public forests, parks, and
grasslands which appear natural and undisturbed to most
visitors are, in fact, under intensive management. It would
be wrong to say that such human control is damaging to wildlife. Any change, whether of natural or human origin, shifts
the balance, favoring some species, penalizing others. The
change that causes a deer population to increase may lead to
a decline of porcupines.

Today's newspaper reports that a hundred thousand acres
of Maine woods will be sprayed with DDT to destroy spruce
budworms. Unlike many decisions to use pesticides, this one
was not made by careless or indifferent men. Those who took
the action, government officials, were told that a tenth of the
region's conifers have been killed by budworms, and that a
budworm plague threatens the remainder. The local lumber
industry was said to be in danger, as well as the jobs of two
thousand men.

The decision was taken with full knowledge that spraying
will affect the forest wildlife for years to come. DDT, a persistent chemical, will remain in the soil, to be concentrated
in the tissues of earthworms, and further concentrated in the
organs of animals eating the worms. Some bird species are

likely to disappear altogether. The full effects on animals cannot be predicted, but there is no doubt that the community
will be disrupted.

Those conservationists who spoke out against the mass
poisoning were ridiculed. Since the budworms are about to
destroy the forest, is not DDT the lesser evil? Who wants to
see the habitat laid waste?

The basic issue was not clearly stated. This is not Maine's
first budworm outbreak. Another, which began in 1910,
killed seventy to ninety percent of the mature spruces. DDT
was not then available, and the outbreak ran its course. The
lumber industry suffered. Yet it is evident that natural recovery followed, for another stand of merchantable spruce is
now endangered.

Budworms are as much a part of the natural ecology as deer
and porcupines. They defoliate trees. Young and vigorous
trees usually survive the assault; older trees succumb. Thus
the budworms take a harvest, preparing the way for a new
generation. There is doubtless some genetic selection of
strains resistant to budworm attacks. In killing the budworms, man is not preserving the forest; he is competing for
the harvest. It does not suit his purposes that budworms kill
the mature trees. He wants them for lumber.

Quite possibly the current budworm epidemic may be
more severe than that of 1910. While budworms are an element of natural forest ecology, the Maine forest has been extensively altered. In managing a commercial forest it is common, for example, to thin selectively, removing unwanted
species to promote growth of sawtimber. As on cropland, this
favors populations of insects that feast on the chosen plant
species. Man-managed ecosystems tend to be unstable, because of such specialization, and drastic measures such as
chemical control of weeds and pests seem essential to their

maintenance. Too often, however, efforts to check one un-wanted consequence of change produce others.

Changes in the plant community inevitably alter animal populations, but profound changes in an ecosystem can also be caused by attacking a single animal species. The decline of the beaver began in the seventeenth century, thanks to the European passion for beaver hats. When beavers vanished, their dams disintegrated and wetlands drained. Many species, including migratory waterfowl, declined in numbers in consequence. On the other hand, extermination of wolves allowed prey species to increase, but to their ultimate detriment, since populations soon exceeded food supplies.

In the four centuries following the landing of Columbus, America's wildlife was assaulted without effective restraint. In Kewanee, Illinois, I was shown a huge, old warehouse from which whole carloads of dead songbirds were once shipped to the food markets of Chicago. Egrets and terns were slaughtered for their plumes. Nests were robbed of eggs. Fearsome weapons were devised, including batteries of cannons that could kill hundreds of ducks with one fusillade. It is surprising that so few species became extinct, as did the heath hen, the great auk, the passenger pigeon, and the sea mink. Many, however, were drastically reduced in numbers. Few species of waterfowl, for example, were ever brought near the vanishing point, but we will never again see the great migratory flights that once darkened the sky from dawn to dusk.

In the main, the most-threatened species were not those sought for their meat or their skins but those which came into competition with man. The bison herds were eliminated, except for a captive few, because their habitat was wanted for cultivation and cattle grazing. Bounties were put on predators because they were thought to prey on animals man used for meat.

A reasonably good balance has been struck in our century, about the best available under the circumstances. While a number of native American species are still in danger of extinction, most of them, such as the beach meadow vole and Kaibab squirrel, were vulnerable because they were never numerous and lived in small areas. Only a few, such as the alligator, are threatened because of continuing exploitation.

The wild species that live most securely today in America are those which have established relationships with man. Some, like the robin and chipmunk, have adapted to us and live in our midst. We have adapted to others, providing refuges and other managed habitats for them and regulating hunting and trapping.

Should one go to Africa, then, to see great hordes of wild animals living free in the untrammeled wilderness? They are not there. Most of Africa's wildlife is gone. The huge herds are history, eliminated in less time than was our American bison. Only scattered remnants remain outside the national parks and preserves. One can see many lions, giraffes, wildebeests, and zebras, but in man-managed habitats.

As new African nations replaced colonies, many white men predicted disaster for the remaining wildlife. Happily, they were wrong. Today there are far more parks and preserves than in colonial times, and many African nationals are being trained in scientific wildlife management. The outlook for survival of rhinoceroses and antelopes is brighter than it was a decade ago. But this is not the case in many parts of the world. Indonesia, for example, has many preserves, and its legal code is well designed to protect native species, but effective enforcement in the field is next to impossible because of difficult terrain, the long coastlines, and economic instability. India, Malaysia, Thailand, and the Philippines also have reasonably good laws, some preserves, and a few dedicated conservationists; but their people are not educated to think of wild animals as a resource worth saving. The situation in most Arab nations seems virtually hopeless.

In South America, I saw at first hand the difficulties of enforcing game protection laws in the field. There is a lively trade in wild animals, and an even larger traffic in their hides and furs, much of it illegal. It would take tens of thousands of wardens to patrol the vast Amazon Basin and to seal off the borders which are now crossed freely. Where game wardens have been posted, they have often become poachers, simply because a few furs would bring them more than several months' salary.

But hunting and poaching would threaten few species if their habitats remained intact. In South America, however, forests and other wild lands are being depleted at a terrifying rate, with only marginal efforts to provide for the future. In Madagascar, Tasmania, Ceylon—almost everywhere, it seems —the explosive increase in human population is driving other species from habitats they occupied undisturbed as recently as a generation ago.

On every continent, the continuous web of life has been broken into disconnected fragments. The Sumatran rhinoceros, the mountain gorilla of Africa, the Brazilian giant otter, the Asiatic lion, the Arabian oryx, the Galapagos penguin, the money-eating eagle of the Philippines, and many other species are making their last stands, hemmed in, under pressure.

It is not impossible that these species will be saved and that their lines will continue for years to come. The European bison, Pere David's deer, the southern white rhinoceros, and Swinhoe's pheasant were once in equally grave peril and now seem secure. But this is not to be accomplished by laws alone. Protection, in the old-fashioned sense, is neither feasible nor sufficient. The modern wildlife conservationist seeks ways to bring about practical patterns of coexistence between man and other species.

It is significant that wild animal species are today most secure in the most highly developed nations, such as the United States. We have, to a considerable degree, stabilized patterns of land use. The United States has many more acres of forested land today than earlier in this century. Millions of acres of land not suitable for cultivation have been retired to grass or trees. We have an extensive system of state and national parks, forests, and preserves; and our system of game protection is financed largely from hunting and fishing license revenues. Further, we have the scientific resources, as well as the economic assets, to invest in such projects as preserving a tiny population of whooping cranes. Development as such is not the threat to wildlife. It is the reckless, extractive, exploitative, unscientific assault on nature, the destructive abuse of land, that brings only brief benefits to man and inflicts permanent damage on natural resources.

Zoo animals were once curiosities, specimens taken from distant places where they roamed free. Today "the wild" no longer exists. There is no longer a dichotomy between cage and wilderness but a continuum, varying degrees of confinement, management, and other human influence. The wild has become less free, while zoos are seeking, with considerable success, to provide conditions which more adequately meet the physical and psychological requirements of animals in their keeping. For more and more species, zoos are becoming survival centers for animals that seem likely to vanish in their homelands.

The study of animals in captivity and semicaptivity sharpens awareness that the human species is also, in our times, confined to managed habitats. Survival in such man-managed settings is not easy, and it places upon the managers a fearful responsibility. The intricate and balanced interplay of natural forces is violently disrupted, yet the needs of the inhabitants are largely intact. The failures in our zoos and in our cities are evidence that our skills are not yet adequate.

The wildlife conservationist is sometimes pictured as an impractical fellow with romantic notions of stemming the tide of progress. He is even accused of treason, of seeking to preserve other species at some cost to his own. Yet we live by the same natural laws as other species, and we depend on the same resources. Destruction of their habitats diminishes our own. As fellow inhabitants of earth, we share today a common danger.

2

Enlistment

I do not remember when I first walked in the deep woods, or when I first visited a zoo. When I was a child, the woods were close at hand and familiar. Parents were unworried if we played there or if two twelve-year-old boys packed in for a weekend. Two weeks after I obtained my first driver's license, at age sixteen, a schoolmate and I were heading west, camping gear stowed in a 1928 Model A. Ten days later I woke to hear a bear snuffling outside the tent and, far off, the haunting calls of coyotes.

When Jane and I married, we traveled together. Within weekend range of Washington, D.C., is a rich variety of natural environments: the seacoast, with its estuaries and marshes; rivers, streams, and lakes; mountain ranges; extensive forests. On vacations we enjoyed more distant places: the Tetons, the Adirondacks, the Everglades, the desert. Always we camped, preferring the quiet places. Our children were accustomed to tents before they learned to walk.

At first it was only for pleasure. We studied the beavers, roadrunners, and dolphins because we were their neighbors for a time, they were attractive, and we wished to know them better, as well as the plants and the soils in which they grew.

Since we are writers, we began to write about animals and their habitats, though we wondered, at first, if having work to do would lessen enjoyment of our outdoor time.

Instead, it enhanced satisfaction by giving each trip meaning and focus. We had to seek and find, and we could not leave questions unanswered. Best of all, we now had reason to work with foresters, wildlife managers, soil scientists, range management specialists, marine biologists, and other experts, and wonderful people they were. We jounced over miles of country in their Jeeps and pickup trucks, learning more than we could find in libraries.

Our cameras were as useful as our notebooks on these expeditions. As we gained some skill in their use, we began producing educational filmstrips for biology and ecology classrooms. Here was a better reason than writing to spend time in the field. The writer can describe an animal. The photographer must learn how to find the animal he seeks and understand the species well enough to capture it on film, at reasonably close range.

Meanwhile, for some twenty years, we pursued our occupations, Jane as an economist, I as an industrial management consultant. This was not, in my case, a career choice based on academic training. I had gone to work of necessity at eighteen and scratched a living through the bleak years of the economic depression at a variety of odd jobs. Later, during the years of World War II, I had been in the federal service, in an equally varied assortment of those unique and challenging posts that exist only in wartime. Diversity of experience was an asset in consulting, and consulting also gave me considerable independence, especially when I established my own practice. I could manage my own time, and Jane and I could plan at least one major field trip each year.

A consultant travels, and my work took me across the country. Carrying cameras and a light field kit, I could often manage a day or so for research on a current book or photography for a current film. When there were just a few hours to spare, I was likely to spend them in the local zoo. The first house Jane and I bought was close to the National Zoo, so close we sometimes found errant peafowl at our doorstep. It was a place to walk, when we had an hour or two. So we came to know the zoo well, its collection and many of its keepers. Traveling, I became acquainted with zoos in New York, Chicago, St. Louis, Cleveland, San Francisco, and a dozen other cities.

At Chicago's Lincoln Park I met Lear Grimmer and renewed the acquaintance when he moved to Washington as Associate Director of the National Zoo. He urged us to join a new organization, the Friends of the National Zoo. We did, and I became its President a year later. The zoo was then in a desperate situation. For years it had had no capital budget. Aged buildings were in poor repair, as were the supporting utilities. The operating budget was far too small, and a cut was threatened. The Friends, an uninhibited private association, could say things publicly which zoo officials could not. We said them. We commissioned a landscape architect to prepare a master plan for complete renovation of the ancient establishment. The newspapers were on our side. The Smithsonian Regents and many congressmen were persuaded. Soon money was found to develop a more detailed master plan, which Congress liked well enough to support. Capital funds were forthcoming, and rejuvenation of the National Zoo began. Later, when I was no longer President of the Friends, Director Ted Reed asked me to become a consultant to the zoo, to help develop its growing organization. Two years later, Lear Grimmer unexpectedly resigned to take up residence in the Bahamas. Several months later, I joined the staff as Assistant Director.

My business colleagues looked at me oddly when they heard about it. Was I leaving the real and earnest industrial life to play with animals? Like most people, they thought of a zoo as an amusement park.

For most people, it is. Yesterday, for example, was a sunny Sunday, the kind of day almost no one can spend indoors. Expecting a crowd, our keepers hastened to complete their morning chores, the police captain detailed extra men to the parking lots, and the concessioner warmed his popcorn machine early. Forty thousand people came to stroll in the sunshine, to picnic, and to see the animals.

Only a few zoo directors are unabashed showmen. Others are sometimes irked because newspapers treat zoos so frivolously. All like to believe that zoos are educational and try to make them so. On weekdays, teachers bring their classes, and our docents lecture to visiting groups. But on crowded weekends, how many people read the cage labels prepared so carefully by the zoologists? How many of them know that we have scientists and laboratories? The Sunday visitors come to toss fish to the sea lions and peanuts to the bears, and to watch the elephants.

We are ambivalent about showmanship, however, because we know who pays the bills. The more popular a zoo becomes, the more support it enjoys—and this is especially true of those zoos that charge admission and benefit financially from concessions. If a zoo pleases and entertains the public, the zoo director may have a better chance of adding a pathologist or a nutritionist to his budget. New exhibits are designed to meet three sets of needs: those of the animals, those of the keepers who service the enclosures, and the qualities of public exhibition.

My new colleagues in the zoo world were no less puzzled than my business friends. Zoo-keeping is an old and honorable profession with traditions passed from generation to generation. More than one zoo director began his career cleaning cages. Until recently, no college offered courses directly preparing men for zoo careers, nor have there been vocational courses for keepers. Keepers and curators acquired their skills and knowledge working in zoos. Yet here I was, an outsider who had served no apprenticeship, named to the second-ranking post in one of the world's principal zoos. Understandably, there were raised eyebrows.

I could have said that managing a zoo and managing a factory have much in common. Of the more than two hundred members of our staff, less than one third are keepers. Those who work with the animals are outnumbered by our carpenters, painters, metalworkers, welders, plumbers, steamfitters, electricians, auto mechanics, stationary engineers, truck drivers, equipment operators, tree workers, gardeners, and laborers. Our maintenance crew equals any factory's in craft skills and excels most in versatility. Like any business, a zoo must have plans and budgets, good financial and inventory controls, a resourceful purchasing agent, and a personnel office. I could have said this; but I did not join the zoo to be its business manager. I came because of the animals.

Some book reviewers, for lack of a better term, have called me a "naturalist." I accept this title as an accolade. One does not earn it at a university. Indeed, in my schooldays one could not become a naturalist by attending classes. Zoology was taught from preserved specimens, with emphasis on taxonomy. Biology students dissected frogs. Animal psychologists baited rats in mazes. It was only the dedicated amateurs, by and large, who went to the hills and plains to study nature as a whole, who were concerned with the lives of animals in their habitats.

This is still true in much of the world. A visiting Israeli scientist tells me that ecology is not taught in his country today. Nor is it yet taught in most South American universities. The Latin American scientists we have met on our travels are, with some notable exceptions, highly specialized in their studies. Much of the basic field work describing native species, their ranges, and their behavior is still being done by field-trained naturalists.

It is only a step from naturalist to conservationist, from student to crusader, an almost inevitable step since one defends what one loves. Fifteen years ago, Jane and I sat on a sand dune, waiting for the moon to rise from the ocean. Just below us, our infant daughters slept quietly in the tent. In the far distance, the lights of a seaside resort town made a dull glow in the night sky. Except for a surf fisherman or two, we were alone on these miles of wave-washed sand. This had been one of our favorite weekend camp sites, but we knew this weekend would be one of the last. Before the next summer, a new bridge would be opened, and the crowds would come.

They came, and for the first two years the state, which owned this land, still permitted people to camp where they pleased. When the filth became intolerable, camping was prohibited. Under pressure, the state then provided a supervised campsite, back of the dunes, out of sight of the sea. We passed it one day: Hundreds of tents and trailers were regimented into neat rows, each assigned to a postage-stamp plot.

We can still escape the crowds and find quiet places, backpacking, or by loading camping gear into our small boat. But we have been driven from our quiet beach, and a hundred places we once enjoyed have been corrupted or obliterated by subdivisions, highways, and new industrial plants. Rivers we once drank from are now too polluted for swimming, and sometimes too offensive for cruising. Few children today have the easy access to the woods I took for granted in boyhood.

When I first came to Washington in the late 1930's, I served for a few years in the Department of Agriculture. My assignment required constant travel. I crisscrossed the continent in a secondhand Studebaker, sleeping in farmhouses, tourist homes, or, occasionally, under the stars. Those were great days, epitomized in Pare Lorentz's magnificent film, *The Plow That Broke the Plains,* and the searing pictures of Roy Stryker's Farm Security Administration photographers. Terrifying dust storms, ravaging floods, and costly crop losses had persuaded Americans that our land was on the brink of ruin. Now the government, through such instruments as the Soil Conservation Service, was doing something about it. My muddy boots tramped over miles of land with farmers and ranchers who were learning how to manage soil, water, crops, and trees in new ways.

There are conservationists, I know, who devote themselves exclusively to the protection of a single natural area, such as the Indiana Dunes, or to the survival of a single species, such as the sandhill crane. While I am not one of them, we have much in common in that we are activists, eager to have effective impact on situations close at hand. The need to conserve, to manage resources intelligently, is worldwide and basically indivisible, but the individual conservationist must choose. For some years I chose writing and film production, changing emphasis with each new project: the forests, the seacoast, rivers, grasslands.

As a writer, I undertook to prepare the first manifesto for the Friends of the National Zoo, in 1960. Though a lifetime zoo visitor, I had never confronted some of the questions the manifesto would have to answer: What is a zoo? Why is a zoo?

What are its missions? The answers were shaped in long talks with Ted Reed and Lear Grimmer, and with leaders of the Friends, many of them professional conservationists. One conclusion was that zoos in general, and the National Zoo conspicuously, should become far more deeply involved in international wildlife conservation. With almost five million visitors a year, the zoo could be highly effective in conservation education. It could undertake to breed in captivity members of species on the verge of extinction in the wild, and perhaps add a large breeding farm in the country when zoo cages and paddocks became too small for growing numbers. Zoo-based research could seek answers to some of the problems of managing wildlife in natural preserves. Finally, zoo leaders should enlist in worldwide conservation efforts.

Ted Reed was in full agreement. Smithsonian's Secretary, S. Dillon Ripley, a world-famous conservationist himself, needed no persuasion. Months later, when the post of Assistant Director became vacant, we agreed to recast it in a new design. Half of my time would be required for zoo management. Half would be reserved for extramural conservation projects.

So it happened that only a few days after I joined the staff, Jane and I boarded a plane for Switzerland, where I was a delegate to the Ninth General Assembly of the IUCN, the International Union for Conservation of Nature and Natural Resources. Even before then, my services had been offered to our national zoo association, the American Association of Zoological Parks and Aquariums, to serve as chairman of its Endangered Species Subcommittee.

Conservation is indivisible, and the strategies of survival for the polar bear, the pampas deer, and the rare bird species of the Seychelles are not unrelated to the plight of our human species. In September 1968, Jane and I flew the Atlantic again, this time to Paris and the World Biosphere Conference at UNESCO headquarters.

Here assembled scientists from sixty-six nations, named by their governments, to piece together their information and unify their concerns. The conference documentation was massive, and the published proceedings are rich in technical detail. The significance of the gathering, however, and its transcendent quality was this: It was the first time such a distinguished body of experts had, in formal conclave, declared man to be an endangered species.

Zoo animals today are no mere curiosities. They are representative of the species with whom we share a small, deteriorating planet, whose lives are bound up with ours by the very nature of life, and with whom we shall stand or fall.

3

The Honorable Tradition

A February blizzard paralyzed our metropolitan area. On Monday morning, most streets were impassable. Government workers were told to stay home. In nearby Maryland and Virginia, private automobiles were ordered to stay off the roads. Few buses were operating. I pulled on my boots, pushed through drifts to the nearest main avenue where plows had passed, and hitched a ride to the zoo.

I reached the Bird House first. Two keepers had arrived by then, of the nine scheduled. Food for the birds was our first concern. The Commissary reported by telephone that half its men were there, and they would soon have the day's supply ready. Transportation reported a less promising condition. The Bird House was cut off by deep drifts. One of the zoo's two plows had tried to clear the service road and was now out of action on the steep hill.

Some stocks of grain and seed were on hand. We worked the outdoor cages first, since the birds exposed to the bitter cold and high winds needed food most urgently. I struggled into the huge outdoor flight cage, and birds gathered about me, some sitting on my arms and shoulders as I scattered seed. Yesterday's food pans were buried deep. I scooped one out and found it half full: the storm had halted feeding activity the afternoon before. The meats and fruits were frozen solid, but we could thaw them and supply some rations until the Commissary truck arrived.

More keepers had arrived now, so I continued on my way. In the valley I saw two men carrying a heavy food basket slung from a long pole held on their shoulders.

The Boiler House is one of our most vulnerable points, and will be until a new gas heating system is finally installed. What we have now is a museum piece: old, down-draft, hand-fired coal burners, supplying steam to most of the zoo buildings. A heating failure in weather like this would be disastrous, and it takes a full crew to manhandle the needed tons of coal. I stopped for a visit. We had a full crew. Two men had slept there on cots, afraid that if they went home they couldn't make it back by shift time. One man was working his second consecutive shift, filling in for a man who didn't arrive.

Our men are federal employees, and radio broadcasts had told all federal employees to stay home, without loss of pay. But they are also zoo men, and none needed to be told to ignore the message. In zoo tradition, the animals always come first.

Each morning emergency calls come in to the central maintenance control desk. Most of them seem minor: a plugged drain, a broken hasp, a loose connection. Minor, but the plugged drain may be flooding a cage that should be kept dry, and the hasp may secure the door of a leopard's cage. Our Zoo Police are on patrol twenty-four hours a day. If a vital electric circuit or a water line fails during the night, they have a list of on-call mechanics. Some repairs can't wait until morning.

We had gerenuks on the way from Africa. A new building,

where they would be housed, was in the final stages of construction. Just before the gerenuks were released from quarantine, federal inspectors declined to approve the building until corrections were made. No other heated shelter was available. Our maintenance men built one in two days, complete with heating unit, feed rack, and other fittings. Further, they built it in panels, assembled with bolts, so it could be knocked down and stored for future use.

Our young male African forest elephant was maturing, and conflict developed between him and the larger African female with whom he shared quarters. For training purposes, they are chained at night, but they could reach each other, and one night the male suffered a broken tusk. Maintenance men were summoned in the morning. A few hours later they had set two steel I-beams in the concrete floor, supports for a chain barrier to be snapped in place at the end of each day. Next morning there was another conference; one of the I-beams had been bent like a soda straw. Out came the I-beams. In went six-inch steel pipes with four-inch pipes nested inside, the interstices packed with concrete. So far they have been elephant-proof.

A few days ago our supervisors watched a training film, one of a series. In this one, the examples were jobs in industrial assembly plants, repetitive, short-cycle operations. Our men watched in evident horror. Some zoo chores are repetitive, to be sure, such as the daily cage-cleaning. But there is also infinite variety, and the unexpected happens daily. A welder may be called off a fence-repair job to work with the veterinarian, fashioning a unique metal cast for a zebra's broken leg.

An animal keeper who did no more than perform his routine chores efficiently would be a liability. In the food preparation center of the Small Mammal House, for example, each cage has a diet card. The keeper preparing food for Cage 15 refers to the card for ingredients and quantities. But zoo men speak scornfully of a keeper who "feeds the cage," rather than the animals inside. Cage 15 houses three marmosets, two adults and their offspring. The keeper knows them as individuals. Did they eat well yesterday? Is each one eating his share? What is their condition this morning? Does one seem listless or overexcited? A zoo tale tells of a keeper who fed an empty cage for three days. He is no longer among us.

The keepers have a special status, of course, because they work directly with the animals; and they are also the zoo employees most seen and talked with by visitors. Among keepers, there is an elite corps unrelated to seniority, pay, or titles. Its members are the men the keepers themselves recognize as outstanding animal men. An old zoo term, seldom heard today, is "nick." The keeper with "nick" had an exceptional understanding of individual animals, exceptional skill, and exceptional courage. If a leopard was out of its cage, he was the man who would quietly walk it back in again instead of dashing for the gun case.

No one knows better than a keeper that wild animals are dangerous. There are inherent dangers in the daily routines, and accidents are rare only because keepers know how to work safely and respond to the actions of their charges. Every keeper is expected to know how to capture animals, at least those in which he specializes, but some capture operations are especially difficult and hazardous. While Clint Gray, our veterinarian, is expert in the use of immobilizing drugs, he uses them only when physical restraint would be impractical. If an animal is being captured for transfer to another cage, or if it needs to be restrained only briefly for medical examination or treatment, old-style capture is safer—for the animal. When a capture team is chosen for a difficult job, none of the

choices are surprising. Almost anyone in the keeper force,
asked to choose, would pick the same men. I asked one vet-
eran what qualities mattered most.

"Quick reflexes," he replied. "A real understanding and
feeling for the animal. Knowing that your first hold has to
be your best one. And, whatever happens, not letting go."

Early zoos were not professionally managed. Several were
offshoots of natural history museums. Some were launched by
voluntary zoological societies. A number were initiated by
city parks departments. A few were established by breweries
and transit companies. America's oldest zoos were founded
in the late 1800's, but there had been zoos for centuries in
other parts of the world.

The museum concept was influential in their development.
Like museums, zoos had "collections," and excellence was
measured by the number and variety of species on display.
The specimens were living, and efforts were made to keep
them alive so they would not have to be replaced frequently.
Often they died, however, and some species were said to be
"impossible" to maintain in captivity.

The superintendent of one of these early zoos might have
been a man with some scientific training, or perhaps some experience in managing domestic livestock. Or he might have
been a career employee of a parks department with previous
experience supervising playgrounds or tree-trimming crews.
It was not long, however, before leaders emerged, some professionally trained, others self-taught, who gave direction to
the developing profession. With healthy infusions from the
older European zoo tradition, they shaped the art of exotic
animal husbandry.

While each zoo has its own traditions, there is a body of
knowledge and lore on which all depend. For example, almost every zoo man keeps a copy of "Crandall" within easy

reach. Lee S. Crandall, General Curator Emeritus of the New York Zoological Park, still active in 1969 after sixty years of dedicated zoo work, is the author of *Wild Mammals in Captivity*.* Opening it at random, I read that the London Zoo received its first orangutan in 1830, that a ten-foot wall is considered high enough to confine this species, and that these apes become sexually mature at eight to ten years of age. Crandall assembled an immense collection of information from zoos around the world: the histories of species in captivity; how they are caged and fed; what diseases and other causes have led to premature deaths; how successful captive breeding has been.

My daily mail brings newsletters and journals from the zoos of Tokyo, Frankfurt, Havana, Barcelona, Sydney, Winnipeg, and many other cities. Zoo men everywhere soon know that Bristol has had a litter of white tiger cubs, that Paris has received the first giant elands known to be in captivity. News travels even more quickly among American zoos. Don Dietlein telephoned from Kansas City to report the birth of a female gorilla. We told Clayton Freiheit of Buffalo when he called an hour later. Clayton, then President of the American Association of Zoological Parks and Aquariums, passed the news to others over the next day or two.

When I was in the advertising business, it often seemed to me that advertisements were not really written for consumers, who merely glanced at them. The copywriter knows that his most attentive, appreciative, and critical audience consists of his fellow professionals: the advertising men employed by his clients, prospective clients, and competitors. They are the only ones who might acclaim his masterpieces. In the same way, we know that only our fellow zoo men will recognize and praise our triumphs and see where we have failed or

* The University of Chicago Press, 1964. Lee Crandall died in July 1969.

erred. A curator of reptiles may make a great effort to obtain a rare snake which, to the visiting public, appears drab and uninteresting. His fellow herpetologists, however, credit him with having the only such specimen on exhibition anywhere.

As in any tight little community, zoo men gossip about each other, sometimes bitingly. There are rivalries, enmities, feuds, and competitions. Yet we are bound together both by dedication to animals and by the nature of the art. Exotic animal husbandry is not yet a science. It still evolves largely by trial and error. Unless we confess our failures to each other, someone else is likely to repeat the mistakes we made. Recently the Prime Minister of New Zealand gave us a pair of kiwis, a species our zoo had not kept for many years. How should we house and feed them? We consulted Crandall, of course, and other library sources. We also telephoned to the several zoos that have had recent experience with kiwis, asking what they had done, and with what results.

We visit other zoos frequently. Ted Reed has, by now, visited more than 150 zoos around the world. On our first European trip, Jane and I were introduced to zoos in Switzerland, Germany, and England. A camera is indispensable on such visits, which are almost never long enough for really thorough study. Last year Jane and I visited nine South American zoos, but had only one day in each. We made more than a thousand color transparencies, however, to add to the more than thirty thousand in the zoo files. These are pulled selectively, for detailed study, when we begin planning a new giraffe house or deciding on the design of a new moat.

One Friday afternoon I received a long-distance call from a superintendent of parks in a medium-size southern city.

"We want to start a little zoo," he told me. "I have to tell the city council on Monday how much it will cost. Suppose we begin with four species of monkeys. How much would it cost to build cages for them?"

"Two thousand dollars," I answered. There was a silence.

"You must be joking," he protested. "Surely it would be more than that!"

"Not for monkeys," I told him. "For five hundred dollars you can build a good cage and shelter. Now, if you want people to see the monkeys, it will cost more."

We talked further, and he quickly grasped the idea. City zoos are built for people. That's where the money goes. Animals don't need massive buildings, impressive architecture, terrazzo floors, and manicured flower beds. If people are to be accommodated, there must be parking lots, access roads, pathways, benches, water fountains, rest rooms, and trash receptacles. The animals must be attractively displayed, and barriers must keep people and animals safely separated. For security reasons, there must be a perimeter fence, so the grounds can be closed at night.

A lavish expenditure of money may produce a zoo that appeals to people but is quite unsatisfactory for animals. Architects understand the needs of people, but few of them know much about animal requirements—which differ markedly from species to species. When a city government hires an architect to design a zoo building, the zoo director and his staff, though consulted, may not have control of the planning. We saw what can happen when we visited a European zoo. Its newest and costliest building had been acclaimed as an architectural masterpiece. Indeed, the designer had received an award from an architectural society. As an animal shelter, it was unspeakably bad. The work of the keepers had been made difficult and time-wasting. The public spaces were far too small for the expected crowds.

The old museum tradition has been persistent in the design of zoo buildings: Specimens were kept in boxes just large enough to display them. With emphasis put on displaying the maximum number of species, it was sufficient to have one of a kind. If both a male and a female were shown, it was more to demonstrate sexual dimorphism than to achieve reproduction. Little heed was given to the fact that many species, in nature, do not live in pairs but in herds, troops, or flocks, and that social interaction characterizes their total behavior.

The idea of a zoo-without-bars originated in Germany years ago, and it has been emulated here. Dispensing with bars was more a concession to the public than an improvement for the animals. Barred cages offend some people because they signify imprisonment. A skillfully designed outdoor moated exhibit gives the illusion, to visitors, that the lions or giraffes are unconfined. For the animals, the chief benefit in such new-style enclosures is simply that they tend to be larger than their predecessors. Similarly, animals are unimpressed by rockwork and decorations intended to suggest a natural habitat. Such theatrical effects are good for exhibition, though it is sometimes risky to make the habitat illusion too specific. One must often shift species from one enclosure to another, and a marsh-dwelling deer looks odd in a simulated desert.

Desmond Morris, former Curator of Mammals at the Regents Park Zoo in London, set off a lively controversy when he published a blistering attack on zoos in general.* According to him, present-day zoos turn their animals into psychoneurotics by confining them in bare, sterile cages that offer none of the challenges and stimuli that prompt their behavior in the wild. Frustrated, they either lapse into sullen indolence or adopt substitute behaviors, such as ritualistic pacing, playing with their feces, or hypersexuality. No zoo

* "The Shame of the Naked Cage," *Life Magazine*, November 8, 1968.

can properly manage more than five hundred widely differing species, he contended. He urged total reform as the only acceptable alternative to abolishing zoos altogether.

Some zoo men responded with roars of outrage. One paced angrily around his living room while his wife read the offending article aloud.

"But, darling," she said on reaching the end, "you've been saying the same things right along!"

A zoo director has a proprietary feeling toward the establishment over which he presides, and he is stung when it is attacked. Yet I can think of less than half a dozen public zoos that approximate what their directors would like them to be. Money is the most common limitation. Another is the expression of the old museum tradition in massive structures, aged but solidly built, so solidly as to defy effective remodeling. In the years since these fine old structures were built, much has been learned about animal-keeping. They are obsolete, but it is difficult to persuade the guardians of the public purse that a building should be razed which, according to the engineers, has a useful life extending into the next millennium.

Every zoo director worth his salt dreams of building an all-new zoo, and a few have had the chance. Even then the result is rarely a fulfillment of the dream. If his zoo is city-owned, the first and most crippling setback is likely to be in the choice of a site. Authorities are likely to insist that the site be within the city limits, which puts severe restrictions on its size. The site may be carved from the city's parkland, which is rarely ample. Even if an understanding architect is chosen who is willing to respond simply and directly to a zoo assignment, he may be forced into a costlier framework by the board or commission that sits in judgment on the esthetics of public buildings. This is not unreasonable; there is no guarantee that a zoo director will have good taste. But inexpensive simplicity is rarely approved, and animal facilities are consequently diminished.

One of my favorite zoos is at Chester, England. The elephant house there is enormous, giving the pachyderms more room indoors than many zoos provide outdoors. The huge barn of a building, and a similar tropical house nearby, will win no prizes for architecture. They are nothing but concrete warehouses with big windows let into their walls. What rescues them from utter bleakness is a profusion of plants, indoors and out. Chester is famous for its gardens and greenhouses. In the tropical building, uncaged birds fly among palm trees and flowering shrubs. Lush mosses grow on the rocks of indoor cascades, and bromeliads bloom on rotting logs. At lunch, Director Mottershead treated us to bananas harvested from the display.

These vast buildings are merely shells, within which arrangements can be changed at will and at minimum cost. Cages can be erected or demolished. Some of the bird cages we saw were made of chickenwire stapled to peeled logs. Most city zoos are expected to be more elegant.

In earlier times, cities were logical places for zoos, since they were centers of social and cultural activity. When the National Zoo was founded, the chosen site was well within the city limits, yet described as being "a pleasant carriage ride from Washington."

The zoo at Buenos Aires, built at about the same time, was also in an undeveloped area. In the European tradition, its buildings were fancifully designed, with much ornate ironwork and bas-relief. The park was delightfully landscaped with ponds, islands, streams, bridges, statuary, and fine plantings. It was one of the hemisphere's finest zoological parks.

When we saw it in 1968, it had been swallowed up by the city, hemmed in by high-rise buildings. Heavy traffic roared just beyond the fence of a deer paddock. For thousands of nearby residents, this zoo is the most convenient park, and each morning mothers assemble here with their baby carriages. Visitors from other parts of the city are well advised to come by subway, bus, or taxi, for there is little parking space on bordering streets. The admission fee is only a few cents, and city officials have refused to approve an increase because of the zoo's function as a public park. So the budget has been squeezed, as is all too evident in the deterioration of the old buildings. It is no longer a great zoo.

For such large, long-established zoos, one of the most difficult traditions to abandon is species-counting. To exhibit a thousand species once put a zoo among the world's leaders. Even today the *International Zoo Yearbook,* our basic reference, published in London, reports annually the number of species of birds, mammals, and reptiles each of the world's zoos keeps. There is no evidence whatever that visitors expect such great variety or derive enjoyment from it. Quite obviously, a colony of twenty gelada baboons can be given far more thoughtful study and expert care than ten pairs of assorted monkeys in separate cages—and such a group exhibit of baboons would offer visitors far more activity, a kind of activity far closer to natural behavior than caged-pairs display.

No zoo director I know is slavishly following tradition. None is devoted to the "naked cage." Some, I am sure, would like to abandon their hemmed-in downtown parks and move their animals to spacious areas beyond the near suburbs, but it is more difficult to transplant a public zoo than a department store. The changes will not happen quickly enough to satisfy zoo critics or zoo directors, but they will come. Rochester, for example, has wisely concluded that rebuilding its decrepit zoo, on a twelve-acre site, would be abortive, and the county has acquired fourteen hundred magnificent acres near an expressway; construction now hinges on authorization of a bond issue.

The honorable tradition has flowered in remarkable diversity, and zoos today come in many guises. In a few cases, private enterprise has innovated where public zoos could not. Roland Lindemann's Catskill Game Farm, a hundred miles north of New York City, is popular and has done more than any American zoo to breed herds of endangered ungulate species. At the Alberta Game Farm in Canada, Al Oeming is doing good work with species tolerant of that cold climate. Busch Gardens, in Tampa, Florida, built by the Anheuser Busch brewery, is excelling in both breeding and colorful exhibition.

Some privately financed animal enterprises are not open to the public but devoted entirely to breeding and management. One of these, which Jane and I visited recently, is Bob Baudy's Rare Feline Breeding Center in Florida. In southern Indiana, C. C. Irving has done good work with several exotic bird and mammal species and is now attempting to establish large herds of zebras. More than a hundred privately owned game ranches, from Florida to California, now have exotic wildlife behind their fences.

The many zoo men who have grown up in the profession respect its traditions, but they have not waited for critics to tell them that this is a time for innovation.

4

Designs for Coexistence

The catching team rolled out of camp at dawn: two Toyotas in the lead, a Land Rover just behind, a big, stake-bodied six-wheeler bringing up the rear. Scouts had spotted zebras the day before. The trapper had permits to collect five, and customers were waiting.

The catcher in one Toyota saw them first, a fine herd grazing peacefully in the early light. He signaled a halt, and the vehicles gathered together. Drivers and catchers studied the terrain, sketching their strategy with descriptive gestures. Few words were needed, for these men were veterans of many chases. The Toyotas moved out first, circling in opposite directions, closing in cautiously lest the herd take flight too soon. The catchers made ready, standing up and bracing themselves inside padded rings, each holding a long pole with a noose clipped to its tip.

Go! A dozen zebras tossed their heads and ran. The Toyotas spurted in pursuit, one on either side of the fresh dust cloud. This is a hazardous, punishing race, demanding skill and controlled recklessness. The terrain is rough, the chase vehicles hard-sprung. Often a driver needs one hand to hold himself in place as his car pounds and lurches. He must avoid the worst obstacles lest it capsize or break an axle, but if he turns too far or slows, the quarry will escape.

Twice the Toyotas almost had position, but the herd swerved at the critical juncture. One car tripped in a tight skid turn, rocked perilously, but recovered. Once the herd almost escaped into brush, but the driver of the slower Land Rover had foreseen the maneuver and cut them off.

Then came their chance, the Toyotas closing on either side of the rear runners. Catchers chose their targets. One dropped his noose and missed. The other neatly caught a straining neck. The driver slowed gently, avoiding the sudden stop that could break a neck or leg, snubbing the zebra to a halt without throwing it. Men leaped from both vehicles, and the Land Rover came racing up with more help. In seconds the zebra was thrown, tied, blindfolded, and lifted to the bed of the six-wheeler. Now all hands relaxed, rinsed dust from their mouths, and lit cigarettes.

This was an operation by experts whose quick reflexes and cool judgment let them crowd the line between foolhardiness and acceptable risk. Their chases are quick and decisive. Zebras cannot withstand the stress of pursuit for more than brief minutes. Even if captured alive after a longer chase, they are likely to die later. A responsible team succeeds quickly or breaks off.

Capture is only the first step. When a wild zebra has been caught, it is helpless and terrified. Back at the camp, it is released into a small corral. The next few days are critical. Careful, understanding management is essential if the zebra is to live.

If it accepts food and water, the adaptive process has begun. If all goes well, the zebra begins to associate food with the man who brings it. Unless frightened by unfamiliar sounds, sights, and odors, the zebra will soon develop a new attitude toward the corral: what was at first a prison becomes an island of security.

Before the adaptive process was understood, losses of wild-caught animals were high, and the causes were ascribed to vague maladies. The signs of stress are not always conspicuous, and they can appear in strikingly different ways: one animal refuses food; another eats compulsively. One cause of stress is exposing an animal to circumstances that demand flight while the animal is unable to flee. It is aggravated by many of the changes incident to capture. For example, the captured animal is fed, but not the same foods to which it is accustomed.

Between the point of capture and its arrival at a zoo, a zebra experiences a succession of unfamiliar adventures. It will be placed in a crate, hauled by truck to an airport or sea-port, sent on a long journey. The crate will be jounced, shaken, tilted. There will be noises of vehicles, winches, shouting men, steam whistles, horns blowing, and strong new odors. Captured wild ruminants must withstand the further stresses of long weeks in quarantine, as well as spraying and dipping to rid them of parasites.

A greater kudu arrived at our zoo one evening, the first of a group ordered to stock a new exhibit. The adult male kudu is one of the handsomest antelopes, more than four feet tall at the shoulder, gray-brown with white body stripes, a white face-bar, huge ears, and long spiraled horns. Ours was a young male. Our veterinarian, Dr. Clinton Gray, accompanied the truck which picked up the kudu at the government quarantine station in New Jersey. We were waiting when the truck arrived at the zoo, after dark.

Four men slid the crate back to the tailgate. The lift-truck operator slid his forks underneath. The crate was raised, slowly tilted, lowered to the ground. As I grasped a slat to help steady it, a soft, moist nose sniffed gently at my fingers.

When the kudu was safely installed in a secluded pen, we put the area off limits except to the appointed keepers for a few days. When the animal was settled into its new home, I went visiting. It was after hours, and the building was closed. Alone, I stood against the cage bars and spoke softly. In a moment, the kudu's head appeared in the stall door. Large eyes looked at me soberly; large ears were attentively cocked. I extended a hand, and the kudu took a step toward me, then another. Finally, neck outstretched, he sniffed my fingers again. Another step, and the nose touched my sleeve, moved up to my shoulder and face, down my body to my shoetips. I touched his neck, and the skin quivered. One more touch, and he relaxed. At last the lovely beast leaned his head against me while I stroked neck, ears, and muzzle.

This is an astonishing transformation in a wild creature whose normal behavior is to take flight when man approaches. According to some writers on animal behavior, flight from man is "instinctive," and wild animals instinctively identify man as a primary enemy. This, they believe, is true even if the individual animal has never seen or smelled a man before. Is it possible that such basic fear could be overcome by confinement and feeding?

Wildlife photographers become more familiar with the ways of animals than do hunters, for the camera is more demanding than the gun. A photographer cannot shoot from any angle or at any instant; he is concerned with light and shadow, and with the motion and pose of his subject; and he must shoot from closer range. While, on rare occasions, I have had the time and patience to sit for hours in a blind, most of my animal photography has been done by stalking. One learns that each species has a characteristic "approach distance." Kingfishers, for example, are notoriously shy, cardinals somewhat less so. Chickadees are curious, flirting just out of reach. Chipping sparrows will pick up crumbs an inch from one's toes. Richardson's grouse, the "fool hen," is so unconcerned one wonders how the species has survived.

Approach distances vary within wide limits, however, depending on the time and place, seemingly the weather conditions, and other circumstances. Early one morning we were lucky enough to make a fine photographic series of a coyote; he had just made a kill and, hungry, was reluctant to be driven off. A thirsty deer, approaching a desert waterhole at night, is timid, ready to vanish at the slightest hint of danger; but once it has begun to drink we have fired flashguns again and again without causing flight. We have stalked pronghorn in the open, approaching slowly but in plain sight to within less than ten yards of a herd; but on other occasions we could not come within range.

Often an automobile is an excellent blind. We spent several days photographing waterfowl at the Brigantine refuge in New Jersey, where one can drive on dikes between impoundments. If one of us drove while the other used the camera, we could come within a few yards of the ducks, geese, and swans—if the automobile remained in motion, however slow. If we stopped, they took flight. Visitors to Africa's national parks find the game accustomed to vehicles; and we found this to be true of hoofed animals on the Wichita Mountain refuge. In the Rocky Mountains, I have ridden a horse to within a few yards of deer that would not have tolerated my approach on foot.

One might expect a Thomson's gazelle to race off in panic at the sight or scent of a lion, but this is not what happens. The lion is a predator, and it will kill when hungry, but only then. In Africa's Serengeti, visitors often see gazelles and lions together, the gazelles grazing with apparent unconcern. A lion rarely if ever feigns indifference, strolling casually, then suddenly attacking. On the kill, the lion stalks a herd, approaching stealthily, flattened, tail switching. These are the signs of danger, and once the gazelles read them they are off.

Fear and flight are to some degree a cultural response, a manifestation of what behaviorists call "living tradition." Visitors to Yellowstone Park see this demonstrated. Generations of animals living in this protected environment have acquired exceptional confidence. Tourists wander among bison. Elk recline undisturbed as amateur photographers snap close-ups. Marmots take peanuts from visitors' fingers. Golden-mantled ground squirrels perch on children's knees. A cow moose wanders through a campground, grazing.

The black bears living in the Teton National Park, a few miles south of Yellowstone, are no less protected, but this sanctuary was more recently established. In Yellowstone, the bears are a nuisance, begging at car windows, snatching food from picnic tables. The Teton bears are shy. The Shenandoah bears are not yet so bold as those of the Great Smokies, but there are marked signs of a trend.

Deep in the Okefenokee Swamp is an island of dry ground called The Pocket. Here, several years ago, the resident warden picked up an injured doe, nursed her, and allowed her to wander. She went into the swamp, but returned for food, and one evening she was joined by another doe. By the time of our visit, more than a dozen deer were coming in each evening. They took food from our hands and allowed themselves to be petted; but away from The Pocket they are as wild as any deer.

When we had need to photograph beavers, several years ago, I wondered if we could do it. We knew where to find active lodges, but beavers are generally active only after sundown. We had seen them occasionally at dawn or dusk, never by daylight. We learned, however, that this nocturnal or crepuscular behavior is an adaptation to disturbance by man. We had only to go into backcountry, where disturbance was rare, find a colony, approach quietly, and make ready.

At Silver Lake, in Delaware, migrating Canada geese often gather by the hundreds. The lake, actually a modest pond, is surrounded by roads and houses. Wild geese accept offerings of bread, boldly coming ashore to take morsels from people's hands. The geese we see in wildlife refuges are less responsive to humans, keeping some distance away, yet showing no fear.

In the coastal marshes outside refuge boundaries, geese are wild and wary. Hunters say the geese "know where they are safe," and their behavior seems to confirm this. The learning process has not been explicated, however. The geese that gather at Silver Lake, or fly into our zoo ponds, are "tamer" than those in protected but quiet refuges. Are they the same geese, responding to environmental cues? Or do certain geese, and their descendants, frequent settled places and accept association with humans?

People who live in isolated places often form close relationships with individual animals: deer, woodchucks, raccoons, porcupines, skunks, and other mammals, as well as birds. Their narratives indicate that it is not always the human who makes the initial contact. A deer appears in the garden; if it is not frightened it comes again; its attitude toward the householder combines caution with curiosity. Soon the deer is a familiar visitor, seeking affection.

Young animals of most species are lively, curious, experimental, and unafraid. I entered our zoo hospital one morning and almost tripped over a young lion the size of a Great Dane. He greeted me, purred thunderously when I scratched his ears, and closed his jaws gently on my wrist. I was rescued by a leopard kitten who leaped from a laboratory bench onto the lion's back, tumbled off, and began chewing the lion's tail. A diapered chimpanzee waddled in, sat on the lion's paw, then retreated in arm-waving mock alarm when the lion yawned cavernously. In these play sessions of young animals, a baboon will wrestle happily with a leopard, though adults of these species are mortal enemies in the wild.

Generalizations about animal behavior are risky. It seems clear, however, that the native psychological endowment includes a mixture of inquisitiveness and wariness. There is no specific fear of man or other strangers but a fear response to novelty, a sight or sound or odor not previously experienced. The typical pattern is conspicuous in a kitten when presented with a new toy: It approaches, alert, tense, ready to spring back instantly. If the toy emits an unexpected squeak, the kitten leaps away. Then, since the squeak led to no hostilities, the performance is repeated, until the kitten, satisfied that the squeak is innocent, touches the toy, at first experimentally, then confidently. Now the squeak makes the toy attractive.

Our young black Labrador, exploring with us in the Adirondacks, found something of interest off the trail. We heard him bark, caught glimpses of him circling, tail-wagging, feinting. Then came a single yelp, and he came running back, stopping every few feet to paw at the porcupine quills in his muzzle. Fortunately, it was a young porcupine, and the quills were easily removed. A few days later we passed the place again, and he stayed on the trail until we were well past.

The young animal is exposed to an endless succession of novelties, many of them repeated. The first exposure may be alarming. In most cases, however, the novelty is neutral, without real effect, such as the sound of an airplane overhead. The initial alarm recedes until, like most environmental factors, it becomes part of the background.

What we are considering, however, are relationships between wild animals and man, and particularly the development of positive or tolerant relationships. In the writings of early naturalists, one finds a few accounts of experiences in places which humans had not disturbed, where a softly moving observer could imagine himself in Eden as the more inquisitive birds flew to perch on his head and shoulders. It is easy to understand that animals should have become fearful when human visitors became more obtrusive, using axes and guns and building fires, and more so when settlers disrupted habitats, clearing and plowing land. At the other extreme, we see patterns of coexistence developing, where species such as starlings and squirrels have learned to depend on human civilization. The limits of coexistence appear to depend as much on our tolerance of the proximity of wild animals as on their tolerance of our nearness.

Suppose one wishes to establish relations with a wild animal. The usual beginning is to offer food. If I offer a peanut to a gray squirrel in my backyard, it looks at me with interest from a safe distance. I must toss the peanut and stand some distance away before the squirrel takes it. In less than a week, however, I can have the squirrel coming to my call and taking peanuts from my hand. In a few days more it will eat a peanut while sitting on my knee. Then it becomes a nuisance, banging and scratching at my window to demand its ration.

Of interest is a squirrel's reaction to confinement. I had bought a new live-trap and needed experience in setting it. With peanut butter on a cracker as bait, I put it out on the lawn. Within an hour, I had trapped a squirrel. Releasing him, I reset the trap. Almost at once the same squirrel was trapped again. After the third trapping, he refused to get out until he had finished eating the bait.

Wild birds are readily attracted by food. So are deer, bears, porcupines, and many other mammals, as well as fishes. Many of them learn to associate food with the humans who provide it. One can easily conclude that feeding forms the basis of relationships, that the provision of food overcomes fears, that feeding is the key to adapting a captured zebra to captivity. This, I believe, is true, but by no means the whole truth. The act of feeding appears to have greater significance than the satisfaction of hunger.

Every zoo visitor sees how animals respond to offerings of peanuts and other morsels. Elephants extend their trunks. Bears set up and beg. Zoo animals recognize individual visitors who come often to feed them. Yesterday I saw a zebra prancing in excitement at the approach of a visitor who always pulls bunches of tall weeds or grass and tosses them over the railing.

In the wild, some animals spend most of their waking hours seeking food, though others feed only at certain times. Food is not always abundant. Hunger is not unknown. Our zoo animals, however, are always well-fed.

Jane and I often tour the zoo at night. In the Monkey House, I fill my pockets with biscuits. As I go down the cage lines, each of the macaques, mangabeys, woolly monkeys, spider monkeys, gibbons, and other primates greets me in its own way and accepts or snatches a biscuit. On the few occasions when I have made the round empty-pocketed, I was still greeted with the appropriate chattering, chirping, or grimacing, but the monkeys made it clear that my conduct was unsatisfactory. The significant fact is that the monkeys take the biscuits eagerly from me, though identical biscuits, left over from the day's feeding, may lie on the cage floors.

When we turn on the lights in the Pachyderm House at night, our first move is to get a supply of day-old bread. Each of the rhinoceroses rouses and comes forward to nibble on slices and accept our petting. Why should a well-fed two-ton rhinoceros be interested in two ounces of bread?

Food is not the only bond. The response of many captive animals to their keepers, and to frequent visitors, is as warm and outgoing as that of a pet dog or cat. It is more than the absence of fear, more than tolerance, and more than desire for food. One could readily explain this were all these animals hand-raised, and thus imprinted on humans, but hand-raised animals are a small minority in our zoo.

The offering and accepting of food have symbolic meaning. Primitive people used food offerings as tokens of peace. Breaking bread together, eating bread and salt, have had significance in most societies. I can think of no convincing analogs in the animal kingdom, at least not between other species, but it seems conspicuous in their relationships with man.

Psychologists use food rewards in animal experiments. They can eliminate the human factor, arranging apparatus to dispense the rewards mechanically. Animal trainers use a different strategy. They begin with food rewards but accompany them with affectionate pats and words of praise. Most trainers of dolphins, sea lions, and elephants continue using the food rewards. Others, including dog trainers, find that signs of approval suffice.

What I am suggesting, somewhat tentatively, is that there is an urge for relationship, exemplified by the initiative shown by many species in approaches to man. I do not contend that it exists in all species, nor can I suggest its biological meaning. It is readily overwhelmed by fear, and, once established, the fear reaction is difficult or impossible to overcome. But the urge is seen too often, in too many species, to be denied.

"Relationship" is not necessarily defined in human terms.

Incautiously extended, the hand of friendship may be bitten. Some animals enjoy fondling, but this is not the essence of relationship. What matters is the possibility of coexistence. Were other members of the animal kingdom basically intolerant of the human presence, the outlook for wildlife conservation would be bleak indeed, for few corners of the earth are uninhabited by man. Wildlife conservation has become a study of designs for coexistence.

Centuries ago, man lived with other animals. He was a hunter, but many species killed for food. Perhaps his grass huts were more sophisticated than eagles' nests, and his spears and arrows were unique, but he needed such aids to compensate for his handicaps. His eyes were not so keen as a hawk's; he could not run so swiftly as a gazelle; and he was more vulnerable to cold than a wolf.

Colonial Americans were farmers, but their impact on wildlife was, for the most part, no more threatening than the Indians'. There were some exceptions, such as the large-scale trapping of beavers and the annihilation of auk rookeries. Some concern was expressed in colonial times that the white-tailed deer was vanishing, but although there may have been some reduction of herds, the chief reason was that deer had become warier and retreated from settlements.

Until the middle of the nineteenth century, most Americans lived with wild animal neighbors, though not always with appreciation. My wife's father, as a young schoolteacher in a Wisconsin town, was followed home one night by a bear. Many people worried about wolves and mountain lions. Rifles were kept ready and within reach. Bounty hunters were well rewarded. To some degree, man was at war with nature, competing with some species for use of land, seeking to exterminate rival predators. Still, there was a daily awareness of participation in the natural complex, dependence on soil and water and sunshine, familiarity with the ways of deer and wild turkeys.

Today our far larger population is urbanized. Millions of rural residents have left their farms and moved to the city. While the population density of many cities has risen to disquieting levels, large areas of farm and ranch land have fewer residents now than a generation or two ago. This does not mean that the land they farmed has been abandoned. Many small farms, uneconomic to work with modern machinery, have been combined into larger units.

If this land-use pattern remains reasonably stable, the United States will be able to support a large and varied wildlife population indefinitely. There are certain qualifications, of course, such as enforcement of sensible hunting regulations and suppressing the illegal collection of alligators and Texas tortoises.

"Survival" is an imprecise concept, however. The sudden return of sixty million bison would be a considerable embarrassment. Indeed, there is no possibility of maintaining bison in the United States except for managed herds in confined areas. The herds must be harvested annually lest numbers increase beyond the carrying capacity of their limited ranges. We can keep a few thousand bison, but no more, with us indefinitely in controlled settings.

Deer, bear, and a few other large mammals are thriving within the design, so much so that annual harvests by hunting are management necessities. Most small mammals are readily accommodated. Looking through the list of native species considered to be in danger of extinction, one sees that most are special cases: the spotted bat, which was always rare; the Utah prairie dog, always confined to a limited range; two voles, each found on a single island; the Columbian white-tailed deer, gradually being displaced from the few north-western river bottoms this subspecies inhabited.

Predators are the most difficult to fit into the design, most difficult for man to accept as fellow tenants. The timber wolf population of the conterminous United States has been reduced to less than five hundred, and these are in jeopardy. Since precolonial times, man has considered the wolf to be an enemy. Wolves were shot on sight. Bounties were offered wolf hunters. Farmers and cattlemen favored total extermination.

Today, well-informed managers of wildlife preserves are willing to accept the wolf as a desirable member of the ecological community. The Fish and Wildlife Service favors reintroduction of wolves to wilderness areas where they have been eliminated. Michigan and Minnesota, the only states (except Alaska) with timber-wolf populations, have at last ceased offering bounties. Men and wolves will never again be close neighbors; farmers and cattlemen will not tolerate their predations. The question is whether wolves can adapt to the design, living and preying where we are willing to have them, learning that they will be killed if they come closer.

It would seem that wild animals and man can coexist in a nation as populous and developed as our own. The requirements for such coexistence are severe, however, and in much of the rest of the world they have not been met. One requirement is rational land-use. A second is a public attitude sympathetic to wildlife conservation and the measures necessary to its achievement. Third is a corps of skilled ecologists, wildlife managers, game wardens, soil scientists, foresters, and other specialists.

Many less-developed nations are now passing through a stage that ended here in the first quarter of the twentieth century: recklessly destructive exploitation of their natural resources. We have little reason to be complacent, however, considering our polluted rivers, dead lakes, smog-laden air, and chemically contaminated soils. We have not yet fully controlled erosion of our soils, and overgrazing still adds to unproductive wastelands. All these are threats to wildlife, but they are equally threats to our own species.

5

The First Challenge: Keeping
Them Alive

A professional trapper offered to collect some mountain nyalas for us, if we would place an order for them. This large, handsome antelope occurs only in the high mountains of southern Ethiopia, a rather inaccessible region. The mountain nyala is protected by law, but the trapper was sure he could obtain permits to collect, if he had orders from reputable zoos. The risks would all be his. We would be obligated to pay his price—a rather high price—only when we received the animals alive and well.

The offer was tempting. No mountain nyalas had been in zoos since Berlin had a pair before World War II. Exhibiting such a rarity is a mark of distinction. Further, we had new paddocks to fill. Even so, we declined.

A few months earlier we would have declined without hesitation, for the mountain nyala was then classed as an endangered species. More recent surveys had raised population estimates to four thousand, about what the restricted habitat can carry, and game authorities were issuing a few licenses to hunters.

Even so, the attempt to capture could become embarrassing to the sponsor. Some mortality is inevitably associated with collecting. Relatively few deaths occur when responsible and competent professionals, operating in country they know well, go after species they have captured often enough to have devised good methods. In less favorable circumstances, disasters have occurred: many dead, few if any living captives.

In this case, the trapper had had experience, but not with this species, and not in the Ethiopian mountains. Capturing a fleet-footed animal in rugged mountain country is difficult and risky. It would be a formidable task to get one down from the hills and back to a holding station.

Articles in popular magazines have given the impression that the CapChur gun has made collecting safe and easy. An immobilizing drug is placed in a hypodermic dart. The dart is fired from an air gun. Aim, fire, and the quarry lies helpless. Experts know better.

Any drug powerful enough to stop a wild animal in its tracks can also kill. Some of the first drugs used for this purpose had to be administered in precise dosages: a trifle too little and the animal escaped, a trifle too much and it died. Dosages had to be calculated in relation to the animal's body weight—practical in zoos but not in the field. Further, different species, even those closely related, differ widely in sensitivity. A dose barely adequate to narcotize one kind of zebra may kill another. When the drugs were newly in use, every shot was a gamble.

Drugs with wider tolerances are now available, but field use is still neither safe nor certain. Recently our veterinarian undertook to immobilize several elephants in Ceylon, to train a Ceylonese team in the technique. He found that dosages adequate to knock down an African elephant had no visible effect on the Indian species. Twice as much was required.

Careless use of drugs can kill animals as readily as incompetent trapping or noosing. For some species, experts still prefer the noose. Further, present dart guns have limited ranges. One must come quite close to place a dart accurately. Even if all goes well, one must still solve the problem of moving the downed animal from where it fell to a point accessible by truck. Beyond this lie the many problems of keeping a captured animal alive.

Such considerations made us believe the capture and transportation of Ethiopian nyalas would be difficult, though not necessarily impossible. A good case could be made for bringing a nucleus herd into captivity and attempting to breed them. But when a species is critically endangered, conservationists are likely to discourage capture attempts, especially if the risks appear high, lest the remnant population be further disturbed. It is better to make the attempt while sufficient members of the species survive, so that losses can be tolerated. An established captive population can become a hedge against extinction in the wild. Further, what is learned about the species through captive management may assist those responsible for protecting and managing the wild population.

In the end, we declined the trapper's proposition, not without regret. Ideally, a capture effort in unfamiliar territory would begin with a field study of the species, assembling facts about its habitat, diet, and behavior. Good logistic support would be arranged. A veterinarian might be included in the capture team. But an entrepreneur must balance his commitments and risks against his potential revenue. In this case, the plans seemed inadequate.

We had no such qualms when we brought back a trio of greater kudus, a species closely related to the mountain nyala. The first greater kudus acquired by a zoo arrived in London in 1861. Since then, many have been captured. The present world zoo population of greater kudus probably exceeds one hundred. Methods of capture, conditioning, and transportation are well established.

When a zoo buys an animal from a dealer—which is the way most animals are obtained these days—the dealer is responsible up to the time of delivery. In some cases, dealer responsibility does not end even then. He may, for a price, be willing to guarantee that the animal will survive for a stated period of time, such as a month, following delivery.

The challenge to zoo husbandry begins when a wild animal has ended its journey and arrived at its new home. Keeping wild animals alive in captivity is the first objective of zoo-keeping. Early zoos were most successful with those wild animals whose needs were most like those of domestic cattle, sheep, horses, pigs, goats, dogs, cats, and poultry. In Roman times countless exotic animals, including lions and leopards, were brought from Africa and elsewhere to be slaughtered messily in arenas. The organizers of these bloody enterprises doubtless learned much about keeping their victims alive until the carnage. Kings and emperors maintained private zoos, receiving gifts of rare species from far away. One surmises that their keepers sought to avoid royal displeasure by success in husbandry.

Imagine the predicament of an early zoo-keeper who received a new kind of animal, one he had never seen before, one he knew nothing about. What to do with it? Feed it corn? Grapes? Wheat?

Suppose it was catlike in appearance, with sharp teeth and claws. Obviously it was a carnivore, accustomed to killing its own food. People were less squeamish in those days. We buy packaged, frozen horsemeat for our zoo cats. Early zoo-keepers were more likely to throw live goats into the cages.

Or it might be an animal with hoofs, horns, and flat teeth. It was reasonable to call it an herbivore, probably a ruminant, and to offer it hay and grain. Observant men quickly learned to deduce from the shape of a bird's bill whether it subsisted on fruit, seeds, or prey. Such rough-and-ready guides were at least a step toward providing captive animals with the proper food.

What would we have done had we obtained mountain nyalas? Today a zoo-keeper who receives a species new to his collection can often get advice from zoos that have kept it successfully. There would have been no one to consult, however, about the care of mountain nyalas.

Little is known about its natural diet. Indeed, this is surprisingly true for many more common species. Our American mountain goat, for example, is vegetarian. On my shelf is a standard reference work on the food habits of native wild animals. It tells me that the mountain goat feeds on mosses, bromegrass, dogwood, alder, hemlock, alpine fir, and other plants. However, this list of plants is based on a very few scattered observations, not on systematic analysis of stomach contents. It is not necessarily complete. The observations were not made week by week throughout the year. Nor does the book tell me whether the mountain goat depends primarily on one or two plant species, others being incidental and nonessential, whether it requires a balanced assortment of plant foods, or whether it can subsist on whatever is most readily available.

An animal in its own habitat has a free choice of the available foods and exercises this choice selectively. Some animals, such as our domestic cattle, are highly selective. I have often seen cattle, muzzles to the ground, cropping the last remnants of their preferred grasses while standing shoulder-deep in other green plants, which they ignored. Only when the preferred grasses are gone will they turn to other plants. The mechanism of choice is little understood, especially where a species feeds almost exclusively on one kind of plant for a period of days or weeks, then shifts to another, and successively to still others.

In the case of seed- and fruit-eaters, this may signify nothing more than harvesting seasonal crops. Browsers may prefer leaves, twigs, and shoots at particular times in their development. The white-footed mouse eats insects and other small animals when they are available, but subsists on a plant diet at other times.

Perhaps because relatively little is known about the nutrition of wild animals, theories abound. It is suggested, for example, that the mating of certain species is stimulated by substances occurring in fresh spring growth. Also, and with somewhat more evidence, it is asserted that food selections are often prompted by hunger for trace elements.

The role of the rumen flora is not fully understood. These bacterial organisms have an essential function in processing ingested food. There are a variety of forms, and the ability of some ruminants to digest coarser food than others indicates a different assortment of rumen flora. There is evidence that a change of diet can, within limits, be accommodated by spontaneous revision of the floral pattern. Such a change might be accommodated more readily if appropriate strains of flora could be introduced to the rumen. I am told that old-time zoo-keepers attempted this by feeding newly-arrived wild ruminants the rumen contents of freshly slaughtered domestic cattle. Supposedly this helped adapt them to zoo diets. I know of no scientific validation for this practice. Nor, indeed, have we adequate comparative studies of this factor in wild species.

Two conflicting concepts of zoo feeding have been hotly,

at times acrimoniously, debated in recent years. One school advocates a scientific, balanced diet, calculated and compounded, frequently produced in cakes or pellets. "Diet A," for example, originally developed at the Philadelphia zoo, is recommended for omnivorous mammals and birds. It includes ground corn, wheat, barley, and oats; peanut, soy, and alfalfa leaf meal; brewer's yeast, dried skim milk, oystershell flour, iodized salt, and vitamin A-D oil. This mixture is prepared in bulk, then combined with a smaller quantity of ground, boiled meat and with liquid. The combination is pressed into cakes and refrigerated. Proponents of such diets argue that all animals need the same broad group of nutrients, such as proteins, fats, and carbohydrates, and have similar needs for vitamins and minerals. They recognize marked differences only among major groups of animals: the herbivores, omnivores, and carnivores.

The opposing school contends that zoo feeding should resemble natural diets as closely as possible. They assert that even closely related mammals are adapted to quite different foods, depending on whether their habitat is humid or arid, tropical or temperate, high or low in altitude, and on its soil types. The form of foods is important, they say, not merely its chemical makeup. Proper nutrition requires biting, tearing, chewing, and grinding. Monotony of diet is to be avoided. While this school recognizes that natural diets cannot be duplicated in zoos, they advocate simulating them as closely as possible.

The "retort theory," with its cakes and pellets, is attractive, especially to efficiency-minded zoo directors. The compounded diets are relatively inexpensive. Using them greatly simplifies zoo commissary operations, reduces the work load of animal keepers, and eliminates most waste. Members of this school have been known to describe natural-food diets as "slop feeding."

No one can deny that they are a bit sloppy. After feeding time, cage floors may be strewn with orange peels, banana skins, and leftover bits of carrots, kale, and fish. But neatness and cost are irrelevant to the central issue of good nutrition, however much they may matter to the front office. Natural diets usually include a variety of items, separately presented, and thus give their recipients at least a limited range of choices. Even within the natural-food school opinions differ on the importance of choice. Some nutritionists believe that an animal in captivity, like one in the wild, will select those foods, in suitable proportions, which supply its needs at the time, if a sufficiently wide choice is available. Others hold that captive conditions distort the choice mechanism, and that even a natural diet must be calculated and balanced.

The two schools are not so far apart as they might seem. The closest possible simulation of a natural diet is seldom very close. A city zoo cannot provide grazers with young, fresh grasses. A single species of commercially ripened banana is not equivalent to the many wild species selected and consumed at varying degrees of ripeness. Slab horsemeat, drained of most blood, is not equal to a whole, fresh-killed carcass, complete with blood, bones, and organs. What near-equivalents to lichens, mosses, snails, termites, thimbleberries, fescue seeds, and hemlock bark are available to zoo purchasing agents?

Further, removal of a wild animal to captivity in a different part of the world alters its nutritional needs. In captivity, it is usually less active. It may be exposed to warmer or colder climates, or both. Especially in winter, if housed indoors, it receives less sunshine. Animals from arid regions are given constant access to drinking water. These and other changes must be compensated for in diet planning.

Neither school of zoo feeding gives assurance against elusive "hidden hunger"—conditions attributable to deficiencies of various vitamins, minerals, and trace elements. Natural foods, including those used in compounding standardized diets, vary in their composition, depending in part on the soils in which they grew. Wild animals living in undisturbed habitats rarely show signs of deficiency diseases, because they have become adapted to the peculiarities of their environment. Thus certain species are able to synthesize their own vitamin C.

Deficiency diseases are a product of civilization, affecting both man and the animals whose food supplies he controls. The adaptation of an organism to its food supply is intricate and subtle. Human nutrition has been studied for many years, yet countless questions remain unanswered. Such severe deficiency syndromes as pellagra and scurvy may be well defined, but it is far more difficult to discover whether marginal deficiencies have long-term consequences. The effects of high-cholesterol foods are still debated. It is quite possible that dietary factors influence emotional stability and vulnerability to stress.

When rickets appears in zoo-born young lions, the indication is an insufficiency of calcium. But what if calcium is added to the diet and signs of deficiency still appear? We now know that the phosphorus-calcium ratio is critical, and that an excess of phosphorus inhibits utilization of calcium.

I compared the diets fed to a species of marmoset by two zoos. Both diets had been designed by capable scientists and veterinarians, yet they were markedly different. Neither had the benefit of a natural model, the marmoset's food in its habitat, for this is not known in any detail. Despite their differences, both diets were "successful," in that both zoos had seemingly healthy animals, and both had recorded births. Quite possibly, however, both diets are sufficiently different from the natural diet to have deleterious effects, though these might not appear for some time.

Like humans, wild animals may be upset by a sudden dietary change. When the stress of capture is compounded by provision of unfamiliar food, consequences can be fatal. Expert trappers often gather fresh food from the animal's own habitat, and this is an excellent reason why haste to ship is unwise. The shift to commercial feed can be made gradually, as part of the conditioning process. We prefer that animals be adapted to zoo diets before they are shipped to us, so there will be no abrupt change when we receive them.

It is reassuring when a newly arrived animal eats. I was at our Bird House last week when a pair of quetzals arrived from Costa Rica. They had made the journey in a wicker basket resembling a picnic hamper, which had been wired shut two days before. The brilliantly colored streamer-tailed male flew to a perch, spied the food dish, and immediately gulped down a whole grape.

The traditional classification of animals as grazers, browsers, seed-eaters, fruit-eaters, carnivores, and omnivores was based chiefly on observation. Wildebeests were generally seen grazing on open plains; therefore they were grazers. Closer and more extended observations, together with analysis of droppings and stomach contents, have revised some earlier beliefs. At least some of the grazing animals do occasionally eat meat. Insects are eaten by a wider array of species than had been suspected. When live mealworms are placed in our large tropical room, where many species of birds are in free flight, a number of the "fruit-eaters" swoop down to get their share.

The earlier observations were not wrong, merely incomplete. The antelope that eats meat doesn't seek it daily. Some animals appear to eat insects only at a certain time of the year. These are dietary supplements, reminiscent of the "spring tonics" once favored by country people. As yet we can only speculate about their significance.

Little by little, zoologists are refining knowledge of natural diets. A wildebeest grazes, but a distant observer cannot tell whether it discriminates among the several dozen varieties of plants growing at its feet. Today a scientist may shoot the wildebeest with an immobolizing dart, then take the fresh plant material from the animal's mouth before it recovers and joins the herd. Thus laboriously gathered, bits of data are pieced together. They show, for example, that a single species of grass may be favored by three grazing species, but at different times: by one when the new blades appear, by another when the plant is mature, by the third when the season's growth is dead and dry.

Can we expect all three of these species to thrive on a zoo diet of compressed alfalfa pellets and dry hay? We can supply a few varieties of insects, such as mealworms, waxworms, and crickets, but are these enough to substitute for the immense variety of larvae, grubs, and mature insects consumed, no doubt selectively, by animals in the wild? Commercial raisers of livestock and poultry keep so many animals, under such controlled conditions, that comparative studies are feasible. Here a deleterious condition affecting whole herds or flocks may be attributed to a tiny deficiency of a trace element such as boron or manganese. Zoo collections are too small to support statistically valid studies. A clinical condition seen in one animal may be anomalous, a matter of its individual physiology. The diagnosticians cannot be sure that it would have appeared in others of the same age and species had they been similarly managed.

The juvenile carnivore, weaned but not yet large and strong enough to kill a zebra or a gazelle, preys on rodents and other small mammals. Is this just a matter of size, mouse meat being nutritionally equal to giraffe meat, or do the smaller prey furnish ingredients significant in the development of young carnivores?

Such questions—and they can be asked almost endlessly—may seem dismaying because satisfactory answers are so difficult to achieve. Yet in many instances the costs of ignorance are marginal. Human nutrition is almost equally fraught with imponderables. From time to time some presumably competent scientist warns of all manner of dangers to health in the consumption of milk, spinach, refined sugar, white flour, coffee, or sugar substitutes; or we are urged to include oysters, blackstrap molasses, and synthetic vitamins in our diets. It is quite obvious, however, that humans who are not impoverished and who have access to ample food supplies live longer and enjoy better health than those who exist at the margins of outright starvation. Hidden hunger is not to be ignored, nor are the obesity and arteriosclerosis commonly associated with overly abundant diets. But until clinical symptoms appear which can be dealt with by experience and experiment, concern about deficiencies can easily become exaggerated.

Zoo diets have improved, year by year, in part as a consequence of sophisticated nutritional research, but more often through experience and experiment. The natural-diet theme has value because it provokes thought and experimentation. Since we know very little about the complete diets of most wild animals, especially about their seasonal variation, literal imitation is presently more an ideal than a guide. Yet the inclusion of natural foods in zoo diets permits observation of the selection process, and it also, I believe desirably, introduces variety. On the other hand, use of Diet A and other formulations provides a basic nutritional foundation. Thus many zoos, including our own, take a middle course, supplementing the standardized rations with fruits, vegetables, meat, eggs, and other items.

We cannot feed a natural diet to the Australian koala, which subsists largely on the leaves and shoots of certain eucalyptus varieties. The San Diego and San Francisco zoos can grow these trees on their grounds, and can thus keep koalas. Other zoos cannot, until a diet is synthesized which the koala will accept and on which they will thrive. Someday this may be done.

North American zoos have not successfully kept the three-toed sloth, although the two-toed sloth is quite adaptable. In Brazil, I saw a captive three-toed sloth eating fresh cecropia leaves and mulberry seeds, items not regularly available to commissaries far distant from the sloth's habitat. We have no alternative diet as yet.

Nutrition is more than an exercise in chemistry. We humans could satisfy our nutritional requirements for a few cents a day and dispense with the complications of supermarkets, Saturday shopping, kitchens, cookbooks, and dishwashing, if only we were willing to live on scientifically concocted ration bars. Wild animals are even more preoccupied with food. They spend most of their waking hours feeding or seeking food, or resting between times. The food quest shapes their psychological and physical development.

It would be convenient for animal keepers to dump fish by the bucketful into the sea lion pool once daily, but this is not the way sea lions plan their meals. A number of zoos have concession stands where visitors can buy butterfish or smelt and toss them to the sea lions. Visitors enjoy it, because the sea lions respond so enthusiastically, often catching fish in midair. It spreads the feeding time over a larger part of the day, which is beneficial. It also cuts the zoo's food bill, though someone must keep track of the quantity visitors feed so that deficits are made up on low-traffic days.

Ruminants have typical diurnal feeding patterns. Commonly there are two periods of businesslike grazing or browsing, morning and evening, and a rest period at midday. At other times, they may be seen nibbling idly and casually, more to entertain themselves than to fill their stomachs. An approximation of this pattern is achieved by supplying food pellets, concentrates, at fixed times and in measured quantities but keeping the hay rack full.

Sea lions, otters, and many other fish-eaters seem satisfied with dead fish. Penguins are less so. Many penguins must be hand-fed by their keepers. Presenting the fishes one by one simulates the motion of a live fish. Most carnivorous mammals will accept dead meat. One wonders if their needs are being fully met.

At a European zoo, I saw keepers toss whole chickens to four clouded leopard cubs. The chickens were dead, but still had their feathers. The cubs pretended they were alive. For almost half an hour they played with them vigorously, stalking, pouncing, wrestling. Only then did they pluck them and eat. A psychological need was being met. In carnivores, the hunt and the kill are important biological functions. Even the plucking of feathers from a killed bird seems to satisfy a psychological need of some felines.

Zoo men would prefer not to discuss the question of live feeding. Many have been scarred by encounters with humane society campaigners. These sincere but emotional people are devoted to mammals and birds. They do not object if live mealworms are fed to mynahs, live crickets to marmosets, or live minnows to diving ducks. They are genuinely horrified,

however, if a live mouse is put in a reptile cage. Some of these
humanitarians consider zoo-keeping a cruel occupation at
best, because animals are confined. Their attacks can be
astonishingly intemperate, laden with invective and threats
of political reprisal.

Predation is no longer a taboo subject in popular media.
Wildlife programs on television and full-color picture stories
in national magazines often show, quite explicitly, carnivores
stalking, killing, and eating their prey. The more sophisticated viewers and readers know that many of these sequences
were contrived, but there has been no outcry of protest. I
have no doubt, however, that zoo visitors would be genuinely disturbed to see a jaguar kill a pig in its cage.

I doubt that any zoo man wants to adopt live feeding as a
general practice. Quite apart from the issue of humaneness
and the probable public reaction, it would make feeding in-
tolerably costly and complicated. The large carnivores are
well-fed. They are generally healthy. Their appetites are
whetted by weekly "starve days," a practice based on the observation that wild carnivores do not eat daily. Lacking is the
stimulation of the hunt and the physical exercise. It should
be possible to develop analogs, substitute activities.

Reptiles are more of a problem. Snakes in captivity often
will not eat. Keepers sometimes resort to force-feeding, but
this takes time, is not altogether successful, and, in the case
of venomous snakes, is dangerous. Many snakes will take live
food—mice, rats, and rabbits—and nothing else. The zoo director must make a choice: accept a high reptile death rate,
feed these snakes in the natural way, or omit from his collection reptiles that take only live food.

Small seed-eating birds cost very little to support. A large
ungulate may cost a zoo three hundred dollars a year to feed,
a large carnivore considerably more. Most zoos, always hard-

pressed for money, are adept at scrounging. Supermarkets may be glad to give away vegetables unfit for sale. Bakeries offer stale bread. Local research institutions may contribute rats and mice. Tree-trimmings are fed as browse. Food plants such as bamboo may be grown on the premises.

Modern zoos have commissaries, where food is received, stored, processed, and distributed. Purchasing agents follow the commodity markets, watching prices fluctuate for such items as horsemeat, grapes, lettuce, fish, and hay. A railroad wreck or a warehouse fire may be an opportunity to make a spot purchase at bargain prices. Refrigerated storage space is valuable, since it enables the zoo to buy in economic quantities and at the most strategic times. Our commissary buys an imposing variety of foodstuffs: horsemeat, fish, mice, rats, chickens, worms, mealworms, crickets, hay, grain, sunflower seed, millet, sugarcane, peanuts, eggs, potatoes, bread, dried milk, carrots, celery, onions, kale, lettuce, apples, oranges, bananas, grapes, canned cherries, and other commodities, as well as prepared chows and dietary additives.

In most large zoos, the commissary is a distribution center, filling daily orders from exhibition buildings and areas. Some processing is done there, but the preparation of food pans for individual animal enclosures is usually a keeper function. The commissary has standing orders, though revisions come in almost daily: so many pounds of meat for the Lion House, certain quantities of fruits and vegetables for the Bird House. As each new day begins, a first order of business is loading the food truck and sending it on its rounds.

The animals always come first in a zoo. Food has a priority claim on budgeted funds, and the daily food delivery must be made regardless of handicaps and emergencies. If a heavy snow falls during the night, members of the snow-removal crew are routed from their beds. Enough plowing must be done for keepers and commissary workers to enter the zoo and park when they arrive. The second priority is clearing the route for the food delivery truck. If the truck driver doesn't arrive, a man is pulled from other duty. Somehow the food will reach the animals.

The food preparation center of our Small Mammal House resembles a restaurant kitchen. Sterilized stainless steel pans are stacked and ready. A bulletin board displays the diet cards. No two pans receive quite the same contents. Nor does a single word, such as "carrots," describe the ingredients. Carrots may be served whole, cut in chunks or strips, diced, grated, or pulped. Meat may be sliced, cut in bits, or ground; it may be served raw or cooked; ground meat may have calcium and vitamins kneaded in. Some animals peel their own bananas; some will not. Placing two scoops of meat at opposite corners of a pan may avoid an argument between cagemates.

A typical food pan may receive a dozen ingredients, including additives. Preparing it is time-consuming. Indeed, a third of the man-hours available in the Small Mammal House are spent in food preparation and serving. We would be more inclined to the ready-mix school if we did not have a group of skilled, sensitive, and observant keepers, who know the habits of each individual in the collection.

The animals' reactions to each day's food are telling signs of their condition. The aardvark is ordinarily clawing at the door when food arrives; today he is listless. The keeper will look in from time to time to see if he eats. In a cage of three fennecs, he will not merely look at what remains in the pan after feeding; he will make sure each of the three has eaten. As he collects each pan, he studies the leftovers. Perhaps one animal has eaten all of the meat but rejected the fruit. Each day, the keeper relates feeding behavior to the activity and appearance of each animal.

I once had a dog who, seriously ill, was cared for by a veterinarian. The illness was arrested but the dog languished, refusing food. I took him home. He sniffed at his usual dog food and showed no interest in dog biscuit, milk, or a raw egg. I cut a morsel of beef from a rib roast and he snatched it, then made a meal of all we had. Next day he refused beef and dog food, but welcomed cooked horsemeat. For several days, as he gained strength, we had to experiment, finding something he would take. Each day, once we discovered something to his liking, he ate well.

In theory, a keeper should follow his diet cards precisely, every day. If keepers were allowed to express their own hunches and prejudices in feeding, we could make no pretense of scientific management, nor could we correlate diet and health. Only the veterinarian (or, if the zoo has one, the nutritionist) can prescribe vitamin additives or diagnose a deficiency of calcium. At the same time, only the keeper is able to respond sensitively to daily changes in the condition of an individual animal. Many a newcomer to our collection has been nursed successfully through its first days at the zoo by a keeper who experimented with foods.

Today zoos have enough knowledge and experience in feeding wild animals so that most species can be persuaded to survive. While most zoos cannot keep three-toed sloths and koalas, the basic reasons for the limitations are known: the right foods cannot be procured. Now the challenge is to refine this knowledge, improving diets in the interests of animal health and reproduction.

At one time, zoos were dependent on wildlife biologists for clues to proper nutrition. Now the favor is being returned. Malnutrition is a serious problem in some parks and preserves. What quantities of food does a given species require? Rough calculations can be made in the field. Zoos can often supply more precise measurements. In a disturbed wild habitat, quality as well as quantity of food may be a problem, especially if the disturbance has altered the assortment of food plants. Both quantity and quality may be inadequate in a marginal habitat to which a species has been pushed by circumstances. Such changes have occurred, in some instances, before the original, unmodified habitat was studied, so we cannot now gather data on the natural setting. Here again, zoo studies may substitute. The modern wildlife manager must often improve the food production of a preserve, even by planting and cultivating crops; but he must first know what needs must be met.

6

Survival in Captivity

My younger daughter, Gale, is raising white mice. One pair is housed in a three-gallon aquarium with a hardware-cloth lid. In this small container, with her help, they have set up living arrangements. The floor is covered with cedar shavings and strips of newspaper. They have an exercise wheel, a forked tree branch, a water bottle, and a food dish. Before the exercise wheel was provided, the mice made a nest in one corner. Now the flat base of the wheel, half an inch above the floor, gives them a tight nest box which they stuff with litter. The food dish is a source of supply, not an eating place. They empty it and hide much of its contents. One corner of the box is their toilet. Usually they remain hidden by day. At night we hear the exercise wheel turning for long periods.

They have raised several litters. Gale tries to remove the male before the young are born. The young are taken out after weaning. The aquarium is big enough for a pair, but she had found that fighting occurs if more are kept in it.

The territory of a wild mouse is larger, measured in yards rather than inches. Behavioral scientists have given much attention to territoriality in recent years, and their studies have illuminated reasons for many patterns of activity in wild populations. Essentially, it appears that a wild animal—or a pair, family, herd, or other social unit—lays claim to a territory and defends it against others of the same species. In many instances, the size of the territory claimed is influenced or determined by food supply. In others, territorial claims are asserted at the time of mating or nesting, and males defend their claims against other males. A wild mouse may spend its entire life-span within its corner of a farmer's field. A marmoset may never venture far from its own tree. In the Okefenokee Swamp, we observed the movements of a striped skunk for several days. Then we set up our cameras on his route, confident he would pass within the next few minutes.

Zoo cages are far smaller than most natural territories. Our Small Mammal House, built more than thirty years ago, has some enclosures no larger than Gale's aquarium. The indoor lion cages are only a few paces wide. The new deer paddocks are much larger, yet far too small to permit growing a natural supply of browse.

Visitors often react to the sight of a caged animal by identifying with it, imagining themselves in a small, barred cell. They feel an urge to set the animal free, an impulse checked by their better judgment and our stout padlocks. "Are the animals happy in cages?" they sometimes ask. It is not an easy question to answer, though some reassuring answers are on tap.

Jane and I entered the Small Mammal House one night, and just as I turned on the lights, a small animal whisked out of sight around a corner. By a bit of maneuvering we drove it into a wing of the building, where Jane stood guard while I called for help. Two keepers soon arrived, and the animal, a cacomistle, was netted. Later we deduced that the little Mexican cat had not really escaped but was enjoying a customary prowl. Able to squeeze through the cage bars, he came out each night, returning before the day shift arrived.

Many animals would do the same if their cage doors were left open. Indeed, most "escapes" in zoos are caused by fright. Some of the antelopes kept in pens could easily leap the eight-foot fences customarily used. At a European zoo, a child tumbled over a railing into a bear pit; the bear, terrified, leaped out! The cage or den is home, a place of security.

Concerned visitors can be told that animals live longer in zoos than in the wild. In the zoo, they are not hunted by predators. The veterinarian treats illnesses and injuries which would bring death to free-roaming animals. In zoos, they have an assured food supply; in the wild, starvation is not uncommon. In zoos, they are safe from such natural perils as forest and brush fires, floods, droughts, ice storms, and hurricanes.

So zoo animals seem to live in peace and contentment. If a male and a female are on opposite sides of a barrier in the mating season, the male may make frantic efforts to get through, butting, battering, or clawing. One almost never sees any such effort to escape from a cage or pen. Such answers may satisfy casual visitors. They do not satisfy zoo men. Captivity does have adverse effects, especially in the small, bare quarters of traditional zoos.

Wild animals are physically active because they must be to survive. Predators must chase; prey must flee. Eagles must soar and monkeys climb. Browsers develop powerful jaw muscles. Beavers gnaw. Ground squirrels dig. Confined in small quarters, protected, their needs supplied, zoo animals have neither the space nor the need to develop their full physiological powers. Too often one sees monkeys in a cage with nothing to climb on and ground squirrels on a concrete floor that frustrates digging.

The same conditions limit or distort psychological development. The point is not that a wild animal has a burning
urge to stalk prey, rip open a decaying log, or huddle in a
howling blizzard. Rather, its wild existence is a series of challenges to which it must respond. Its natural environment is
rich in stimuli, most of which zoo cages exclude.

No one knows this better than an experienced zoo man.
The very fact that this is today the focus of self-criticism is
evidence that they have learned, at least, to keep most animals alive. This has been no small task. A zoo cage, large or
small, is an artificial environment controlled by zoo managers. Within this enclosure they must provide everything
the animal organism needs for survival, at the same time excluding or compensating for influences that might cause
death.

Next to food and water, most people think of climate as a
threat. The typical zoo assembles animals from many climates, hot and cold, dry and humid. How can tropical animals withstand northern winters? The fact is that many tropical species readily adapt to cold weather. If allowed to do so,
elephants, giraffes, tigers, and jaguars will go outdoors when
snow lies on the ground. Some species from warm climates
develop markedly heavier coats when kept in the temperate
zone.

Zoo buildings are kept warm in winter, but this is chiefly
for the benefit of visitors and keepers. Since, in older buildings, cage temperatures cannot be individually controlled, a
satisfactory average is chosen, and this is usually a temperature
that people consider comfortable. Most wild species have a
much wider temperature tolerance than we do. Even in habitats nearer the equator, the nights are often cold. We humans
like to heat our indoor shelters if the temperature drops much
below 70°F, and we welcome artificial cooling if it rises above

80°. Out of doors, we compensate for temperature variations by wearing a minimum of clothing in the heat, muffling up in the cold. Wild animals, as adults, are commonly exposed to greater variations.

Trees of a given species may be planted far outside their natural range, yet live and grow—but their seedlings may not. Survival of an individual animal in an alien climate does not demonstrate viability of its species. In the wild, natural reproduction cycles commonly arrange matters so that births occur at the most favorable season. In captivity, and in a different climate, this advantage is lost, unless wildlife managers take control.

If, in a zoo, a male zebra is segregated at certain periods, births may be timed propitiously. Often this cannot be done. The alternative is to confine the pregnant female indoors if she will deliver in the dead of winter. A remarkable sight in our zoo is to see the Australian black swan sitting on a clutch of eggs when the ground is snow-covered. Though she has been with us for several years, her biological clock still runs on Australian time! Her body heat is sufficient to hatch the eggs, and she has raised several cygnets.

Many of our birds, including tropical macaws, are kept in outdoor cages the year around. In winter they can take refuge in open shelters, under heat lamps, and their perches are electrically heated to prevent frozen feet. Squirrel monkeys can be maintained under similar conditions. We do not heat the shelters occupied by our deer, zebras, gnus, Cape buffalo, elands, and llamas, although heat lamps provide spots of radiant warmth. The Dorcas gazelles, scimitar-horned oryxes, water bucks, kudus, and white rhinoceroses are in heated buildings, but nighttime temperatures may fall below 50°F. In the past, more heat was thought necessary. Recently I saw our white rhinos wandering placidly outdoors while snow fell. At such times in the past, they would have been kept indoors.

Polar bears seem unaffected by our hot summer days if they have access to a cool swimming pool. On the whole, however, tropical species are more successfully maintained in the temperate zone than animals from the Arctic and Antarctic. We have had indifferent success with our reindeer herd. At one time climate was thought to be the problem, so their shelters were air-conditioned in summer. Now we are more concerned with their nutrition. While the ranges of animal species are affected by climate, this is not primarily because of their tolerance for heat or cold. Much more influential is the effect of climate on plants, determining their distribution, which in turn determines the kinds of food available to herbivores.

Broadly speaking, insects, parasites, and many disease organisms thrive best in warm and humid places. This causes management problems when animals from cold climates are moved to zoos in warmer regions, or from a dry habitat to captivity in a humid place. Even the translocation makes the problem of disease a critical one, however, for animals are adapted to diseases endemic in their habitats. Moved elsewhere, they are exposed to different organisms against which they may have no resistance.

Some new zoos have cages that are hospital-like in appearance: tiled floors and walls, glass cage fronts, fittings of stainless steel. A wild animal looks incongruous in such a setting, and it is easy to believe that the animal is both physically and psychologically uncomfortable. Yet there is reason for such sterility. In nature, the body wastes of animals are elements of a cycle in which organic matter is synthesized by living plants, utilized by animal consumers, and ultimately decomposed, enriching the soil in which plants grow. Most wild animals scatter their droppings as they move about. The droppings of arboreal creatures fall out of their living space. Burrowing rodents often include a defecation chamber in their underground structures.

Zoo visitors sometimes see a chimpanzee pick up fecal matter and play with it. In the wild, a chimpanzee would not ordinarily encounter its own feces. In the confines of a zoo enclosure, urine and feces accumulate on the cage floor, often in close proximity to food. The result can be a recycling of parasites and other organisms, causing serious health problems. Many parasites and bacteria are killed by exposure to sun and air; an indoor zoo cage may receive no sunlight, and it may have cracks or pockets in which wastes accumulate.

Thus sanitation is a most stringent requirement in keeping wild animals alive in captivity. Daily cage cleaning is one of a keeper's principal chores, occupying as much as a third of his working time. The variety of procedures used is surprising. It is most convenient, of course, if cage occupants can be shifted out, to other cages or to sleeping quarters, so the keepers can work without risk or interference, but this is not always possible.

In some cases, cages must be cleaned from the outside. Especially in winter, when some animals cannot be shifted outdoors at will, the keeper may not be able to enter a cage to work with scrubbing brushes and other tools. When he works from the outside, his primary tool is the hose. Many zoos, including ours, make use of apparatus that supplies a controllable water jet which, at the flick of a lever, will carry a detergent or other cleaning compound with it. Even if animals can be shifted once a day, for a thorough cage cleaning, flushing from outside is useful. More often than once a day, the keeper will use his hose from outside, flushing away urine, feces, and partially eaten food.

Surfaces such as those of glazed tile, stainless steel, and epoxy-coated concrete are highly desirable for sanitary purposes. They are nonporous and nonabsorbent. They flush clean. If, after cleaning, the water drains away or is removed by squeegees, such surfaces dry quickly. Thus they satisfy the sanitarian, though they offend the behaviorist, who points out that animals living wild are accustomed to walking on turf, duff, sand, and other natural surfaces. Tile and concrete are cold and hard. In Europe and South America, I saw zoo cages floored partially with concrete, partially with wooden planks. The animals almost invariably chose the wood to lie on.

Some animals are disturbed and put under stress by the daily cleaning. Many mammals are scent-markers, defining their territories by urinating on or rubbing scent glands against selected spots. Thorough cleaning removes these claim marks, and the animals scurry about afterward, sometimes almost frantically, reasserting their claims.

We have yet to find a really satisfactory material for a cage floor. Ideally it would be warm, as wood is, and at least as resilient. But wood absorbs moisture and is inclined to rot. Monkeys pick at wood so persistently that it must eventually be replaced. Cats and canines scratch at it, with similar results. Because wood absorbs moisture, it retains odors—although this seems to offend only people—and it can harbor disease organisms. Heavy linoleum is as vulnerable as wood, as are other resilient materials thus far tested. Undoubtedly many of the animals would prefer to be kept on dirt, tanbark, sawdust, or sand, but such materials present obvious sanitary problems. We continue our search for something better than concrete, and several materials are under test. Even an "ideal" material, however, were one found, would not approximate natural conditions.

The need to scratch one's back would not seem to be a life-or-death matter, but a persistent itch becomes preoccupying. Almost all animals need more than bare boxes for comfortable living. The necessary furnishings may include rubbing-posts, wallows, or dust baths. Cats need places to sharpen their claws. Birds need perches, and arboreal mammals a substitute for living trees and vines. Nest-builders need building materials.

The need to scratch, or to satisfy other behavioral needs, may be a matter of life or death. Stress is the most pervasive threat to survival in captivity. Stress causes animals to succumb to illnesses or injuries they would otherwise withstand. It can provoke fatal fights among cage-mates, or cause parents to destroy their young. It accounts for deaths otherwise unexplained.

"Stress" is a catchall term covering a multitude of psychosomatic upsets. An animal is subjected to stress when it cannot find sufficient food. Fear causes stress in a spectrum ranging from blind panic to marginal insecurity. Stress may be brief and passing. It is most insidious when it is low-grade but prolonged.

Should a dog enter a zoo antelope paddock, an antelope may dash blindly into a fence or wall, breaking its neck, whereas in the open it could run freely and escape. Species typically have flight distances. The boundaries of zoo cages are smaller than these invisible circles of security, but most species come to accept partitions as substitutes. A cage front is a different matter, since it is open to sights, sounds, and odors; yet once accustomed to their cages, few animals show fear when visitors approach. This may take time. For several months our colobus monkeys stayed close to the rear of their cage whenever visitors were near. Spider monkeys, on the other hand, quickly welcome attention.

A cage open on one side only provides a greater sense of security than an island exhibit, open on all sides. While many species adapt well to such free-standing open cages, others do not. Zoo men now generally agree that most species experience at least occasional stress if they cannot, at times, escape from public view. Modern designs generally include retiring dens, sleeping quarters, or other off-exhibit spaces.

Some small mammals feel most secure when they have physical contact with their environment on all sides. Our scientists were working with one such species, the long-tailed tenrec from Madagascar, which had never before reproduced in captivity. They supplied a small nest box, so small it seemed barely large enough for the animal to enter. The female packed this tiny area with litter, squeezed in, and there delivered her young. Animal mothers have a special need for privacy and security at such times. Bears, for example, need secluded cubbing dens. An insecure mother may destroy her young or fail to nurse them.

The "naked cage" cannot be made into a duplicate of a wild habitat, but improvements are being made. The most significant improvement, and the most difficult for established zoos to make, is increased size. One must, at a minimum, have the necessary real estate or be willing to reduce drastically the number of species on display. Open-air enclosures are the easiest to enlarge, if space is available, at least for species that can be confined by fences. It is more costly and difficult to provide large outdoor enclosures for such species as gorillas and tigers, for which a fence is no barrier. Even indoors, it is often possible to enlarge true living space by better design. A nest box, for example, may add only a small fraction to the actual cubage, but it is more of a gain than doubling the size of the cage itself. In an outdoor paddock, building a mound in the center may have the effect of enlarging effective space, since junior males will be able to get out of the herd bull's sight.

Designing an artificial environment for a wild species imposes an awesome responsibility on the designers. So many things can go wrong. An antelope can slip and break a leg on smooth, wet concrete; the surface must be sufficiently rough to prevent this, yet not so rough as to frustrate cleaning. Sharp edges and corners can cause injuries. Fence lines should never meet at an acute angle, forming a trap. Fence mesh and cage bars should be so fashioned as to minimize the risk of snagging heads, horns, or legs. One zoo confined its bears successfully behind vertical bars, but one pair produced cubs, which easily exited between the bars.

Adjacent paddocks should be double-fenced, with an aisleway and visual barrier between, to prevent fighting through the fence. Lead-free paint must be used on any surface an animal might lick or gnaw. Any new enclosure must be carefully inspected before it is used for animals; one of our contractors left fence-wire clippings strewn about, which could have had fatal consequences if ingested. Yet while animal welfare must be paramount in cage design, two other sets of needs must be integrated: those of keepers and visitors. If inept design makes needless work for the keeper, he will have less time to devote to animal care.

Before an animal is introduced to a new cage, another question needs to be answered: How will we recapture it if we must? Keeper safety needs careful consideration. I have seen poisonous snakes kept in cages with blind service doors. The keeper had to open them without knowing where the reptiles were. In some cases, he could not see the entire cage even with the door open, and leaning in would expose him to danger.

A few months ago we had to move two white rhinoceroses

from our Pachyderm House to new quarters some distance away. They had been young and small when the zoo received them. Now the male weighed almost five thousand pounds, the female almost four thousand. The problem was like having built a yacht in one's basement.

Methods of transfer were suggested and debated. Some were too chancy. Had we asked them to do so, I'm sure the keepers would have undertaken to walk the rhinos between them, since they had always seemed docile. A few of the suggestions bordered on fantasy. The one finally chosen was conservative and laborious, but effective. Welders built a steel cage on the bed of our heaviest truck. The bars of the outdoor pen and visitor guardrail were cut and fitted with slip joints. A steel bridge was built across the moat, measured so precisely that its side rails engaged matching rails on the truck-mounted cage. A ramp was excavated at the new enclosure.

Early one morning, veterinarian Clint Gray fired his dart gun at the first rhino. It was down within a minute, and a countering drug was injected in its ear. Soon the rhino was on its feet, well tranquilized. Pushing, pulling, coaxing, ten keepers inched the mammoth beast onto the bridge and into the truck. It took almost as long to ease it out at the end of the line. In four hours, both had been moved.

The daily report that comes to my desk from the Animal Department records each birth, accession, and death. Rarely does a day pass without a few entries on the death list. No zoo man takes these deaths lightly. It saddens us when a favorite animal dies, and we are troubled by the loss of a rare specimen or one essential to continued breeding. Yet all animals die, and in a population of three thousand, deaths will not be uncommon. We must relate our deaths to some criteria to judge our husbandry.

Until quite recently, a low death rate was considered a mark of excellence. It had taken years of effort, with discouraging failures, for zoo men to learn how to keep wild animals alive. Now there were successes on every side, new longevity records being set each month. One could say with confidence that animals live longer in zoos than in the wild. Today, zoologists are asking whether this is an unmixed blessing. Are zoos keeping too many animals alive?

A dairyman who tried to set longevity records with his cows would soon be bankrupt. So would a commercial breeder of pigs or poultry. While zoos are not engaged in producing milk, meat, or eggs, we can well ask ourselves what results we are seeking to achieve. In a zoo conceived as a living museum, longevity is an asset, since it conserves specimens, reducing the rate of needed replacements. But if the aim is to approach natural conditions as closely as possible, saving lives can become detrimental.

Zoos that keep, on the average, less than three or four individuals per species tend to become geriatric institutions. More and more cage space is occupied by individuals or pairs beyond the age of reproduction. A reduced death rate is matched by a reduced birth rate. One may also question the genetic effects of keeping alive young animals or adults that would have perished in the wild. Survival of individuals is not equivalent to racial survival. Indeed, the viability of a race depends on elimination of those least able to withstand environmental challenges.

We humans think of diseases as our enemies. We would like to eliminate infectious diseases altogether, or at least immunize everyone against them. We are concerned with the life of the individual, even one that is physically or mentally defective at birth.

In the wild, disease organisms are as much a part of nature

as bluebirds and palm trees, and they are as vitally involved in the complex of life. In any population of a species there is an assortment of physical qualities. In response to such environmental challenges as disease, some individual will succumb, others survive. Thus there is selection of qualities in those that live and reproduce, and the next generation will be composed of a slightly higher proportion of individuals adapted to the prevailing circumstances—which are themselves subject to constant change.

Of course, if certain members of a wild population are translocated to another habitat, they may not survive, for the new set of challenges may be unlike those to which they are adapted. Thus we cannot, in zoos, accept disease organisms as part of the zoo environment, for we are gathering together animals from around the world. We must attack disease, suppress the organisms, immunize animals against them, and treat them if they fall ill.

Yet how far should we go in life preservation and extension? A dog breeder inspects each new litter carefully and promptly euthanizes any puppies that fall short of his standard. Cattle breeders are highly selective of their herd bulls. Zoos, however, which generally have few members of a species, exercise little selection.

A leopard cat delivers two kittens. She does not care for them and seems likely to destroy them. So we take them from her and raise them by hand. Our zoo hospital has incubators and a list of volunteers eager to serve as foster mothers, even though this means bottle-feeding every two hours around the clock.

Are we compensating for the abnormalities of the captive situation? Mothers in the wild sometimes reject their young, any they may do so because the young are unfit. Such rejection is a factor in genetic selection. Significantly, when we fail in our hand-raising efforts, autopsies often show congenital defects which had not been apparent.

Such questions had no great significance so long as zoos could replace most of their losses with new wild-caught specimens. As more and more species become rare in the wild, we must propagate them in captivity, generation after generation, if we are to keep them in our collections. Zoos have succeeded admirably in achieving survival. Many of our practices must be radically changed, however, if "survival" is to be of species rather than individuals.

7

Zoo-Born

Young animals have irresistible charm. Visitors gather around cages where monkey mothers nurse young, where a sloth bear plays roughly with her cub, where a newborn gnu stands on shaky legs. Distinguished gentlemen make absurd gurgling noises to attract the attention of a baby rhinoceros. News photographers demand animal baby pictures when there is a shortage of photogenic fires or auto wrecks.

Zoo-keepers puff up with pride when a new baby arrives. Our secretaries go to see it at lunch hour. The carpenters and welders seem no less pleased and find occasions to stop by. Our recent crop includes a gorilla, an orangutan, a rhinoceros, golden marmosets, leopards, a Nile hippo, black-footed kittens, and many more. Another giraffe is expecting. We hope the white tiger is pregnant again. The colobus monkeys have been mating. We have emu eggs in the incubator.

Among humans, it is commonly believed that proximity provokes sexual response. Courts have held that if a man and woman have spent a single night together in privacy, they have presumably had intercourse. According to folklore, a male and female cast up on a desert island would inevitably mate. Whatever the truth of the matter, they could never persuade others they had not.

Gale can pair mice at random, with confidence that they will produce young. Dog owners know the magnetic attraction of a bitch in heat. The tomcat's promiscuity is proverbial. Many species are more selective, however. Compulsory pairing does not assure mating.

Pairs of apes have been kept together for years without result. We had such a pair of orangutans. They lived together amicably, but neither exhibited sexual interest in the other. Eventually we shipped the male away to another zoo, where he promptly sired young. We acquired another male, and our female was soon a contented mother.

Eager moralists may leap to a conclusion from such evidence: The judges and folklore are wrong. That desert island story was just a joke. Only the lower forms of life are inherently promiscuous. The great apes, more closely resembling man, choose their mates with discrimination. In the absence of true love, they repress base impulses.

The student of comparative behavior does not shun analogies, but the evidence permits other interpretations. Indeed, study of such cases suggests that our orangutans failed to mate because they knew each other too well. In nature, this limits inbreeding. In a zoo, the inhibition also affects unrelated individuals kept together from an early age. On the other hand, if brother and sister are separated as juveniles, they may well mate if brought together as adults.

For mice and men, two is enough for mating. For a number of other species, sexual behavior is a social activity. Many ungulates are herd animals, and herds have definite social structures headed by senior males. They monopolize the females, warding off rivals, some of whom may form bachelor herds. Junior males spar with each other, practicing combat and determining which of them will ultimately challenge the old man. Such fighting is usually ritualistic. Even the final contest that displaces the boss is seldom fierce enough to cause mortal injury. For the senior male, there appears to be a close relationship between his rivalry with other males and his sexual interest in the females of the herd.

A zoo acquiring a new species of deer or antelope is likely to buy a trio: one male, two females. This is often satisfactory and propagation ensues. Numerous cases have been recorded, however, wherein the male of such a trio failed to cooperate until a second male was added. Then, once they had decided which was dominant, all went well. Actual combat is not essential to the process; the presence of a rival male in an adjacent pen provides sufficient stimulus.

A zoo-keeper's pride in a new birth is justified. If captive animals reproduce, we must be managing them reasonably well. Often we do not know what made the difference, however. A quarter-century ago, many species had never reproduced in zoo collections, and it was then thought that most of these never would. The fact of captivity was believed to be enough to prevent either mating or conception. Our American Association of Zoological Parks and Aquariums makes annual awards to zoos for notable births. Even today, the award is sometimes made for a "first," but the list of possible "firsts" grows shorter. Many "firsts" have been scored by zoos that have made no systematic efforts to propagate the new species, and to this extent they can be called lucky. Such luck occurs, however, only in the context of good husbandry.

Success in reproduction is a natural aim, in part because it demonstrates the results of proper care. Baby animals attract visitors and make fine publicity. The past decade, however, has compelled men in the zoo world to take a harder look at results which have, in total, been less than satisfactory.

In the first place, animals have become more and more expensive. Today it costs $3,000 to $5,000 to buy an orangutan, $1,000 or more to buy a zebra. A number of antelope species are available at $10,000 or more for a trio. Replacing losses, even the number caused by normal mortality, digs deeper and deeper into zoo budgets. Unless losses are offset by births, many zoos will have to limit their collections to relatively common species they can buy for modest prices. On the other hand, a zoo that breeds successfully has surplus animals to sell or trade. A zoo-born orangutan is a considerable asset.

Money is not enough, however, to assure replacement of losses. As wild populations of many species decrease, collecting becomes more difficult and less certain. It is a commercial enterprise these days. Animals move from trappers through dealers to zoos or other customers. Most entrepreneurs prefer to deal in species they can obtain and sell with reasonable certainty rather than take the risks of speculation. More and more rare species are coming under the legal protection of governments, so that none can be taken from the wild. A number of the species now represented in zoos will vanish from collections unless captive breeding is successful.

Such success means more than an occasional birth. The white rhinoceros reproduced in captivity for the first time in 1967, in Pretoria. This is encouraging, but we have no reason to believe the present zoo population of this species, well under a hundred, will maintain itself. A very few cheetahs have been born in captivity, and until 1960 none of the infants survived more than a few weeks. A pair born in 1960 did survive, but there were no further successes for several years. About a hundred zoos have cheetahs today, but only two can boast of recent success.

The record of the National Zoo is comparatively good. In a typical recent year, 126 mammals were born, while 214 died. We had 158 reptile births, 341 deaths. Birds are generally most difficult, and here 528 deaths were offset by only 128 hatchings.

Such figures do not tell the whole story, however. To take an extreme example, we had, in that year, over 400 bird species, of which 3 accounted for almost two thirds of the hatchings. Mallard ducks are dependably prolific; we can hatch as many as we choose. Only 22 bird species appeared on the hatchings list. Obviously we were not able to replace more than a small fraction of our losses.

Of the mammals, 1 species in 5 reproduced that year. This is a better showing than among the birds—1 species in 18— the more so because mammals have longer life expectancies and lower natural reproduction rates. Even so, it is far from sufficient to replaces losses. We produce surpluses of a few species and have little or no success with others.

Lions are so prolific in captivity that it is sometimes difficult to find homes for maturing cubs. Most deer reproduce well in zoos, as do llamas and Cape buffalos. We have supplied other zoos with Dorcas gazelles, Barbary apes, black leopards, Nile and pygmy hippotamuses, and Cape hunting dogs. We have a fast-growing herd of white-bearded gnus.

Such good results are welcome, but we judge them cautiously. It sometimes happens that wild-caught animals reproduce well but their progeny do not. Some records appear to show declining fertility with succeeding captive generations. Inbreeding is also a concern, especially if a zoo beginning with a pair or trio attempts to maintain the species indefinitely without introducing new blood.

These are not our foremost concerns, at least not yet. What seems, statistically, to be declining fertility may have a simple and remediable cause, such as overcrowding. Zoos concerned about inbreeding can exchange males or females.

Such matters will receive more attention when we have solved the problems of consistent first- and second-generation propagation.

A few outstanding success stories give encouragement. Pere David's deer, for example, has lived only in captivity for centuries. Further, all of the 450 specimens living today are descended from a tiny group brought to England almost a century ago. Przewalski's horse, once believed extinct, may indeed be extinct in its native Mongolia today; but by careful husbandry, a surviving captive nucleus has been increased to 150. The wisent, Europe's bison, and our own are both thriving under close management.

Unfortunately, with notable exceptions, zoos have had their best breeding success with species not yet endangered in their native habitats. To some degree this may be attributable to the fact that naturally prolific species are least likely to be pushed toward extinction. It is also generally true that endangered species, because of their rarity, are not numerous in captivity. For example, less than ten Chilean pudus are now in zoos.

Why have zoos had such poor success? With respect to the mammals, there is no evidence demonstrating that captivity, as such, inhibits propagation. Some species do require special arrangements which zoos do not always provide, such as secluded cubbing dens for bears. We are not yet sure why we fail with cheetahs. A current theory, backed by slender but suggestive evidence, holds that breeding is inhibited when the sexes are kept together; the male should be kept apart, out of sight, smell, and hearing, until the female is in season.

While some such puzzles remain, the poor breeding record of zoos generally has a far simpler explanation. Sexual reproduction requires, at a minimum, the presence of one male and one female of breeding age. More often than not, this basic requirement is not met!

The reason why is best illustrated by a case history. A zoo —and it could be almost any zoo—once acquired a pair of oryxes. They were not readily obtainable. The male came first, so the record book shows no reproduction the first year. A female arrived the following summer. Zoos generally prefer to acquire young animals, since they adapt better. The newly arrived female was a juvenile, not sexually mature, and a year younger than the male. Mating was not observed until the third year, and the calf arriving the following spring was stillborn. In the fifth year, a healthy calf arrived. It was a male. The records therefore show this zoo kept the species for five years with only one successful birth.

When a female calf was born a year later, the young male was traded to another zoo. Now the zoo had a trio. The third calf, born before the second female reached puberty, was another male. It had to be traded before the ninth year, since both females were pregnant and the small paddock would be too crowded when the calves were born. The ninth was a banner year, however: two healthy youngsters were produced.

For three more years, this zoo did well with the species. At least one was born each year. For lack of space, they had to be sent to other zoos. They were good trading material, however, and desirable animals of other species were received in return. The basic "herd" remained the same: the original male, the original female, and their first female offspring.

They were aging now. It might have been wise to dispose of the older animals and keep selected calves. But the bull was a proven sire and both females had produced. If calves were substituted, no births could be expected for two or three years, and they might then prove to be unproductive.

And how could the older animals be disposed of? No other zoo would want aging oryxes.

So the breeding line came to an end, but the oryxes lived for several more years. The male died first, at age fourteen, but there was no point in obtaining a younger male for the over-age females. Then a female died. Now efforts were made to obtain a juvenile pair, but it was more than a year before they were delivered.

The records show that one enclosure was occupied by this oryx species for seventeen years. Propagation occurred in eight of those years, and ten of the young lived to sexual maturity. Had all of the young been kept, the zoo would have a fine herd, since third-generation births would have occurred by the tenth or eleventh year and fourth-generation births a few years later. But the young were not kept, and the species died out—not only in this zoo but in those that received the offspring, since their conditions were similar.

The case is typical. Many are even less favorable. The male of a trio may die prematurely, and the zoo may be unable to find a replacement male approximating the females in age. For two years we sought a mate for a handsome male drill. Finally we obtained a female, not yet sexually mature. Before mating could occur, the male died unexpectedly. Now we have an unmated female.

Some species are capable of reproduction by their second or third year. If we acquire a young orangutan, however, we must wait six to eight years before the first hope of breeding. A female emu may lay dozens of eggs in her lifetime, and a feline may give birth to two dozen kittens. No captive gorilla, however, has yet given birth to more than three offspring, and only two have produced this many.

Clearly the problem is one of numbers. If a single enclosure is assigned to oryxes or gorillas, and if it will accommodate only a pair or trio, births will occur in a minority of years, and the species cannot be continuously maintained. What does the record show?

According to a recent *International Zoo Yearbook,* the Regents Park Zoo in London had 762 mammals of 254 species, an average of 3 individuals per species. Its satellite zoo-in-the-country, Whipsnade, had 1,063 mammals of 80 species, an average of 13.5 individuals per species. These are radically different types of collections. London, in the old tradition, exhibits far more species. Whipsnade has a far better breeding record. Most city zoos conform more closely to the London pattern. Some of the larger zoos in the United States report these average numbers per species in their mammal collections: New York (Bronx), 3.7; San Diego, 3.4; St. Louis, 4.2; Chicago (Brookfield), 3.6; National Zoo, 3.0.

Even these averages are somewhat higher than they were a few years ago. Some of the large zoos are selecting a few of their many species and assigning to them a disproportionate amount of space. In our new hoofed stock area, we have a number of reasonably large paddocks, which now accommodate herds of fifteen or more white-bearded gnus, Dorcas gazelles, red deer, and sika deer. If we are successful in breeding some of our rarer species, such as the scimitar-horned oryx and sable antelope, we will make room for them at the expense of more common species.

Some of the younger zoos, which have not yet made heavy commitments in bricks and mortar, are specializing somewhat more, not seeking to exhibit the maximum number of species but to maintain breeding groups wherever possible. While their averages are somewhat higher, they are not impressively so, for the most part ranging between 4.0 and 5.0 individuals per species. A number of private zoos are well ahead of this. The Catskill Game Farm in New York has a tremendous mammal collection, with almost 1,500 individuals, averaging 12.8 individuals per species. Goulds Monkey Jungle, near Miami, is more specialized but maintains 12 individuals per species. Rare pheasants, such as Swinhoe's, are maintained and raised in considerable numbers by private breeders.

A trend seems to be in the making, but there are formidable obstacles to the establishment of many self-sustaining captive populations. Were endangered species the only concern, zoos might well become the means of saving a number of mammals, birds, and amphibians from extinction. Even relatively common species may disappear from zoo collections, however, if imports should be halted, and the constant threat of disease makes such an import ban all too possible.

In 1967, Great Britain was hard hit by a fast-spreading epidemic of foot-and-mouth disease. Cattle had to be slaughtered on several thousand farms to bring it under control. Not long before, Italy suffered a costly outbreak of swine fever. African horse sickness has spread to the Iberian peninsula. None of these diseases presently occurs in the United States. Foot-and-mouth disease has been stamped out nine times here, most recently in 1929. Strict quarantine procedures are maintained, but these only reduce the risk of an outbreak. They are not complete safeguards.

The quarantine period is long enough for an active infection to become manifest. Official veterinarians still worry about the possibility that a seemingly healthy animal may be a carrier of a dreaded disease. Zebras, for example, are apparently resistant to African horse sickness. Might they carry it? There is no evidence that they do or proof that they cannot.

From time to time, quarantine authorities have considered halting all importations of zoo animals, or of all ruminants or equines. They are charged with protection of the livestock industry, which is more important economically than zoo collections and hence wields greater political power. Thus far zoos have had a persuasive defense: no epidemic has been caused by zoo imports. Should an outbreak occur, or if circumstances intensified the risk, a ban would surely be imposed.

Recently a ban on equine imports was suggested. Zoos hastily took stock of their zebras, wild horses, and wild asses. Most of us had assumed that the position of Grant's zebra, at least, was rather good, since it is by far the most common zebra in our zoos. The quick census found almost two hundred of them, in forty zoos. But only twenty of these zoos had pairs of breeding age, and there were only fourteen proven sires!

We should be alarmed. Bactrian camels are neither rare nor endangered, but the number in our collections is dwindling. The camels are considered a domestic species which, under the rules, cannot be imported unless from a country known to be completely free of foot-and-mouth disease. Will American zoos someday be empty of zebras, giraffes, and gazelles?

Several years ago, a group of leading zoo directors organized the Wild Animal Propagation Trust to promote captive breeding of endangered species. The first thought was that zoos should pool their resources to establish rural breeding farms, where selected species could be raised in satisfactory numbers. Since few zoos have any resources to pool—other than some of their animals—no farms have been established, but the Trust has achieved limited results. Even a small zoo might make arrangements to keep a reasonably large herd or group of one species, or possibly several; or a traditional zoo committed primarily to exhibition could make room for a few special breeding groups. Unless such efforts were coordinated, however, several zoos might elect to work with the same species, while other species in need of such attention would be ignored. Through specialist committees, the Trust has sought a sharing of responsibilities.

Surveys of zoo collections disclosed that in a surprising number of cases, rare species were widely scattered in zoos. One zoo might have a single male, another two unmated females. The Trust sought to bring about voluntary transfers and exchanges, and has had considerable success. The Galapagos tortoise, for example, an endangered species, is so strictly protected by Ecuadorian law that very few have come into collections recently. Only three zoos—Bermuda, San Diego, and Honolulu—have provided the conditions requisite to egg production and hatching. We cannot do so, and we have agreed to send two female tortoises to Honolulu on deposit. The next step may be to establish a larger breeding site at Honolulu, and to invite all zoos with tortoises to deposit potential breeders there in a Trust-coordinated pool.

In a few cases, the Trust has been able to go farther. The situation of the orangutan is especially critical, and zoos wishing to obtain orangutans for breeding purposes have been asked to submit their requests to the Trust's Orangutan Committee. Most have been willing to do so and accept the priority order set by the committee. Further, several zoos with surplus orangutans, and several dealers, have agreed to offer their animals to zoos listed by the committee, in order of priority.

Publicizing the list of endangered species, compiled and revised frequently by the International Union for Conservation of Nature, has in itself had useful results. Most zoos are giving greater attention to these species. They are more eager to pair them, and more concerned with successful propagation. If a zoo, having had some breeding success, has more members of an endangered species than it can house, the director is likely today to give some thought to their disposition rather than advertising them and selling to the first buyer.

While zoo breeding records improve year by year, and while zoo men recognize the need to maintain larger breeding groups, performance still falls far short of the need. Populations of most species are not self-sustaining in zoo collections. While I have no data, I doubt that as many as twenty-five species have been self-sustaining in zoos for as long as twenty-five years. Most others would have vanished without frequent replenishments by wild-caught stock.

If only endangered species were considered, the need might be met even within the framework of existing zoos, with only modest rearrangements of facilities. Of all the endangered mammals, there are probably no more than fifty or sixty species suitable for long-term zoo maintenance. It would not be impossible to make provision for these. This might satisfy the conservationists, although more species will surely be added in years to come. It would not meet the needs of zoos, however. If imports of ungulates were cut off, American zoos would have to become entirely self-sufficient, in one way or another. Even if import bans are not imposed, the fast-rising prices of imported animals and the greater difficulties of obtaining desirable species are compelling arguments for self-sufficiency.

It will not be achieved without radical and drastic revisions of zoo policies. If a zoo cannot double its animal spaces, it can reduce by half the number of species on exhibition, thus doubling the facilities for those retained. Animals beyond breeding age and those unsuitable for breeding can be culled, making room for breeders. Any zoo can choose one or more species in which to specialize and give them an extra share of space and an extra share of skilled attention.

Few zoo directors are free agents, it is true. Most are accountable to parks commissions, city councils, or other political entities. Those that are publicly owned and publicly supported must satisfy their visitors. Some zoo directors feel they would face strenuous opposition if they tried to eliminate species and increase herds and flocks.

Some might, but chiefly because they or their predecessors boasted so often about having many species on display. It was justifiable at the time, but it equated great variety with excellence in the minds of people on whose support the zoos depend. In our own appropriations hearings, legislators often ask how the National Zoo stands in comparison with others. It is difficult to avoid mentioning that in numbers of species we stand among the leaders. Zoo men can redefine their aims in more modern terms and win popular acceptance of new goals. Certainly in terms of public interest a zoo with five hundred species can equal or excel a zoo with a thousand.

No zoo visitor counts the number of species he sees, and he passes most with a glance. A relatively few high-interest exhibits draw the crowds. If I were designing a zoo strictly for good showmanship, it would be built around perhaps half a dozen major attractions. These would be planned for action. They would be large, for each would be intended to draw large crowds. Some of the subsidiary exhibits would also be large, but these would hold animals such as antelopes which are lovely to look at but not continuously active.

The resourcefulness of zoo men has solved many of the problems of individual survival in captivity. Survival of species is no less a challenge.

8

The Third Objective: Action

At night, I enter the darkened Monkey House. At the sound of the door, a macaque begins leaping about his cage, battering loudly on the sheet metal. Other monkeys rouse as the lights are switched on. Jane is often with me, and we supply ourselves with monkey biscuits and go down the line. One female spider monkey greets me with chirping noises and extends her prehensile tail. She never takes a biscuit by hand. Her female cage-mate always takes biscuits by hand. One of the woolly monkeys always hangs upside down while accepting our offers.

The monkeys know us, even though we are not daily visitors. The female spider monkey greets me if I appear at the rear of a crowd on a busy day. We know them, too, well enough to know which ones will snatch at our hands instead of taking biscuits politely, and which one will snatch off our eyeglasses if we come too close.

The monkeys disturb me, and I never leave the Monkey House without an uneasy sense of guilt. I felt the same way once on a visit to an orphanage, where well-fed but lonesome children looked wistfully at me, hoping for more attention and affection than I could offer. Perhaps even an administrator should set aside several hours a week to work with these demanding primates, yet I know this is not the answer to the problem.

We are not proud of our Monkey House and look forward to its replacement. In the old style, it is lined with bar-fronted cubicles. A visitor who leans over the guardrail can hand a peanut to one of the larger monkeys, if the monkey extends his arm, but the visitor cannot reach within biting range. The original cage walls and floors were wooden. Moisture from cage-flushing rotted the wood, and some of the monkeys picked at it incessantly. Picking eventually opened holes between several of the cages through which neighbors made unofficial visits. Eventually we had to pour concrete floors and replace the side walls with sheet metal.

Technically, this is an improvement. Fewer visitors complain about odors now that the urine-soaked floorboards are gone. The new floors flush clean and drain well. The cockroach population has been greatly reduced. The changes benefit the monkeys, in that sanitation is better. I doubt that they appreciate them. While picking at wood is neither an admirable nor rewarding pastime, it was one of the few available, and we have deprived them of it.

Monkeys are active by nature, inquisitive, curious, and dextrous. Their psychological need for activity may be no greater than that of other species, but we can recognize it more readily, since their patterns of exploration and play resemble ours more closely. Some wild species are inclined to lie about except when feeding or escaping. Monkeys are among those which are active much of the time. Their natural habitats are rich in stimuli.

Caged, they have little to occupy their minds and bodies. In smaller cages, furnishings seldom include more than a dead tree with several branches, or an array of pipes to climb on, plus a shelf for resting or sleeping. Deprived of normal outlets, they respond in several ways, most of them unsatisfactory.

One sees ritualized behavior in many zoo animals, including some of the monkeys. The macaque who began leaping around on my arrival almost always leaps in precisely the same way, bouncing off the wall at the same point. Lions tend to pace back and forth, back and forth, in a monotonous pattern. Monkeys are somewhat less likely than other mammals to lapse into indolence, unless they are unwell. They are more likely to play with their feces, bite their own feet, pluck hairs from their tails, rub themselves raw against some projection, masturbate, or fight with cage-mates until one is injured or dead. Several zoo gorillas regurgitate food and eat it again.

Visitors who recognize this say we should give the monkeys something to do, and a sympathetic visitor may bring in toys for the monkeys. We have yet to find a toy which lasts more than a few minutes. If it is small enough to pass through the bars, it is quickly tossed or dropped outside the cage. Objects of wood, rubber, or other soft materials are chewed or torn to bits. Some keepers object to ropes or chains, fearing that animals might injure or hang themselves.

Certain European zoos provide their large primates with quantities of excelsior. Young gorillas and chimpanzees have a great time with it, piling it on their heads, hiding under it, rolling in it. The result is a mess for the keeper to clean up, and keepers are understandably resistant to such added work. Orangutans love to play with green branches. This also makes a mess, and it is not easy for most city zoos to obtain such branches, which are also in demand as browse.

A few of our monkeys are more happily situated, because they have each other. This is conspicuously true of a group of Barbary apes inhabiting one large outdoor cage. The group is not as large as a typical wild colony, but it has the proper age-sex distribution: a boss male, adult females, junior males, juveniles, and infants. Their complex interaction compensates, in part, for the relatively barren environment.

Monkeys have a lively interest in visitors, finding them most entertaining. Their behavior is markedly different when visitors are present. They beg for and accept food, but, as noted earlier, this is not because they are hungry or because the visitors offer items more appealing than zoo food. They ask for peanuts long after they have eaten all they can consume for the day. They show off for visitors in many ways. They recognize them, too. I saw several of our monkeys react with obvious recognition when a favorite visitor returned after a six-month absence.

This is one reason why the design for the new Monkey House worries me. Instead of bars, the planned cages have glass fronts. They will protect the monkeys from any diseases visitors may carry, some of which are far more deadly to monkeys than to humans. They will also prevent public feeding, which many zoo men would favor, believing it best to control diets. It is true that a few visitors offer food that is quite unsuitable, including some things that could prove fatal. Glass fronts will also protect monkeys from the few malicious idiots who shoot paper clips at them or who poke at them with umbrellas. But the glass fronts will isolate them from relationships with people and eliminate the bars on which they now cling and climb.

In the Small Mammal House, a little jerboa jumps back and forth, always in the same way. The red fox runs from wall to wall, placing his feet each time in the same spots. The muntjac has worn a track along one side of his pen. The river otters manage a surprising amount of gymnastic swimming in their small, shallow pool, but they soon stop, as would a virtuoso limited to a single string on a cheap violin.

It is not confinement that punishes animal psyches. It is the artificial limitations placed on their activity, their psychological development, their learning through varied experiences, the frequent testing of alertness and response. Veterinarians can observe the consequence of malnutrition and infections. They are on shaky ground in assessing the causes of languor and depression. Even if some organic condition is found, did it cause the psychological state, or vice versa?

Neurotic states can be induced in animals. A classic method in laboratories is to condition an animal to obtain a reward or avoid pain by certain actions, then change the rules confusingly. Neurotic behavior can be induced by overcrowding, by exposure to incessant bright light, by loud noises, and by other offenses to peace of mind. The behavior of many zoo animals seems neurotic.

One need not demonstrate psychopathology to assert a need, however. Beyond survival and beyond reproduction is a third challenge to captive management: that a captive animal be enabled to develop and use all of his physical and mental capabilities. To the degree that an animal is capable of learning, it should be exposed to learning experiences.

Such a goal is easily justified, even in terms of exhibition. Visitors like action. Active animals draw crowds. Occasionally our police collar juveniles who were tossing stones at animals, and I believe their explanations: They weren't trying to hurt them, just to stir them up. Interaction among cage-mates is more entertaining than the activity of a single animal. But is the goal reasonably attainable? It takes more than stirring up the animals or devising indestructible playthings.

To be sure, highly important aspects of behavior are implicit in survival and reproduction and in the rearing of young. In the wild, obtaining food, finding a mate, courtship, and rearing are primary activities. In the young, play is no less important. The conditions of the wild cannot be duplicated in zoos, even if we enlarge enclosures substantially; we cannot have stalking and killing of prey, for example. But it should not be beyond our intelligence to find analogs.

The different but not irreconcilable objectives of exhibition and animal husbandry may cause some confusion here, so it is necessary to make a point sharply. If we encourage more elaborate behavior by an animal, it would be good exhibition if this behavior resembled the actions characteristic or suggestive of the animal in the wild. If our concern is with the animal's psyche, however, such resemblance is not necessarily relevant. Our task is to devise challenges to which this species can and will respond, to offer stimuli that enrich its environment and promote activity. The resulting behavior may appear bizarre, but it is nonetheless a valid and useful response—unless, of course, we have resorted to pain and punishment, as old-fashioned animal trainers did.

Consider, for example, the behavior typical of bears in zoos. They sit, stand, wave, beg, and perform other antics when visitors offer food. Several of our regular visitors can put the bears through a complete repertory of such tricks. It is a lively performance, pleasing to visitors and bears. It offends some purists who consider it unbearlike and demeaning. It is bear behavior, nonetheless, adapted quite appropriately to the situation. The bears are challenged, and they respond rather resourcefully.

Zoo men differ sharply, even violently, on the virtues of circuslike performances in zoos. Several zoos have animal trainers, and they present shows with performing elephants, sea lions, chimpanzees, and felines. This offends some of my colleagues. They are most offended when wild animals are dressed in costumes and trained to carry umbrellas, eat at tea tables, and ride bicycles.

If we conceive our mission as presenting simulations of nature, such performances are incongruous. If we are more concerned with animal welfare and the understanding of animal behavior, training has an important and valid place. Is it better to have a listless, neurotic animal weaving back and forth in a bare cage, or one that enters into a circus act with unmistakable enjoyment?

Psychologists who study animal behavior achieve remarkable results. Their concern is with adding to human knowledge, however. Once they have completed a study, the animal subject is relegated to his barren cage again, denied further opportunity to demonstrate his talents. An animal trainer never finishes work on an act—if he's any good. If he is working with species such as sea lions, they won't let him stop "training." Many of the most impressive tricks are invented by the sea lions themselves. The trainer's skill lies in seizing upon the new behavior, rewarding it, and encouraging repetition. It's the same with my dog, Tor. The only visible limit to his repertoire is fixed by our time together and by the willingness of Jane and myself to recognize and praise his improvisations.

I prefer the Budapest string quartet playing Bach to "Yankee Doodle" blatted off-key on bulb horns. But the trainer supplies the horns and calls the tune, not the sea lions. A good trainer should be able to develop acts that please human visitors and listeners without displeasing his performers. I saw a delightful chimpanzee performance at London's children's zoo, which explained and demonstrated what apes can learn, and which included much humor. The bird performance at Busch Gardens in Tampa is impressive, in part because the birds are free-flying and in the open air.

Whether one favors or opposes such performances in zoos, they are not the answer to the psychological needs of most animals. How many animals could one trainer handle? In a zoo with five hundred species, it is unlikely that he could work with more than a dozen. Further, the psychological needs of many species do not lend themselves to circus-type acts.

This last point needs a bit of explaining. Because they seek food and avoid unpleasant stimuli, most animals can be trained to repeat simple actions, and a skillful trainer can link such simple actions together in combinations that impress the viewer. He can, indeed, make it appear that the animal has a much greater problem-solving ability than is actually the case. For example, an animal can be made to seem to read words in print. In trying to please the public this way, the trainer may neglect other and more important aspects of the animal's intelligence, which do not lend themselves to theatrics.

The chief limitation is time. Suppose that we trained every keeper in our zoo in the techniques of animal training, and that animal behaviorists could show us how to devise challenges suitable for such diverse species as anteaters, hyenas, and ostriches. Even if we doubled our keeper staff—a fiscal impossibility—the time available for training would be only ten minutes per animal per day, far too little to accomplish anything of significance.

So we return to the bear dens, where much training has resulted from people-bear interaction. Can still more be done? We might provide in each den a stout tree, which bears could climb. Before long, some visitors would have taught some bears to climb trees to obtain rewards. We might borrow ideas from experimental psychologists, who have devised many kinds of training apparatus. In a typical laboratory setup, an animal presses a lever to obtain a food reward, but the lever works only at certain times. For example, a panel may successively display geometric shapes, such as noughts and crosses, and food is dispensed only if the lever is pressed when a cross is shown. By such means psychologists discover which particular species can recognize different geometric shapes, or discriminate between colors. In a zoo, similar apparatus could be devised to achieve programmed learning. Sequences could be actuated by visitors, perhaps by dropping a coin in a slot.

We should not commit ourselves to apparatus, however, until less artificial means have been fully explored. Here, again, size of enclosure is critically important. Larger spaces permit more complex activity patterns, especially when they permit social animals to live in groups.

One of the most successful exhibits in our zoo is the prairie dog colony. Years ago, a deep hole was excavated, more than thirty feet across. It was lined with concrete walls, and the bottom covered with a layer of stones, so the prairie dogs cannot dig their way out but drainage is good. The pit was filled with sandy soil. Here the prairie dogs have built their own underground homes, which they have maintained for years. Except for the fact that we provide their food, they live much as they do in nature. The population has remained quite stable, deaths offsetting births. No burrowing owls or ferrets are associated with them in the zoo, but the wild hawks keep them alert. Pigeons fly in to compete with them for food, and there is some interplay between the species.

It should be possible to provide comparable facilities, perhaps on a smaller scale, to other ground-burrowing species, and this could be done even indoors. Several zoos, for educational and display purposes, have prepared glass-fronted cross-sections of underground burrow systems, which ground squirrels occupy and use as if they had made them.

One Saturday I spent several hours watching our herd of white-bearded gnus, consisting then of eleven adults and five calves. They occupy one of our largest paddocks. Nothing much happened. For a time, they ate. As the sun grew hot, they slowly gathered in the shade of a tree. Some of them lay down. It was obvious, however, that they were a herd, not just sixteen individuals, and that each was aware of the others. Numerous bits of minor interplay occurred, a small action by one causing small actions by one or two others.

This might seem to be a satisfactory situation, and it was, at the time. When males begin sparring, however, keepers may have to intervene. In nature, such sparring is playful, in some cases, and in others helps establish patterns of dominance; fights between males occur, but the combat is more ritualistic than mortal, and it usually ends when one male submits. The zoo paddock which is large enough most of the time may be too small to accommodate rival males, however. The junior male may be unable to retreat far enough, or to escape from his rival's view. A fight may continue beyond the point at which it normally would end, and the junior male may be killed or severely injured. For this reason, we have holding pens, so rival males can be segregated. This prevents fighting, but it also interferes with the natural evolution of herd social structure. We come closer to the natural pattern than would be possible in pens holding only pairs, but one would come still closer in a forty-acre paddock.

Jane and I were leaving the zoo one evening, after dark, when the police relayed a visitor's report that our male yak was killing a calf born the day before. We met the night keeper at the pen, and another keeper, homeward-bound, stopped to help. With flashlights, we spotted the calf lying near the front fence, which was constructed of three heavy horizontal bars. Just then the bull tossed the calf through the fence.

One of the keepers quickly grabbed the youngster. We carried him to the rear door of the shelter, which has several stalls. By quick and careful work, the keepers were able to admit the cow to the stall, shutting out the bull.

Was the bull trying to kill the calf? I don't believe it. In the wild, newborn ungulates are vulnerable to predators. Evolution has equipped them to get to their feet within minutes after birth. A giraffe born in our zoo yesterday was standing, somewhat shakily, forty-five minutes later. In the wild, these youngsters are soon able to run with the herd if danger appears. I have often seen a bull prodding a calf, urging it to its feet, urging it to use its legs, walk, run. In a confined pen, however, such instinctive urging can become too violent, so keepers prefer to isolate mothers and young.

Variety of terrain enlarges effective space, if the variety is consistent with species characteristics. One small zoo provided its otters with an oval concrete trench, about three feet wide and deep. A pond of equivalent water surface would have been little more than eight feet across. The trench provided a waterway almost seventy feet around. River otters will make use of any facility given them. In this zoo, I watched the otters swim the circuit, change direction, cut across overland. The best otter enclosures I have seen provide deeper ponds, underwater tunnels, slides, and diving places, all of which the otters use inventively.

Gibbons are the arboreal counterparts of otters. Given space and facilities, they easily outperform circus aerialists. I saw one gibbon launch himself from a flying trapeze, perform two giant swings around a horizontal bar, and soar upward, in one smooth motion, to catch the flying trapeze again. Often several gibbons enter into the play.

One zoo man built a fence around a big, well-branched tree and ran several strands of electric fence wire inside, to deter monkeys from climbing out. This was an enclosure for squirrel monkeys, and what a time they had that summer! It was only one tree, yet it offered many times more opportunity for action than the few bare branches that can be fixed inside a cage.

When I visited the late Fred Stark at San Antonio, he showed me a large island exhibit, a dry moat surrounding a rugged rockpile, where he kept Barbary sheep and gelada baboons. Both species had reproduced that spring, and they were a delight to watch. Grooming is a characteristic baboon activity. They groom each other. I was once flattered to have a baboon sit on my shoulder and groom me. In the San Antonio exhibit, the baboons also groomed the sheep as both relaxed in the sun. Young baboons played with each other and with the lambs, and they rode the backs of the adult sheep.

Such exhibits of mixed species have become increasingly popular in zoos, yet some zoo men have reservations about them. While assorted species live together in nature, with no fences between them, unexpected accidents can occur when they are confined together. An individual of one species who, in the wild, would be inclined to move away a few yards if challenged by a larger, stronger animal may feel it necessary to stand and fight if a fence is at his back. Or, in his haste to move off, he may collide with the fence.

The simplest combinations are achieved when species can share a cage but occupy different territories. Finches and quail have no conflicts, because the finches prefer the branches while quail remain on the ground. At Busch Gardens, lions share a moated island with baboons. Lions have little interest in predation when they are well-fed, and the baboons have trees to climb. I saw two of them on the ground, but screened from the lions by a clump of brush.

The lions are aware of the baboons, however, and their presence makes the baboons more alert. It is possible, of course, that they are too alert, that the lions keep them under stress. But unless experience demonstrates this, it is probable that both species benefit somewhat from the proximity, although there is no conspicuous interaction.

Symbiotic relationships offer possibilities. Several zoos now keep cattle egrets in their rhinoceros exhibits. In the wild, the egrets eat insects stirred up as the rhinos move about. While this doesn't happen in zoos, the egrets are attracted anyway, at least to the extent that they often perch on the rhinos' backs.

Different species of ungulates are often kept together, sometimes out of necessity when a zoo is crowded. If a paddock is large enough, they tend to remain in separate territories. For a time we kept a few Dorcas gazelles with our scimitar-horned oryxes. A horizontal bar across one gate kept the large oryxes out of the indoor quarters of the small gazelles.

One must be cautious and observant, however. Fights can be caused by semantic confusions when species are not accustomed to each other. In one species, for example, lowering the head may be a signal of submission, which ends a fight when males of that species conflict. In some other species, lowering the head signals attack! Among the smaller mammals, some seek and welcome body contact. They like to snuggle. Such species would not mix well with others that shun such contact.

Is anything to be gained by combining species that appear

to ignore each other? I recall a morning at Blacktail Pond, near Jackson, Wyoming. The beavers were active, cutting green branches and towing them back to their lodges. A moose appeared on the far shore, wading in the shallows to feed. Young ducklings swam after their mother, scattering suddenly when a beaver surfaced close by. A kingfisher made forays from a nearby perch. A splash, marked by spreading ripples, marked the strike of a fish. Was the moose aware of the great blue heron fishing nearby? Had the beavers any interest in the ducklings? Evidence is lacking, yet I believe such associations enrich their total living experience—as they enrich ours.

A red squirrel darts near a browsing deer. The deer lifts his head, snorts, and resumes grazing. A coyote prowls through the tall grass, sensing and interpreting countless odors. When my dog and I take a weekend walk in the woods, he is fascinated and excited by the scents he never encounters in the city. Does the soaring hawk see only his prey, far below? Do the delicate ears of the kit fox respond only to sounds of danger?

Still, we must guard against applying our own tests of what seems natural. A number of zoos have built large outdoor flight cages which visitors can enter. In small cages, birds can do little more than hop from branch to branch with a single wingbeat. In these big cages, they can make extended flights, circling high above the heads of visitors. Such cages are heavily planted with trees and shrubs, and they usually have ponds and waterfalls. Thus there is great variety of terrain, an abundance of cover. Feeding points can be widely scattered. It is a delightful experience to walk among the birds, with no intervening wires or glass, and the illusion of nature is heightened by the fact that not all of the birds are immediately visible. The longer one looks, the more one sees.

The management of such a large cage demands high skill. Which species can be kept together in this way, and how many of them? Birds are territorial, sometimes aggressively so. The tiny hummingbirds can be fierce toward their own kind, so much so that two pairs of a species may be all a large cage can hold. Male pheasants may live together harmoniously if no females are present. Add a female, and cage capacity, for that species, may be reduced to a single pair. Some birds are aggressive toward other species, although they are not predators, harassing them, driving them from every perch on which they light.

One bird begins to build a nest, gathering twigs. Another steals the twigs as fast as they are put in place. If a nest is built and eggs are laid, they may be broken or eaten by a nest robber. The curator of birds has no guidebook to tell him which species are incompatible. He learns by close observation. He must also know which species can withstand the extremes of climate in the area, since recapturing birds in such a huge cage is next to impossible.

Mixing species is not likely to be successful in zoo enclosures which are really too small for a single species. In designing a new zoo or a new enclosure, however, the idea is well worth considering. It is far less expensive to build one large enclosure than to build five one-fifth as large. If species are kept together whose territorial requirements do not conflict, each will have more real space than could otherwise be provided, the sum of the parts exceeding the whole.

Even if species are not to be mixed, the behavioral characteristics of each should be carefully considered before any new cage or pen is designed. Even today, zoo architects are much inclined to follow the old museum traditions, confining their modern touches to roof lines and facades. A small mammal house or feline house is likely to be arranged as a series of cages, perhaps in two or three sizes but otherwise identical. The different sizes are intended to accommodate species of different sizes. Only after these boxes have been built can zoo men attempt to compensate for their inadequacies.

There is no necessary relationship between the body size of an animal and the size of the enclosure it should have. The bushbaby is quite small, for example, but it is capable of wonderfully graceful long leaps. Nor should cage shapes be all the same. For terrestrial animals, vertical height has little significance. For those that climb, height adds living space.

I have just been reading a passionate book, *Man and Monkey*, by Leonard Williams.* On the Cornish coast he has established a colony of South American woolly monkeys. The facilities include heated indoor shelters, outdoor pens and shelters, a tall column surmounted by a platform, and rope bridges to nearby trees, with passageways connecting the elements. He employs two full-time keepers and devotes much of his own time to the monkeys. Further, the monkeys, on invitation, associate with other members of the Williams household, including the Irish wolfhound.

Williams' chief hate is the pet trade, with good reason. For every woolly monkey brought to market, several dead are left behind, and few of those sold live long. He is almost as bitter about zoos. No zoo, in his opinion, provides woolly monkeys with facilities equal to his, nor does any care for them as well.

He is right. While many zoos provide superior facilities for one or two monkey species, none have offered twenty or thirty species the elaborate arrangements Williams has built. Nor can any zoo assign two or three men to the care of each species. More often one finds ten men caring for more than

* J. B. Lippincott Company, Philadelphia, 1968.

a hundred species, none of which have the varied challenges and stimulations the woollies enjoy at Cornwall.

But zoos are not a lost cause. Far from it. I had lunch with three of our keepers today, just listening. They are as passionate as Williams, and no less devoted to their animals. Nothing would delight them more than having time to do what he is doing. There is a ferment. Zoos are changing, perhaps not as rapidly as one would wish, but changing. It was no mean achievement to solve the problems of survival, and much has been learned and applied in the fostering of reproduction. Williams is himself a former zoo-keeper. Men like him and like the keepers I lunched with will shape tomorrow's zoos.

9

Are They Like Us?

Reviewers of books about animals keep a handy epithet loaded and ready to be fired: anthropomorphism. The writer guilty of this sin is dismissed as hopelessly unscientific. Some trigger-happy reviewers even blast away at innocent tales for little children, whose animal caricatures are intended to be no more realistic than Peter Pan or Joe Palooka. Their favorite targets, however, are fair game: the sentimentalists whose animal world is a Garden of Eden, where no wolves tear at the flanks of ailing deer, and baby animals appear as if by magic.

Some critics stalk their game through the pages of popular books by competent naturalists. In describing the life history of a coyote, for example, a writer may choose a prototype, call him "Pablo," and recount his adventures from puppyhood onward. Pablo has more experiences than ever befell one real coyote, but each is within the scope of coyotehood.

The writer's problem is that in conventional literature Pablo must be a hero. If he moves about like an automaton, the reader will become bored. Readers want to know why Pablo does what he does, how he feels when hungry or in danger, and how things seem to him generally. A few writers try to escape the sin of anthropomorphism by depicting animals as if they were mental retardates—"Pablo dimly sensed that . . ." "Driven by a mysterious inner urging . . ." Others play the game skillfully, satisfying readers, making critics read some sentences twice, but never presenting a good target.

The horror of anthropomorphism can be overdone. American Indians and frontiersmen were incorrigibly anthropmorphic in their interpretations of animal behavior, but their conclusions met a scientific test: ability to predict. They found game where they expected to find it, hunted it successfully, and succeeded with traps and snares. While they ascribed human qualities to animals, they recognized that other species have senses differing from ours. Some have superior vision, others keener hearing or sense of smell.

We cannot know, directly, how things seem to other species. Nor do we know by actual experience how they seem to other humans. Among ourselves, we are sure we are on common ground because we can communicate and thus repeatedly test correspondence of perceptions and responses. Much of our communication is not verbal. We interpret each other's smiles, frowns, nods, and other deliberate signals, as well as countless involuntary signs, such as tensing the shoulder muscles.

My Labrador cannot speak to me in words, but he can communicate. No one could misinterpret his leaping prance when I put on my coat and take down his lead, his invitations to play, or his apologetic cringe when he has misbehaved. He can tell us when he needs water, ask us to retrieve his ball from under the couch, or object to being left behind. He understands and responds to an even larger assortment of messages from us, by no means limited to the formal commands which entered into his training.

It would be surprising if at least some other species did

not have reactions and responses resembling our own. We share with other mammals a common if remote ancestry, as well as similar biological processes. Not very long ago we shared their habitats, coping with comparable needs for food and shelter, defense and flight. Other species have different social and family organizations, but there is great diversity in this respect among human tribes.

Indians and frontiersmen could interpret animal behavior because of their intimate association. But who could misinterpret the signs of threat, despite their great variety: hissing, spitting, growling, crouching, bristling, tooth-baring, pawing, head-lowering, wing-brandishing, and so on?

It is easiest to grasp the meaning of animal expressions, gestures, and sounds when they occur in relationship to us. Indeed, perhaps the most significant step in interspecies communication is mutual recognition. Zoo-keepers give names to many of their charges. Many animals recognize not only individual keepers but people who visit them less often. Recognition may be expressed by signs of hostility or fear, if the visitor has offended the animal in the past, or by joyous greetings.

Species show recognition in different ways. Our elderly shoebill clattered his bill when a friend approached. A male Dorcas gazelle makes an odd growling noise. A lion rubs sensually against the cage bars. Such recognitions and relationships are not peculiar to zoos. Humans living in wild habitats often cultivate relationships with resident species. Wild birds and mammals often learn to recognize and respond to park rangers or other frequent visitors in the woods.

Anthropomorphism offends science chiefly when human value judgments are imposed on animal behavior, so that a species is characterized as "cruel," "cowardly," or "noble." Yet scientists themselves are often guilty of anthropomorphism in studies of animal behavior, by using human psychology as a frame of reference or by generalizing from data based on studies of a single species. At times this verges on hypocrisy or outright dishonesty. Recently, for example, a psychologist read a paper before a gathering of social scientists and administrators. He reported a series of laboratory experiments with rats, which yielded some interesting data. He did not assert that his findings were valid for the human species. Yet he was well aware that his audience had no interest in rat behavior. They had convened to discuss programs benefiting disadvantaged youths. The paper was relevant and appropriate only if they believed the psychologist was saying what he did not openly declare: that people behave as his laboratory rats did.

Some time ago I reviewed a book about behavioral research, an anthology of landmark papers which, according to the preface, summarizes the main line of psychological investigations. Almost without exception, the authors had conducted their research in laboratories, the great majority of them with rats and mice. Yet the editor's preface assumed that the findings were valid for the entire animal kingdom, including man!

Is the behavior of laboratory rodents, descended from many captive generations, typical even of their own species in the wild? Through many successive generations of controlled breeding, they have been adapted to close confinement in sterile boxes, deprived even of social interplay. It was once assumed that all species other than man behave "instinctively," that they are equipped at birth with all of the behavioral skills and responses manifested in life. Much animal behavior is built in. The ovenbird needs no instruction to build its characteristic nest, nor do bees need teaching in the engineering of honeycombs. A kitten taken from its mother and hand-raised will respond to a dangling spool as other kittens do.

A large share of animal behavior must be learned, however, although the capacity to learn is inherited and species differ in their aptitudes. Young animals learn from their parents, from others of their species, and from experience. This can be demonstrated in two ways in zoos or other captive situations. The hand-raised animal, isolated from others, fails to develop behavior they exhibit. On the other hand, the captive animal can be taught responses never seen in the wild, thus showing its ability to learn.

A male gorilla raised in captivity responds to the sex urge, but some such males haven't known the appropriate response. If the female attracting him was also raised in the absence of elders, the two may have quite a problem. Among gorillas, a social species, such behavior as mating and maternal care are learned; the young are raised in the group and learn by observation. A number of captive-raised gorillas have delivered young and, lacking the educative experience, didn't know how to respond. Some were terrified at the appearance of their infants. One held the baby to her breast—upside down. I watched our gorilla for several hours after her third delivery. We hoped she would care for this baby, though she had not nursed the first two. She held it for a time, then laid the newborn on the floor and ignored it. Again she picked it up, carried it about, then again placed it on the floor. In the end, we had to take the baby and hand-raise it.

Among the felines, such as the lions, mating and maternal care seem to be built-in behavior. Lions raised alone react appropriately when put together. But the story of Elsa, the lioness of *Born Free,* tells of the difficulty in releasing a captive-reared predator who had never learned to kill.

Tor, our Labrador, came to us at about eighteen months

of age, and we know nothing of his background. As we took
our morning run one day, near our suburban home, wild
geese flew overhead, honking. Tor froze, pointed, quivered.
Here I can only speculate. Was he trained to hunt before we
acquired him? A few days later he flushed a rabbit on the
school grounds and raced off in pursuit, behavior no trainer
would approve.

Deer do not chase rabbits, and it would be extraordinarily
difficult to teach a deer to do so, or to teach a porcupine to
point at honking geese. Bears learn how to hold up passing
automobiles, seeking food rewards—and I once met a tribe
of donkeys that had mastered the same art, first blocking
the road, then thrusting their heads through open car windows—but they do not construct lodges as beavers do. Behavioral differences among the species are dictated by physical
characteristics and sensory apparatus, and also by built-in
aptitudes.

Can it be called "intelligence"? A special kind of anthropomorphism has handicapped investigations of animal intelligence: the assumption that human intelligence provides an
appropriate standard for measurement. Many studies are designed to determine how other species compare with us. We
come out quite well. No other animals can beat us at our own
game.

More thoughtful investigators question the meaning of the
word "intelligence." An impressive group of behaviorists has
broken away from the rat-mouse school, calling themselves
"ethologists" to emphasize the distinction from conventional
animal psychology. Ethologists are concerned with systematic and imaginative studies of species behavior, working in
natural habitats as much as possible. They are more interested in the differences among species than in similarities,

though studies of differences often converge in more illuminating generalizations.

"Dominance" and "pecking order" are familiar terms; and dominance behavior has been noted in many species, from elephants to barnyard fowl. It is readily observed that many species, including various ungulates, primates, and canines, live in groups, that the groups have social structures, and that the typical social structure is headed by a dominant male who has a following of females and juveniles. Subordinate males keep a respectful distance.

This arrangement suggests a sexual monopoly, which it is in certain species. The herd bull mates with the eligible females; junior males may be excluded and form a bachelor herd. Thus each generation is sired by the most vigorous male. When he flags, he is challenged and displaced.

But dominance does not always take this form. At Chicago's Brookfield Zoo, a wolf pack has been under close observation for ten years. Well-defined dominance patterns appear in both sexes, and a high-ranking female is dominant over junior males. Courtship and mating are strongly influenced by dominance, but there is no monopoly. Indeed, while the dominant male is courted by many of the females, he is less inclined to mate than are the lesser adult males. When he does mate, it may be with a peripheral female who is not courted by the subordinate males.

Dominance has significance far broader than mate selection. It maintains a coherent social structure, leadership in attack and defense, and an educative process. The patterns of behavior observed at Brookfield—far more complex than this summary suggests—also revealed a population-regulating mechanism. One may question whether behavior observed in a captive pack, especially a pack of predators, closely approximates behavior in the wild. The wolf enclosure is more "natural" than a laboratory cage, since a pack can be kept together, with sufficient space to act out at least a part of normal activities. It would be impossible to observe wild wolves so closely, day by day, over an extended period.

Field observation is difficult, especially when the subjects are small, or when they range widely, inhabit wooded, brushy, or rugged terrain, or conduct much of their activity after dark. It is easiest to study large animals on open plains by daylight. Further, in our country a disproportionate amount of field work is conducted during the summer months, a circumstance partly attributable to teaching schedules. In a case such as the wolves, about the best that can be done is to test correspondence. If most of the fragments of wild behavior observed fit neatly into the comprehensive model built up by captive observation, one can have considerable confidence in the model.

However intelligence is defined, certain primary factors are involved: the kind, quantity, and quality of information the organism gathers from its environment; the sophistication with which this data is processed; how much of it is stored in memory; and the results. Beyond this are somewhat murkier areas such as ability to learn, complexity of communication, and transmission of "knowledge" from generation to generation.

Human investigators are severely handicapped in studying the information-gathering of other species, because we have no counterparts for many of their faculties. Birds of prey perceive small objects at great distances; we find it difficult even to comprehend such acuity. Bats have superb echo-locating ability. Some reptiles detect and interpret infrared radiation. Certain fish have light-sensitive skin cells. Many animals obtain information in ways not yet identified.

An investigator may suspect that a species has a certain

capability. The physiologists may have provided a clue by describing a puzzling organ or adaptation. With such a clue, the investigator may be able to extend his own sensory abilities by using special apparatus. It was observed, for example, that certain Madagascan tenrecs, small hedgehog-like creatures, have specialized quill patches that vibrate at times. By electronic means, the sound generated was picked up, amplified, and translated into a visible recording. This showed that the quills were producing a sound signal of high frequency, well above the range audible to humans. Were the sounds audible to other tenrecs? Was information communicated? To demonstrate this, it was necessary to observe that one tenrec responded, by some typical action, when another produced the signal. The finding was confirmed when the recorded sound, played back, produced this same behavior. Working with another tenrec species, investigators made a remarkable discovery: the adaptation that serves one as a communications method is used by a related species as a means of echo-location!

How do migratory birds navigate over long distances? Many hypotheses have been advanced. By landmarks? They often fly at night, when the earth is obscured by darkness, clouds, and fog. By the moon or stars? They fly on moonless nights, under thick overcasts. Investigators have tested other hypotheses, including sensing of the earth's magnetic field and the detection of radiation outside the visible spectrum.

Painstakingly, laboriously, scientists seek to discover the kind of data gathered by quivering antennae, darting tongues, and independently moving eyes. What attracts sharks to a bleeding fish? Does scent-marking announce only "Someone was here"? Is the scent as recognizable as a face? Or is even more information conveyed? The dance of the honeybee was translated by brilliant and devoted research.

Is this the only case where apparently random movements spell out a coherent message?

I met my first marmot by chance, in South Dakota, as I lay on my belly photographing wildflowers. I saw him some distance away and crawled forward slowly to come within camera range. Then he vanished. Disappointed, I stood up. At once came a chorus of whistles, and a dozen marmots ducked into burrows. To my surprise, I saw that one remained, out in the open, sitting on a rock. To my greater surprise, he stood fast, whistling unhappily, as I moved closer and closer, snapping picture after picture, until I was no more than ten feet away.

The same pattern was repeated in later encounters with marmots. An obvious conclusion is that the whistle is an alarm signal. But is that all? A serious investigator would not be satisfied until he had tested other possibilities. Does the whistle vary in length, pitch, pulse, or other dimension, depending on circumstances? Is "Alarm!" the only word in this language? Are there frequencies or overtones we cannot hear? How is the one sentry chosen?

An animal mother utters a certain sound. At once her brood scatters. An investigator who has heard the sound and witnessed the scattering tentatively decides that this sound means "Get lost, kids!" His belief is reinforced by repeated observations of the same sequence. He may then test it by recording the sound and playing it back. If the playback has the same effect, he has confirmation.

Investigators are discovering more and more ways in which animals communicate. Most such research suffers from a severe limitation, however: To interpret a signal, or even to be sure it is a signal, the investigators must link it to some responding action. Even in seemingly conspicuous cases this may not be easy. The white flag of the Virginia deer is lifted in flight. Does the flag signal "Danger!" to other deer? Or is its chief function to provide a visible patch to deer that are following in partial darkness?

We cannot assume that all animal communication is elementary, with immediate action responses. Suppose that two people are sitting and talking with a dog at their feet. The dog is sensitive to certain of their inflections, but—if his responses are indicative—most of the conversation conveys no meaning to him. We cannot exclude the possibility that there are forms of discourse among other species beyond those that cause immediate, observable reactions.

This is not to suggest that other species have languages as elaborate as our own. My point is that we may be unable to detect and decode their communications. They may occur in forms, such as odors, which we cannot interpret. Further, most scientific experiments are made in laboratories. A wild animal in a laboratory cage is likely to be under stress, and its responses may be suppressed or distorted. Indeed, in establishing the conditions of confinement, the investigator may, unwittingly, have excluded some factor which is essential to the process under study.

A favorite technique of investigators is conditioning an animal to press a lever to obtain a food reward. Once this is accomplished, the animal can tell the experimenter something he cannot discover by direct means. For example, the animal may be conditioned to press the lever when it hears a musical tone. Thereafter, the experimenter will vary the pitch, thus testing the ability of the animal to hear high and low frequencies. Similar methods can be used to test memory.

In other experimental situations, animals are confronted by problems they must solve to obtain food. In all such experiments, however, it is assumed that the hunger drive is imperative. This can be reasonably established by withholding food for a time before the experiments are conducted, but it is not quite so reliable as it might seem. One series of experiments was designed to compare the problem-solving abilities of several species, including the domestic cat. The cat scored lowest. Anyone who has kept cats will hoot this one down. Cats are notoriously self-possessed and independent, choosing their own times to act. Another comparative series used raisins as the food reward. I wondered whether the results measured intelligence, or whether they simply showed that one species likes raisins more than the others do!

We have owned three dogs since we were married. The first, a big cocker spaniel, was intelligent but independent. He learned what he chose to learn. The next, a dachshund, was affectionate but a hopeless pupil. Tor is a genius by comparison. Keepers recognize equally wide variations among members of the same species in zoos. Since experimenters are usually limited to a few individuals, how sound are their conclusions? On my desk is a paper reporting experiments with seven gorillas, eight chimpanzees, and five orangutans, "a very large group when compared with previous studies."

All this is said not to denigrate behavioral research but to note the great difficulties under which experimenters work. Animals are usually tested in settings alien to their natural surroundings and are challenged in artificial ways. If a gorilla or orangutan is available to an experimenter, one statement about it can be made with virtual certainty: It was not wild-born and raised by its mother. Almost all wild-caught great apes are taken as infants. How severely have the experimental subjects been handicapped by subsequent years in confinement?

Physical scientists, studying inanimate objects, have long been aware that their presence and actions affect the phenomena they observe. The human presence cannot help but influence animal behavior. We are impressed by the dog's intelligence because we live with dogs, and we learn most about their behavior not in laboratory settings but in the course of unstructured relationships with dogs.

Tor stands by the hall closet and points to the shelf, where his lead is kept. He wants to go for a run. We did not teach him that the lead is kept on the shelf, nor did we teach him to point. For that matter, we do not use the lead, except in occasional refresher training, but we always carry it, and it symbolizes a run. He points to the roof of the garden shed, where someone has left his ball.

He was trained to stay out of the dining room while we are eating. Soon we yielded to his passionate fondness for cookies and, at dessert time, allowed him to join us for a few morsels. Now he has learned to interpret events around the table. At dessert time he quietly appears, expectantly, before any cookies are produced.

A collie who lives half a block away is confined by day but allowed to run free each evening. Soon after we moved to this neighborhood, Tor and I met the collie on our bedtime run. Tor was enthusiastic until I petted the collie, then showed jealousy by excessive playfulness, by thrusting between the collie and me, and by biting playfully at the collie's legs. Now the collie waits for us each evening, whether we appear at nine or at midnight; and he was waiting on the evening I returned after a five-week absence. Tor is no longer openly jealous. The collie makes the rounds with us back to our doorstep, then quietly goes home.

Our cat, Shan, is Tor's companion while Jane and I are away at our offices. Shan took the initiative in a relationship with the noisy, excitable beagle who lives across the fence. Once Shan understood that the fence was a safe barrier, she teased the beagle at close range, driving him into a fury of

barking. The next steps occurred so gradually that we were
not aware of them, until we saw Shan across the fence, chas-
ing the beagle. As we watched, the roles reversed, and the
beagle chased Shan. It was all in fun, and they were soon
sparring and wrestling together. Having tamed the beagle,
Shan is now working on the Scottie who lives on the opposite side.

When a relationship such as this develops between man
and dog, or between dog and cat, it is necessarily based upon
establishment of communication, mutually understood signals. Such interspecies communication is common in the
wild, even within the limits we can see. The vocabulary is
severely limited. I often fail in my communications with Tor,
and there are times when he is obviously dissatisfied at my
inability to understand.

We will never discuss philosophy together. If he has an
opinion of my intelligence, it is based on the tiny fragment
of my behavior which relates to him. While I rate him high
among dogs, and while I see many signs of sensing and interpreting which I cannot understand, I do not believe the
unknown regions of dog mentality are large.

It would seem logical to base gross estimates of animal intelligence on the complexity of their natural behavior patterns. Except among juveniles, with whom "play" is evidently
a learning process, these patterns generally seem stereotyped
and restricted to such survival requirements as food-finding,
defense, courtship, mating, maternal care, and so on. While
some animals can obtain information from their senses which
we cannot from ours, it seems to be used in highly specialized
and functional ways, such as pathfinding or prey-catching.

It is not strictly true that one generation of a species cannot transmit new knowledge to the next generation. As in
the case of the bears in national parks, behavior may change

over successive generations in response to environmental changes. But this merely substitutes one set of stereotypes for another. Thus I am not persuaded that turkeys are any brighter than they seem, or that tortoises think great thoughts.

But then we come to the bottle-nosed dolphin. The dolphin was credited with extraordinary intelligence more than 2500 years ago, and dolphin legends have persisted ever since. They have been credited with saving drowning humans, guiding ships through narrow channels, and other feats. Aristotle wrote an excellent account, summarizing what was then known or believed about them.

The dolphin must indeed be remarkable to have attracted such attention, since it is not easily observed. Naturalists can enter the habitats of elephants and gorillas to study them at length, but the dolphin habitat is inaccessible. Even a scuba diver can expect only glimpses. Substantial discoveries began only when dolphins were brought into captivity. John C. Lilly, principal contemporary student of dolphins, described his feelings when it seemed that communication between men and dolphins was taking form: *

The feeling of weirdness came on us as the sounds of this small whale seemed more and more to be forming words in our own language. We felt we were in the presence of Something, or Someone, who was on the other side of a transparent barrier which up to this point we hadn't even seen. The dim outlines of Someone began to appear. We began to look at this whale's body with newly opened eyes and began to think in terms of its possible "mental processes," rather than in terms of the classical view of a conditionable, instinctually functioning "animal."

Dolphins can be kept in captivity, though not as readily

* John C. Lilly, "Productive and Creative Research with Man and Dolphin," *Archives of General Psychiatry*, 1963.

as monkeys or antelopes. Antelope behavior can be studied
in paddocks of ten or hundreds of acres; but even were a
dolphin enclosure of such size made, as by placing a net
across an estuary, no human vantage point would permit full
observation of the underwater arena. Studies of dolphins in
close confinement are disclosing that they have remarkable
intelligence, the limits of which are not yet known. The
dolphin's brain is larger than man's and as complex in its
circuitry. Dolphins' responses in test situations are noteworthy not merely because they make high scores but because
they frequently show initiative, even what we consider a
sense of humor. They appear to mimic human speech.

A question troubles me. What do dolphins do with their
intellect? So far as we know, they swim about, eat fish, defend
themselves, maintain social groupings, propagate, rear young
—essentially what small-brained animals do. They have been
credited with high intelligence because of their responses to
situations most dolphins never encounter. They have built
no cities, produced no artifacts or literature. Yet it seems
most improbable that so complex a brain could have evolved
without use. Could evolution have produced an intellectual
mechanism passed on from generation to generation which
functions only on those rare occasions when a dolphin meets
a man in provocative circumstances?

Do they know something we don't? Is is conceivable that
"intelligence" has meanings and dimensions quite alien to
any we comprehend? I am human enough to speculate, skeptical enough to reserve belief until solid evidence appears.
As yet, there is not the slightest evidence that we share the
earth with Einsteins and da Vincis wearing fur and feathers.
Not even wild speculation would seriously call into question
our confidence in man's uniqueness. Nonetheless, fascinating
discoveries remain ahead.

Many of them will be made in zoos, on game ranches, and in other settings intermediate between laboratory and wilderness. If the desired observations and test situations cannot be arranged in the jungle or the swamps, the best alternative is one that simulates the natural setting as closely as possible, consistent with the requirements of the experiment. The ethologist who can alternate between field studies and zoo experiments has unrivaled opportunities.

Zoos have every reason to promote and support such behavioral research, out of sheer self-interest if not devotion to pure science. From such studies, we can learn far more about animal management. Why, for example, have shoebills not reproduced in captivity? Those now in collections were taken from their habitat soon after hatching and hand-raised. Thus they were "imprinted" on humans, relating to our species rather than their own. Aware of this, scientists at the Patuxent Wildlife Research Center guarded against such imprinting when they undertook to hatch and rear whooping cranes. The nestlings were not handled, nor even allowed to see humans.

Better understanding of animal ways can also suggest ways to save endangered species, possibly by altering their behavior. By skillful manipulation of circumstances, a migratory bird species may be induced to become a year-around resident of a safe refuge. Sea turtles may be adapted to return to a safe beach for egg-laying, rather than to a beach traditionally used which has become unfit or unsafe. An antelope species may be introduced to an alien habitat. A predatory species may be so managed that it will remain within the limits of a public park, not preying upon farmers' animals outside.

While in South America in 1968, I talked with men who are attempting to develop national parks. In the United

States we are worried about the damage to our parks caused by the ever-mounting visitor load and consequent demands for more and more highways, camping grounds, service stations, and other tourist facilities. In South America, I was told, they cannot hope to obtain the needed support for park management and protection until the parks have a public constituency. They must attract more tourists.

"But visitors rarely see animals!" several park men complained. "We don't have the zebras and giraffes people see in the African parks, or the elk and bison you have in Yellowstone."

But most of the park areas have a considerable variety of birds, mammals, and reptiles. Their habits and the nature of the habitat make it difficult for casual visitors to see them. I suggested that this could be changed. If a suitable area were chosen around a visitor center in a park, its ecology could be manipulated so that a satisfying variety of animals could be seen. This would be a new and exciting kind of zoo, and one that would be a challenge to planners and managers. The animals would be conditioned by circumstances, managed but not confined.

Still another product of behavioral research is its extension of our own perceptions. We know that many species perceive the world in ways we cannot. If we can, by electronic or other means, detect and analyze the stimuli which they sense and interpret, these environmental dimensions may not remain beyond our grasp.

Finally, the study of other animals underlies much of our self-knowledge, and in recent years behavioral studies have moved closer to illuminating our characteristic weaknesses and vulnerabilities. We are unique in many ways, not only in our language and literature and artifacts, and our ability to innovate. We are unique among the social animals in that our social orders are unstable, often rebelled against, often overthrown. We are unique in our bellicosity, devoting a huge proportion of our capabilities and resources to the means of self-destruction. We are uniquely prolific, multiplying our population despite the restraints that keep other species in rough balance with available support resources. Perhaps all too finally, we are unique in our ability to destroy our own habitat.

Why are we the only species which practices self-destruction so consistently, in warfare, in violent crime, and in numerous other ways? Ethologists studying aggression in other species have suggested reasons, though not yet remedies.

10

Zebras in Texas

I stood on a hill in northern Mexico, looking out through a thin, golden haze. Near Nuevo Laredo the land is gently rolling, broken here and there by upthrust rock masses. It is moderately arid, chiefly grass-covered, except where overgrazing has replaced grasses with shrubs and cacti, but with many groves of trees in spots where moisture gathers. The air was still on this morning, and no birds sang. A slight motion caught my eye. A hundred yards away, two giraffes were browsing on a treetop.

Hunters speak of buck fever. I have felt the same surge of excitement when hunting with my cameras. This was a different kind of thrill. The scene was utterly peaceful, the giraffes at ease, moving unhurriedly as they fed. My long lenses were useless at this range, because of the haze, but I had no impulse to move closer and risk disturbing the tall ones.

Later, I climbed back into the rear of a pickup truck and braced myself against its steel stakes as we bounced over rough ground. Nilgais, fallow deer, and red deer retreated as we approached. Axis deer raised their heads to stare. Herds of zebras, gnus, and blackbucks, as well as a few leaping springbok, raced across a grassy plain. We saw occasional dromedaries, elands, oryxes, yaks, Cape buffalo, pronghorns, ibexes, white elk, sambars, and mule deer. A male ostrich blocked our way, performing a lurching, antic dance as if courting the truck. I saw African crowned cranes, rheas, chukar partridges, vulturine guinea fowl, and other exotic birds, all free.

These animals, most of them alien to our continent, live on a private ranch owned by a wealthy Mexican industrialist. About fifty species have been introduced on several thousand acres bounded by an eight-foot fence. The ranch is isolated. The gates are locked, and there is no gatekeeper. No visitors are received, except guests. The owner himself seldom visits the ranch, and the resident caretaker has no direct responsibility for the animals.

There are no barns, no artificial shelters. Food is not provided. No one, indeed, knows how many exotic animals are on the ranch, since births and deaths occur, and the preserve is large and rugged. They are on their own, as their ancestors were in Africa and Asia.

It was thrilling to see them, exhilarating to realize that such species survive and reproduce here in near-freedom. To a careful zoo man, however, the experiment seems bold to the point of recklessness. Animals were bought, trucked to the ranch, and released. Little attempt was made to match species to habitat, or to predict how the species would interact. Indeed, a great opportunity was lost because no scientists were present to observe how each species behaved when first released and over the next few weeks.

The rancher took risks, and he had had losses. While needless losses are deplorable, the experiment demonstrates that his concept has merit. Exotic species can be translocated. Perhaps even more significant, the ranch was stocked with zoo-born animals, not with animals from wild habitats. Until they came to the ranch, they had been fed on hay and grain and feed pellets. They had been kept in small paddocks with shelters, and few of them had ever encountered a member of another species.

A female beisa oryx, for example, had been raised by her mother in a zoo. She had been a favorite of her keepers, who petted her daily. The only home she had ever known was a zoo cage with a small outdoor pen. In the winter following her birth she was never allowed outside. She was accustomed to people and to the zoo odors and noises. Passing trucks and motor scooters and noisy lawnmowers did not disturb her—not even the welders who came one day to repair a fence post. Hay was placed in the rack each morning, pellets in a wooden trough. She had never had a drink except from the automatic waterer.

Then, one day, she was coaxed into a crate. The jouncing of the truck, the highway noises, and many of the odors were unfamiliar. Now and then, when the truck stopped, a friendly human would speak to her, pet her through the slats, and supply more water and hay. Nonetheless, it must have been a frightening journey.

Then came a final stop and the crate was lifted from the truck. The slide was opened, and the oryx stepped out into the brilliant sun. The truck went away. She stood alone in an utterly strange world. Nothing was familiar: the turf under foot, the odors, the absence of city noises. There was no pen, no shelter, no hay rack, no water trough. The oryx was tense, uneasy, her actions halting and uncertain. She was startled by a grasshopper that whirred up from between her front feet.

Night came, and there was no stall in which to sleep. Dark shadows passed her in the night, trailing unfamiliar scents, and she remained awake and alert. Next morning, hungry, the oryx nibbled on the dry grass and found it good. Wandering aimlessly, she found a shallow lake and drank from it. During the morning she encountered a herd of zebras and another of blackbucks, but they ignored her and she did not run from them. The most alarming moment came when a strange creature, a brindled gnu, turned and charged at her, apparently attacking, but he wheeled and tossed his head at the last moment, then departed.

At some time in the next few days she found members of her own race. I have yet to witness such a first encounter, nor have I talked with anyone who has seen it occur. One can only speculate about the nature of recognition, the part played by shape, marking and coloration, pattern of movement, odor, or other signs. When next seen, however, the oryx was in the company of others. They had chosen a part of the ranch as their territory. Their daily movements had taken on a pattern.

Private game parks have existed for centuries. Once they were pleasure grounds for kings and emperors, where commoners were forbidden to hunt. Many held only native game animals, but exotic species were occasionally introduced. In the United States, the first large private collection of exotics was assembled by William Randolph Hearst at San Simeon, in California. Most of them have been removed now, but a few were never captured, and descendants of some escaped animals roam the nearby hills.

Texas game ranching originated in the 1930's. One version of the story is that the late Dr. William Mann, then Director of the National Zoo, while visiting a Texas industrialist commented that his ranch resembled parts of East Africa. The idea fascinated his host, who soon bought a number of exotic animals from zoos. A few species thrived, notably the blackbuck from India. This ranch has changed hands several times since, but exotic species are still maintained.

The observation attributed to Dr. Mann was perceptive, though the account does not say whether he knew the ecological history of southeast Texas. Like much of Africa's grazing land, its biotic community was fragile, easily disrupted by abuse. One reason is the extreme variation in seasonal and annual rainfall.

"Take half, leave half" is a rough guide to grazing management. Grasses, like other green plants, manufacture food in their leaves. The food is utilized in growth. In most cases, if grazing removes no more than half of the green blades, a grass plant still has sufficient food-making capacity to maintain itself and to produce full growth in the following year. If, through overgrazing, the blades are cropped shorter, the growth process is inhibited, and this will soon be reflected in a reduced root system. Were grazing stopped in the following year, grasses would regenerate. Successive years of overgrazing, however, cause progressive decline of the grasses. Drought compounds the damage.

A typical grassland area has a variety of plants. Cattle are specialized feeders, and good grazing land has a predominance of the grasses they prefer, which provide good nourishment. If these grasses are heavily grazed, so that their regeneration is inhibited, the composition of the plant community changes, since the advantage is now with grasses and forbs the cattle have thus far ignored.

Eventually, hunger compels the cattle to take second best. This sets in motion another and more sinister change, in which forage plants are replaced by "invaders," plants the cattle cannot eat, such as cactus, mesquite, mockorange, sagebrush, and scrub oak. These shrubs have already been favored by suppression of fire. In the past, prairies were maintained by frequent natural burning, fires which usually occurred after the growing season when grasses were brown and dry. Such fires left grass root systems undamaged and increased the supply of available nitrogen, so the prairies greened rapidly after spring rains. At the same time, the fires destroyed or suppressed the growth of woody perennials. The plains Indians understood this, as do the Masai and other African tribes, and often fired the dry grasses. Ranchers, however, found such fires threatening to their herds and checked them when they could. Overgrazing also reduced the supply of dry fuel, so fires did not spread so readily.

Once shrubs become dominant, they tend to remain so, even though cattle are necessarily moved off for lack of food. Many invader plants are water-hungry and send out wide-spreading root systems which collect available moisture. Certain shrubs growing in especially arid regions appear to secrete toxins in their roots or leaves which prevent competition within their growth radius. Between these shrubs, soil is exposed. When grasses grew, rainfall was absorbed and held. Now it puddles, runs off, evaporates. When dry, the soil is exposed to wind erosion. Throughout the world, hundreds of millions of once-productive acres have, by human mismanagement, become desert wastelands.

These acres are now largely useless for grazing or other human exploitation. They lie abandoned. An altered biotic community invites colonization by wildlife. But even if populations of original native species border on the wastelands, little colonization will occur, for the altered community is no longer hospitable to its former inhabitants.

Some of this wasteland can be made productive. I saw fields that had been cleared of shrubs, plowed, fertilized, seeded, and irrigated. This is costly, and the supply of irrigation water is limited. I saw other fields which had been laboriously cleared by grubbing out the shrubs or crushing them with sheep's-foot rollers, but grasses had failed to grow well, and the shrubs were becoming reestablished.

Some of the altered portions of Texas, no longer suitable for cattle ranching or for native wild game, seem suitable for exotic wildlife, and the early experiments have encouraged other ranchers to introduce foreign species. By now it has become fashionable. More than a hundred ranches, from Florida to California, have introduced exotics.

On one visit to Texas, I saw dramatic evidence of the difference between species requirements. It had been a dry winter, and spring growth was late. One afternoon I saw more than a hundred native white-tailed deer gathered on the bed of what had been a shallow lake. They were "yarding," a sign of distress. Indeed, they were conspicuously thin and in poor coat. Some would surely die, and the fawn crop would be small.

Not far away I saw zebras, wildebeests, nilgais, blackbucks, and oryxes, all looking sleek and vigorous. This was not because they withstand hunger better than our native species. Rather, they are adapted to survive in dry places, and dry plant matter is much to their liking. They make better use of the food available under such conditions. The oryx, indeed, can survive without access to drinking water.

Game ranching has met the first test of animal management: survival. More than thirty species of exotic ungulates have been introduced, and lived. Losses have occurred, deaths attributable to fighting, parasites, predators, severe weather, and accidents, but there is as yet no evidence that the death rate is high enough to threaten extinction.

A few species have been on ranches long enough, and in sufficient numbers, for the test of reproduction to be applied. Blackbucks, zebras, fallow deer, elands, sambars, nilgais, aoudads, red deer, and axis deer have multiplied through several generations. The gnus seem fairly well established. Several other species have reproduced, but both their numbers and their period of residence are still short of a meaningful test.

The King Ranch has built a large herd of nilgais. The blackbuck has reproduced so well there may now be more of them in Texas than in their native India. On a recent visit to Argentina I was told the blackbuck is thriving there, also. In both areas, some have gone over the fence, and wild-living populations are established.

These are short-term results, for survival of a species—as distinct from survival of an individual—is limited by the extreme and exceptional conditions of its environment. If the species cannot withstand several days of deep snow and bitter cold, the kind of blizzard that occurs only once in fifty years may eliminate it. The species must be able to withstand (perhaps with considerable loss of numbers) the worst droughts, the most prolonged heat waves, and the minimum food production the environment can present, as well as assaults by insects and diseases that may reach high intensities as a consequence of climatic events. One of the risks of game ranching is a buildup of parasites, some of which may be introduced by the exotic species themselves.

While such risks exist, they are as yet only speculative, and the available evidence argues for a favorable outcome for many of the new species—with one major and possibly fatal exception. Ranches are not wildernesses. The largest of them qualify only as modest game preserves. The animals are confined, unable to migrate or disperse in response to overcrowding. Predation is minor and kept so by deliberate extermination of coyotes and cougars. Almost all of the ranch operations will, I believe, deteriorate over time unless the present lack of scientific management is remedied. As did the cattle, the wild game will deplete the food resources.

How would an experienced wildlife manager administer a game ranch? First, he would have the prospective site studied thoroughly by competent botanists, soil scientists, meteorologists, parasitologists, and other specialists. What are the means and extremes of the microclimate? How dependable is the surface water supply? Can it be supplemented by reliable wells? What are the principal forage plants, and what is the minimum annual forage supply? Are any toxic plants present? Do cattle ticks, screwworms, or other pests occur? Could the site be improved by establishing new ponds or by modifying potentially hazardous gullies? Should there be any changes made in the vegetation by seeding grass or planting trees? Will it be necessary to provide additional shade artificially, or perhaps loafing sheds which combine shade with shelter from storm winds?

With such information in hand, and satisfied that the site was a good risk, the manager would select species whose requirements would be approximately met. His selections would differ from those made by most ranchers, however, for he would have different aims in mind. Why invest so much effort and money to establish herds of species that are still numerous in their native habitats, species neither rare nor endangered? Further, because of his viewpoint and his training, he would not hesitate, other than for reasons of cost or practicability, to bridge a gap between the requirements of a desirable species and the qualities of the site, by including winter shelters, regular feed supplements, or other "artificial" supports in his program. Supplemental feeding would permit regular administration of medications, for parasite control and perhaps other purposes, such as correcting a trace element deficiency. Only when the site was deemed ready

would animals be introduced. The first few would be expend-
ables, probably surplus males.

The zoo-trained manager of one private ranch was able to
begin development in this manner. Riding the range with
him, I could see his skill expressed in the placement of fences,
patrol roads, and feeding stations. Newly arrived animals
were held for a time in well-designed pens and fed their familiar zoo diets for a period of conditioning. Then fresh cut-
tings from ranch plants were offered, the plants on which
they would largely subsist. When they had made a transition
to this diet, the pens were opened and the animals were free
to leave, but they were not driven out. Food was still provided at the pens. At the time of my visit, the giraffes were
leaving their pen each morning, spending the day on the
range, then returning each evening, almost like dairy cows.

As we inspected the pens, we were surrounded by a mixed
group of llamas, elands, zebras, nilgais, and mouflon sheep.
One male llama had a small cactus thorn stuck in his lower
jaw. He allowed me to remove it, then spat in my face. These
were all zoo-born animals, accustomed to association with
humans. Their offspring will be warier.

Supplemental feeding, I soon realized, is a most useful
technique in this setting, even if not nutritionally necessary.
The manager's aim was to see every one of his animals every
day. Even a giraffe can vanish in this ravine-cut terrain, while
species inclined to remain in brushy areas are usually invisible. Before we left the holding pens, the manager filled buck-
ets with feed and set them on the truck. He drove slowly
along the perimeter road. Soon I saw a beisa oryx ahead,
evidently awaiting us. She moved off a little when we
stopped, watched as a few handfuls of grain were dumped
on the road, then came in to eat as we drove off. From time
to time my escort tapped the horn lightly, a signal that

brought zebras and wildebeests into view. Several times we stopped though no animals were in sight, but, looking back, we saw them come to the feed.

Such close observation is vitally important if management is to mean more than random experiments with unknown outcomes. On one ranch, for example, a zebra was killed by a male gnu. The two species are commonly seen together in East Africa, but gnus are often aggressive in zoo enclosures. Did the killing mean that gnus could not safely mix with other species in ranch-size enclosures? Was the aggression an expression of territoriality? The gnu was immobilized by a dart gun. Examination disclosed a deeply imbedded, festering thorn which must have caused intense pain. It was removed, and the wound was treated. In the few months since that incident, no further attacks had been noted.

This quality of management has not been present on any of the other game ranches I have visited, except the King Ranch, whose resources and professional staff are unique. Even so, a zoo man would be critical. Daily observations are made, but systematic records are not kept. Autopsies are not made routinely, nor are there routine checks for parasites. Since my visit, the professionally trained manager has left, and no replacement has yet been announced.

Other ranches I have visited seem to be almost unplanned and unmanaged. Species are ill assorted. Animals apparently were bought on impulse, chosen for their trophy appeal or interesting appearance, or at an owner's whim. In several cases it was all too evident that a few of the species, known to be highly competitive, would multiply until they displaced the others.

Why does a wealthy rancher introduce exotic game animals? Most of the game ranchers had hunted in Africa and Asia. Their ranches were deficient in native game. Why not remedy the lack with something even more glamorous? Would it not be exciting to hunt African antelopes right at home?

Much of the expense could be written off their taxes, since ranches are used to entertain good customers. Exotic game would add much to the entertainment, especially if an important guest could take back a handsome trophy to hang on his office wall. A few ranches have commercialized exotic game hunting. Even if their rates are high, an African safari would cost far more.

Though I do not hunt, except with a camera, I am not opposed to legal hunting. It amuses rather than horrifies me that some "sportsmen" on game ranches shoot from comfortable blinds at animals lured to feed troughs thirty feet away. (One rancher told me that he had bought a fine red deer with a magnificent rack, anticipating the arrival of a very special customer. The day before the guest arrived, the buck shed his antlers!) Controlled hunting is essential to good management of some wild species. Having eliminated other large predators, man must take their place.

But man is a clumsy predator because of his desire for trophies. Most hunters want to kill the males with the finest racks, and these are usually the herd bulls, the very ones most needed for good breeding. Hunters ignore the sick, weak, and aged, which nature would cull. There is a deep-rooted prejudice against killing does, the effect of which is to unbalance sex ratios in herds. On our national bison ranges, herds must be reduced periodically, but this culling is planned to retain the normal age-sex distribution.

In our country, a man can do much as he pleases on his own land. The game ranchers are exercising the privileges of wealth and ownership. I have no wish to criticize them. Indeed, in a somewhat hit-or-miss fashion they have demonstrated possibilities, shown what could be done in this kind of setting by an enterprise with different objectives.

Here is the spaciousness that zoos and wildlife conservationists need. Here we could establish and maintain large herds of species that may otherwise become extinct. Here we could breed other species, not so critically endangered, and keep zoos supplied, so there would be less need to continue capturing wild stock.

The research possibilities are challenging. It is deplorable that the wildlife ranches have not been studied by scientists, for here we could learn much that is difficult or impossible to study in native habitats. Here is a setting that approximates a natural preserve, yet which permits considerable manipulation.

The ranches are fascinating and frustrating. It is an unforgettable experience to ride a morning patrol just after dawn, to see so many animals at large. Some of the ranches are so spacious that the fencelines are out of sight. A conservationist is thrilled by the possibilities, dismayed that they are as yet unrealized.

The ranch "survival center" has been a special passion of mine for almost a decade. Two federal agencies have considered sponsoring such projects. One went so far as to prepare plans, budgets, and authorizing legislation, but the plans were dropped when congressional support could not be found. Zoo leaders banded together in the Wild Animal Propagation Trust, with the initial aim of founding such centers cooperatively. Unfortunately, zoos have money problems of their own, and the Trust has not yet found a way to assemble the necessary resources. The National Zoo has a site in Maryland, land owned by the Smithsonian Institution, where a useful beginning could be made; but we have thus far not found money to develop and operate the farm.

I have talked with a number of the ranchers, hoping to find one who would work with us. Two or three have generously said we could put our animals on their land. Our terms are necessarily more demanding. Five or ten years have little significance when the issue is permanent survival of a species. Should the generous rancher lose interest, sell his land, or die, what would become of the animals? Further, rare animals should not simply be released in the hope that they will survive. There must be professional management.

One of the early game ranches is now a ruin, for lack of such management. Hardly a blade of grass remains, and the trees have been cropped to a high browse line. Much of the soil has eroded, exposing a rubble of stone. Today this ranch is a feedlot. The resident herds must be fed daily or they will starve.

Someday, I hope, a rancher will see it our way. Perhaps his tax lawyer will persuade him that there would be advantages in putting a few thousand acres of his land into a permanent trust and in contributing sufficient money to the trust to provide for managing its assets. If not this, we will find some other way.

11

Strangers Among Us

Before two bridges connected it to the mainland, Assateague Island was one of our favorite weekend refuges. The island is long and narrow, a barrier beach, bisected by the Maryland-Virginia state line. Its only residents were Coast Guardsmen. The federal refuge manager lived on shore, where we would launch our boat. Crossing the bay was always interesting, for the sea was usually choppy and the channels were poorly marked. Oysters are cultivated here, and unless a helmsman was careful he could ram a mound of sharp-edged shells, especially at low tide.

Mooring at a decrepit pier, we would go ashore and cross the salt marshes to the dunes, sometimes fighting off clouds of mosquitoes until the sea breeze carried them away. Assateague is rich in wildlife: migratory waterfowl and shore birds in season, raccoons and rabbits, snails and ghost crabs. It also has a population of wild horses.

How the horses came to Assateague is a mystery. Local historians say they swam ashore from the wreckage of a Spanish sailing ship more than two centuries ago. The island might seem a poor home for them. Until recently it had no surface supply of fresh water, except for ponds formed after rains.

The salt grasses are tough rather than succulent. Storms often batter the ocean side, and only limited shelter is afforded by the dunes and low-growing trees. Hurricanes have driven blue water across the island. A number of horses were killed by a hurricane a few years ago. Even so, the horses have survived and multiplied, and a surplus is taken from the island each year to be sold at the annual Pony Penning, a local festival.

Several years ago, wandering among Assateague's dunes, we saw a herd of the wild horses. We made our way toward them slowly, interested in learning how close an approach they would permit. The mares were curious, rather than shy, but the stallion watched us uneasily. When we came within fifty feet, he tossed his head, snorted, and drove his wives away over the dunes.

A few hours later we saw the herd again, grazing near the bay shore. White birds sat on the backs of three of them. Our binoculars gave us our first look at African cattle egrets, then a recently arrived species on the Maryland coast, now numerous. The two introduced species had formed a relationship.

Assateague has still another introduced species: the Asiatic sika. How this deer became established is also uncertain, since the stories told conflict. Someone obtained and released a pair, or possibly two pairs, on Assateague or on the mainland nearby. They multiplied rapidly, spreading up and down the coast, displacing the native deer, for whom this habitat was marginal. A current estimate of the sika population along the coast is ten thousand.

It is in the nature of living things, plant or animal, that they seek to extend their ranges. Tree seeds are scattered into bordering pastures, and grass seeds blow into the woods. Range boundaries are determined by limiting factors. Beyond the boundary it is too cold or hot, too wet or dry. A boundary may mark a change in soil chemistry. Teachers call their students' attention to the plant zonation of drainage ditches: certain plants grow only in the water, others where their roots are occasionally submerged, still others on the moist banks, while some occur only on the dry land above. A boundary may mark the limits of tolerance of a species, or it may be the point beyond which other species are better competitors for space.

Such boundaries shift constantly. In Kansas, gaillardia advances up hillsides in wet years, retreats in dry years. In the East, the mixed deciduous forest moves northward and higher up mountainsides as a long-term warming trend continues; the conifers yield ground.* Ranges of animal species also change, in response to changes in food supply and such other factors as the prevalence of parasites and diseases. A 1946 field guide states that the eastern glossy ibis occurred in Florida but was not common there, and that a few individuals might fly farther north in late summer. Twenty years later, hundreds of them were appearing on Assateague Island each spring, and many continue north to Jamaica Bay, near New York City. The coyote has extended its range far to the east of its nineteenth-century limits, probably because agricultural development has increased the supply of rodents.

An animal species will invade any favorable habitat unless a barrier stops it. Ranges are abruptly terminated by mountains or oceans. Madagascar has a unique fauna because it is an island. A species native to the northern temperate zone is unlikely to migrate through the tropics into the Southern Hemisphere. When such a barrier is crossed, by accident or by human intervention, an "introduction" occurs. Thus the

* Recent reports suggest that the warming trend may have been reversed in the past decade by increased air pollution.

cattle egret was introduced to the Western Hemisphere; the glossy ibis and coyotes merely extended their ranges.

Most introductions fail. If we were to take the lions, elephants, golden marmosets, roseate spoonbills, and Galapagos tortoises from our zoo and release them in the Appalachian Mountains, few would long survive, and none would establish populations. State fish and game departments have spent hundreds of thousands of dollars attempting to introduce the coturnix, a migratory quail from overseas, without success. Camels were brought to the United States in 1856 to be used as desert beasts of burden. Some escaped and others were released, but they did not become established.

Some introductions have succeeded all too well. If an exotic species finds itself in a favorable habitat, with little competition, it may multiply explosively. The mongoose was introduced to Jamaica to exterminate rats and became more of a nuisance than the rats. In addition to killing poultry and other farm animals, it preyed upon iguanas, waterfowl, frogs, turtles, crabs, and other wildlife, thoroughly upsetting the ecology of the island and threatening some native species with extinction.

Rabbits multiplied explosively when introduced to Australia, becoming a costly pest. In Argentina, national parks officials entertained us at an *asado*. The venison spitted beside the glowing coals was European red deer, just killed by an authorized hunter. Here, too, an introduced species had multiplied to the point where it became destructive. Systematic reduction of herds had become a necessity.

Construction of a navigable route from the Great Lakes to the sea breached the barrier which had previously excluded the lamprey from the lakes. Within a few years this aquatic predator had multiplied to the point where it had heavily damaged commercial fishing.

One of the more recent "successful" introductions to the United States is the South American nutria. As has often been the case, this one was helped along by promoters who published exaggerated accounts of the animal's virtues, chiefly as a source of fur. The first known escape occurred in 1940. By 1960 the wild population exceeded two million. They are most numerous, and most destructive of crops, in the Louisiana wetlands, but others have become established as far away as New Jersey and Oregon.

It now seems almost incredible that European immigrants to the United States so cherished house sparrows that they went to great trouble and expense to bring them here, releasing them in the fond hope that they would soon decorate their lawns and gardens. No one could have foreseen the ensuing population explosion. This little sparrow is the world's most successful bird. City folks are largely indifferent to them, but not to another introduction from abroad, the noisy starling.

Federal law now prohibits importation of a number of "noxious" animals, such as the mongoose, fruit bat, and Java finch. Authorities are concerned about the possibility that some might be released or escape, and that they would multiply and become destructive. One shudders at the thought of piranhas becoming established in our rivers! Zoos can still import such species, but only if authorities are satisfied that the zoo asking permission to do so has adequate security.

One session at IUCN's Lucerne General Assembly was devoted to papers on the subject of plant and animal introductions. Conservationists are conservative, regarding any human tampering with nature as fraught with danger. It was pathetic and shocking to hear scientists pleading for the protection of a few tiny islands in remote corners of the world. A few generations ago they could have had whole continents as their biological laboratories. Today, they can find only these few island acres on which to study the pure state of nature.

Introducing any exotic organism to such a setting would be pointless and mischievous. Nor is there any doubt that ill-conceived introductions have caused vast and largely irreversible damage on every continent. Introductions of various insects and disease organisms have cost millions of human lives. Entire species, such as the American chestnut tree, have been eliminated, and others, currently our American elms, are threatened.

In Brazil, we were told about the frightening consequences of introducing a species of bee from Africa. The species was of interest to farmers because it is a prodigious producer of honey. It is also phenomenally aggressive, making unprovoked attacks in swarms on cattle and other mammals, including humans. Newspaper accounts told of children killed when a swarm suddenly descended upon a playground. Losses of cattle had been reported with growing frequency. The large bees were spreading, displacing native species. Our host in São Paulo was especially distressed, since he had spent years in the study and cultivation of a small native bee, quite stingless and an excellent honey producer.

The concern of scientists for unique island flora and fauna is amply justified, for there have been numerous cases of heavy damage. South Sea islanders succumbed in large numbers to bacteria and viruses introduced unwittingly by the first explorers. Sailors occasionally placed pigs and goats on islands they visited with the hope that they would multiply and provide meat to ships touching there in the future. Multiply they did, in many instances, often to the point of stripping these islands of vegetation on which native species subsisted. The Survival Service Commission recently reviewed a proposal to clear a Chilean island of such damaging intruders. Even a seemingly innocent introduction can upset a fragile balance: the near-disappearance of one rare rodent species, found on a single island, has been blamed on a lighthouse-keeper's cats.

It would be absurd, however, to adopt "No introductions!" as a battle cry. All of our domestic farm animals came here as aliens. Many of our valued plants are introduced species, among them Kentucky bluegrass, white and red clover, orchard grass, Bermuda grass, and common lespedeza, as well as many trees: the horse chestnut, Norway maple, Scotch pine, sycamore, maple, and weeping willow. Most farm crops are introductions. The brown trout was brought from Europe. The ring-necked pheasant, introduced from Asia in 1880, has been beneficial rather than destructive.

Most introductions fail because of the same limiting factors that confine plant and animal species to more or less well-defined ranges. In the case of plants, the test region may have too much or too little moisture, or the rains may fall at the wrong season; the growing season may be too short, or the winters too severe. The soil chemistry may be unfavorable. A native plant may be a more successful competitor. A puzzling failure of pine tree introductions in Puerto Rico was finally explained by the absence of certain fungi in the soil.

An equally complex array of limiting factors confines animal species to certain habitats and causes most random introductions to fail. But limiting factors are also operative in a species' own habitat, factors which keep its population in check. This is why the alternative to failure may be explosive multiplication. Only by chance would a species find, in a new habitat, a set of checks and balances precisely matching those of its homeland.

Introducing a carnivore is obviously risky. A farmer may be pleased at the idea of having resident mongooses to kill the rats, mice, and ground squirrels that plague him. But the mongoose, as Jamaican farmers learned to their sorrow, does not confine its predations to these hungry rodents. As the rodent supply diminishes, mongooses are forced to find other prey.

Rodents present a different kind of risk. Our country is well supplied with rodents now, although we have nothing as large as the three-foot-long capybara of South America. Rodents are the most numerous of the mammals, occupying a wide variety of niches, from the seacoast to mountains and deserts, from treetops to a few inches below ground. A number of the more familiar species, such as the house mouse and Norway rat, were introduced here years ago. While they do much costly damage, and millions of dollars are spent each year to suppress them, their presence is not a cause for grave concern. We have achieved a kind of balance, though with some discomfort.

Only a highly specialized exotic rodent would now find a vacant niche here, but it is quite possible that one might compete successfully with an established species. The nutria, for example, is said to have displaced the muskrat in some areas. The danger lies in the tremendous reproduction potential of most rodents. A newcomer could multiply explosively before established predators learned its ways and before we devised control methods. Studies have shown that a single rodent species may become as numerous as ten thousand individuals per acre in prime habitat! Because of their size and elusiveness, small rodents are less easily eliminated than bison.

On the other hand, what are the risks presented by introducing an ungulate species, an exotic deer or antelope? We have had some limited experience, one example being the sika population which now seems well established along the Maryland-Virginia coast. So far as I have been able to discover, this situation has not been studied by scientists. My information comes from local residents, including refuge managers, farmers, and hunters. One refuge manager believed the sikas were becoming too numerous, to the detriment of vegetation in his refuge, but he thought this would be readily controllable by opening a hunting season. Most of my informants thought the sikas had displaced native white-tailed deer. The hunters were ambivalent. Two said they preferred native deer as game, because the sikas were "sneaky," moving quickly and invisibly through the brush, rarely breaking into the open. Others thought the sika were just fine because there were more of them. The farmers reported no increased crop damage since the sikas appeared.

A few months ago I crossed the Andes from Puerto Montt, in southern Chile, to Lake Nahuel Huapí in Argentina. This is a day's journey, chiefly by boat, and by bus between the several lakes. The country is spectacularly beautiful, like a mixture of Switzerland and the Canadian Rockies: snow-capped mountains, glaciers, forested hillsides, deep blue lakes, roaring streams, and handsome waterfalls. Few tourists come this way, and human settlement is sparse.

We saw no mammals, and their absence seemed incongruous. Time and again we saw places where it seemed that animals ought to be: Here was just the place one would expect to find beavers. Over there one really should see a moose. Bears would seem in place here, but there are no bears. Nor are there elk, or wolves—indeed, no large mammals whatever.

This was not always the case. At one time both North and South America had a rich assortment of mammals, as varied as those seen in Africa in modern times. We are at a low point

of the cycle, for reasons having to do with the glacial periods
and the rising and falling of land. For several thousand years
American wildlife has, in a sense, been impoverished, and
there is little doubt that vacant ecological niches exist. The
rapid multiplication of the red deer in Argentina so illus-
trates.

Seeing that splendid landscape with no large mammals
made me sympathize with people who have tried to fill seemingly empty niches by importing animals from elsewhere.
Why not introduce bears? Would not beavers enrich this
habitat as they have done for so long in North America? And,
if beavers, why not moose as well?

Then I looked again. A landscape is not just a pretty picture of water, trees, snow, and sky. These trees were not the
species of the northern Rockies, nor were the understory
plants the same. The climate differs. The bears and elks
might thrive here, but one could not be sure without pains-
taking study and experimentation. Further, niches are not so
easily demarcated. In other parts of South America, a large
variety of small mammals occupy portions of niches filled by
a few large mammals elsewhere. An introduced large mammal, should it become established, might have destructive
impact on smaller native species.

A number of exotic hoofed animals are living wild in California, some of them offspring of animals that escaped from the
Hearst ranch. The latest available estimates say there are about
three thousand wild boars, three hundred Barbary sheep, five
hundred fallow deer, and small herds of zebras, wildebeests,
sambar deer, mouflon sheep, axis deer, tahrs, and possibly
others. Texas has wild populations of sika and axis deer,
barasinghas, sambars, Barbary sheep, mouflon sheep, nilgais,
elands, wild boars, and blackbucks. Several species have been
introduced on coastal islands, including sambars, elands, and

zebras. New Mexico's game department is breeding kudus, ibexes, and gemsbok in captivity, hoping to produce enough for introductions. As yet, none of these species are multiplying explosively, and no damage to native species has been reported. On the other hand, numbers are still so small by comparison with native species that none of the exotics can, as yet, be considered firmly established.

In a nation as well populated as the United States, it seems unlikely that the population of a species of large mammal could get out of hand. Should undesirable effects appear, it would be enough to summon the hunters. This might not be so effective in the southern Andean region, because of the rugged terrain and the thin scattering of people.

Still, the fascination of introductions is not easily put aside. The arguments marshaled against such experiments are not entirely persuasive. What are "native species"? The moose, caribou, mountain sheep, elk, and even the bison are immigrants to North America, though they have been here long enough to develop distinctive characteristics. Yet it may be wisdom to avoid tampering with habitats that are still little disturbed.

No such case can be made for the "protection" of manmade wastelands. Are these, by any criteria, lands whose integrity we must now protect in the name of conservation? We once camped on a desert in the shadow of tall saguaros and spent a week photographing desert fauna and flora. This had not been a desert until the great cattle drives came through. Before that time, the land supported grasses.

I will happily join in campaigns to preserve the Grand Canyon, the Indiana Dunes, and Padre Island. But the despoiled lands cry out for creative tampering. Such wrecked areas can be found almost everywhere, from New England to the Southwest, from Colombia to Saudi Arabia. Should we not challenge our ecologists to try their hands at designing new ecosystems? May it not be possible to piece together a new fauna and flora, from species chosen in any part of the world, whose interactions would hasten the rehabilitation of these lost acres?

Here an ecologist critic penciled on the margin: "Think of the knowledge gap! Do we dare?" To which my response is: "Where is the risk? On this land the damage has been done. What better way to close the knowledge gap than to experiment?"

The processes of life are dynamic. The challenge is not to create a stable new ecosystem but one whose trends point in the right direction. The action of grazing animals eliminated grasses, allowing woody shrubs to take over. What would happen now if an area were populated with browsers? Might not the trend be reversed so that grasses might ultimately grow again?

It seems possible that some of the endangered species of the world could be translocated to new habitats where they could renew their vigor. It is even conceivable, though perhaps beyond our present textbook knowledge, that a habitat could be remodeled to make it suitable for a displaced species.

Introduced species could also be used to alleviate human hunger. Someday we must face the fact that cattle were a poor invention. This is in part because of their specialized feeding habits, but also because men have made them a specialty, assigning large acreages of grazing land to their exclusive use. The consequences have been destructive everywhere. In past centuries there was always more land, and the cattle were often moved to lusher pastures before the land they had grazed was beyond recovery. In our time there is no more land. Continued abuse progressively curtails food production, while human needs continue to mount each year.

Recent studies in Africa have demonstrated that a mixed population of grazing and browsing animals can yield ten times more edible meat than cattle would supply in the same area. Each species has its own eating preferences, so that several can occupy the same physical space without competing. In the natural situation, grazing and browsing pressure is spread rather evenly over the assortment of forage plants, tending to maintain rather than to distort the distribution of flora.

Experiments with game ranching have begun in Africa, and early results are promising. The taste for beef is acquired. Jane and I have eaten the meat of goats, deer, water buffalo, bison, and other wild hoofed animals, and while none appealed quite as beef does, we can well imagine that early training could have given us a different bias. Antelopes and other wild species have supplied African natives with animal protein for centuries. It will be tragic if "development" leads to imitation of error, if wild species are eliminated to make room for a domestic animal that yields less meat and ultimately impairs the land's ability to support meat producers.

By coincidence, just as I am writing these words two of our zoo-keepers are at Kennedy Airport, in New York, standing by until two crated elands are loaded on a jet freighter that will deliver them to São Paulo, Brazil. Their arrival will be the first step in an experiment that may, some years from now, increase Brazil's meat supply. They will go first to the São Paulo Zoo, then to an experimental enclosure at Campinas, in the interior, which I visited a few weeks ago. Five additional elands are expected there by the end of the summer.

This project was conceived by Dr. Paulo Nogueira Neto, a prominent Brazilian scientist, lawyer, businessman, and conservationist. A large portion of Brazil consists of dry savannahs, where the vegetation will not support domestic cattle. Dr. Nogueira visited us a year ago while he was seeking a meat-producing species which seemed suitable for the habitat. He finally settled on the eland, largest of the African antelopes. Its meat resembles beef. It has been semidomesticated in parts of Africa as a meat animal, and a milking herd was established in the Ukraine before 1900. Since it is more of a browser than a grazer, and because it can live without free water, it seems a good choice for the savannah country.

It will not be Brazil's first supplement to beef. The water buffalo was introduced some time ago, and by 1968 there were said to be sixty thousand of them there, some feral, most on farms. They thrive in places too wet for cattle, and they are said to be resistant to ticks. We ate water buffalo meat in a good restaurant and enjoyed it. Italy has also found the water buffalo to be a good meat producer. Perhaps the eland will do equally well in dry places.

Nogueira is far too careful a man to think of turning elands loose. Further, they are not easily obtained, since Brazil's quarantine laws have the effect of excluding any elands other than those born in the United States. We found this first pair, and kept them at the zoo for medical tests and conditioning prior to shipment. They and the others to follow will be kept under close observation in the experimental enclosure, a representative section of the savannah. How will they respond? What plants will they select for food? How rapidly will they gain weight? Will they be adversely affected by local insects and parasites? Will they reproduce?

If the indications are favorable, the next step, several years from now, will be establishment of a ranch herd. We drove several hundred miles through the savannah region where this trial may be made. It is rolling land, for the most part covered by a dense, dry growth of scrub and trees, with little grass. Even if the elands thrive, there will still be problems to solve. How will they be rounded up when it is time to take them to market? Ways can be found, I am sure.

While such projects have great possibilities, they are not magic answers either to world hunger or to the preservation of endangered species. The worldwide food shortage is critical now and becomes worse year by year. No workable countermeasures can reverse the trend sufficiently to keep pace with the terrifying increases in human population. The eland, water buffalo, nilgai, banteng, gayal, musk ox, and other species could, however, with good husbandry and land-use planning, make useful increases in animal protein production where cattle-raising is uneconomic or scientifically unsound.

Africa has the best chance to achieve a stable ecology, because the commitment to domestic cattle, sheep, and goats has not yet passed the point of no return. In some regions, cattle-raising has been deterred by diseases to which wild species have adapted. Enough original habitat has thus far escaped irreversible change to permit testing and applying a thesis: that man can, today, best satisfy his desire for meat by organizing and managing, rather than abandoning, his traditional role of predator on wild prey.

Elsewhere, where original habitats have been almost totally altered, even to the soil itself, the challenge is to construct new ecosystems. The planners cannot reconstruct, nor is there any compelling reason to imitate the old model, which in any case was but a stage in a continuum. For the myriad chance introductions of ecological history they can substitute deliberate choices, from among any of the world's floral and faunal species. While the vast majority of chance introductions fail, scientific selection should have a better yield.

Granted that the ecologists cannot guarantee results. The challenge asks them to make theirs an experimental science. Granted that results will be slow, far slower than the brute-force landscape alterations made by bulldozers, plows, and power saws. But what is sought here is not short-term exploitation of the land, quick profit too often followed by ecological bankruptcy. What is sought is scientific evidence, actual demonstration that our species can adapt its behavior to natural laws, can modify the environment constructively as well as destructively. And if the experiments begin on wastelands, what are the risks that cannot be controlled?

12

Survival Centers

Kerry Muller, who manages our Bird Division, wrote to a colleague in Hawaii—offering to send him a number of Hawaiian ducks! A close relative of our common mallard, this Hawaiian subspecies has never been so abundant, and a few years ago the wild population had declined to a precarious two hundred. It reproduces well in captivity, however, and this year we hatched more than we could keep. Kerry offered his surplus for restocking in the duck's own habitat.

Another Hawaiian bird, the nene goose, was even closer to extinction a few years ago, only about fifty remaining at large. Captive breeding was undertaken at the Waterfowl Trust establishment at Slimbridge, England, by S. Dillon Ripley at Litchfield, Connecticut, and at a third survival center in Hawaii. Restocking has helped bring the wild population up to about five hundred.

Swinhoe's pheasant, near extinction on Taiwan, has become a relatively common species in public and private collections, and some have been sent back to Taiwan. White rhinoceroses have been translocated from Zululand to southern Rhodesia, restocking part of their former range. Captive-bred ibex have been returned to the Swiss Alps. Chimpan-

zees bred in European zoos were released on Rubondo Island,
a sanctuary in Lake Victoria, in 1966. The first island-born
infants were sighted in 1968. The rare aye-aye of Madagascar
is being colonized on a safe island, in hopes of saving it. Przewalski's horses may be returned to Mongolia once the captive
herds increase sufficiently. Israel has established a wildlife
station in the Negev as a base for returning desert species
eliminated years ago.

Saving a species in the wild is the first aim of conservationists, but it cannot always be done. The heath hen became extinct in 1932. A closely related subspecies, Attwater's greater
prairie chicken, had declined to a few hundred in coastal
Texas when the World Wildlife Fund and Nature Conser-
vancy took options on several thousand acres of prairie land,
to provide a refuge. The whooping crane has been protected
as effectively as any migratory species can be, and it has persisted year after year but without significant gains in the tiny
remnant population. It would have taken only a small disaster to wipe them out, and the Fish and Wildlife Service
decided to intervene. Eggs were taken from the Canadian
breeding grounds in 1967 and again in 1968. Most of them
hatched, and the chicks are being raised.

It is not always possible to save the habitat of a species, nor
is it always possible to protect a remnant population from
hunting and poaching. Even if there seems to be some chance
that the free animals may survive, it is frequently wise to
hedge against the unforeseen, to establish a sufficient number
of the species in survival centers to assure they will not be
lost. Return to the wild may then be possible, if circumstances change for the better. A depleted wild population
may be bolstered by additions of captive-bred stock, or a
vanished species may be returned. This assumes, of course,
that these captive-born individuals would survive if turned

loose to fend for themselves—that captive life has not unfitted them.

Some years ago I heard a prominent zoologist speak scathingly about zoo breeding.

"Zoo animals aren't real," he declared. "They may look like real ones, but only superficially. You're breeding domesticated animals. What good are they?"

He was right in saying zoo animals are different. If they do not eat as they do in the wild, if they do not kill their own prey, if they need not escape or ward off enemies, and if their mate selection is limited or controlled, their development will differ from what it would have been in free life. Some individuals that would have been eliminated by the tests of nature will live and propagate in zoos, and such differences in natural selection will, no doubt, over many generations, adapt the species to captive existence.

This is not necessarily a grave matter, however. If zoo-born animals are taken back to their ancestral homes, and if they can survive and propagate there, the changes caused by captivity will be reversed. The key question is whether they would survive. Does zoo life unfit them for free life?

In *Born Free,* Joy Adamson told the story of Elsa, a lioness taken into her home as a cub and raised as a pet. It became necessary to return Elsa, now adult, to the wild, and this posed difficulties. Elsa had no desire to go. One attempt failed when a wild lioness jealously fought to exclude Elsa from a pride. But the chief problem was that Elsa had never learned to kill.

In the end, the Adamsons succeeded. Elsa learned to kill and found a mate. Here is evidence that it can be done, though in this case the effort required was great. It is a reasonable assumption that predators would make the transition with greater difficulty than herbivores, since they would not, while confined, have learned to hunt and kill prey. The Adamsons' difficulties, and Elsa's, were compounded, however, because return to the wild had not been an early aim. If a skillful animal behaviorist were given a number of cubs to train for ultimate free living, he could have prepared them for it more readily.

Many species have gone wild with no preparation whatever. The United States has a substantial population of feral dogs and cats. I became acquainted with a band of feral cats when I lived in the Hell's Kitchen section of New York years ago. They were completely wild, utterly unapproachable. I trapped one, and it fought fiercely, hissing, spitting, clawing, until I released it.

IUCN's *Red Data Book* lists the wild Bactrian camel as an endangered species, but questions whether any still exist. Bactrian camels do live free, but it is believed that most of them, perhaps all, are feral: domesticated stock gone wild. If so, this is one example of a species that became extinct in the wild state and was successfully reintroduced, though not by design. Various parts of the world have thriving populations of feral water buffalo, sheep, goats, hogs, and horses, all thriving independently after generations of domesticated existence. In many of these situations, the animals have not "returned" to the wild; in some cases, indeed, we are not sure just where the original stock came from. The feral animals have established themselves in new habitats, adapting to them successfully.

As mentioned earlier, many zoo-born hoofed animals have been released, often with no conditioning, onto fenced rangeland, and have successfully made the transition to subsistence living. Some have been released to open rangeland, or have escaped, and now live free. Wood ducks hatched in our zoo incubators and raised in nursery cages have been released in our waterfowl ponds without pinioning. They now populate the creek valley which extends far beyond the zoo.

Thanks to a bit of vandalism in the zoo, one of our African fish eagles escaped. He was in no hurry to leave, possibly because his mate was still caged. Much of the time he spent in the trees nearby, and he ate the food keepers placed on the cage top. He had been netted several times before and would fly off whenever the keepers produced nets. One day he vanished. A day later we heard he was down by the river, several miles away, and keepers went to see. There he was, attracted by the fishermen, catching fish they tossed up for him. One said he had seen the eagle stoop and kill a pigeon in midair.

He was beyond catching now, and later reports placed him downriver, catching his own fish. Then there were no more calls. Since he had little fear of men, unless they had nets, he may have come too close to someone with a gun. Otherwise, he may still live, though a solitary male.

Most species seem able to make the change from captivity to self-support. Many people have picked up fledglings, raised them, released them, and watched them take up wild ways. Infant raccoons, opossums, squirrels, chipmunks, woodchucks, and skunks have been hand-raised and made the transition successfully. Two opposite notions confuse the issue: that all caged creatures yearn for freedom, and that caged animals become dependent and unable to fend for themselves. Neither is strictly true. The cage is security. Food is attractive. If the environment outside the cage is frightening, the animal may not leave it or may soon return. It may well return for food if it finds none outside.

Hand-raised animals released in a congenial environment may not immediately desert their foster parents. They may take to the woods but return now and then, possibly for all of their adult lives, possibly until they mate. A friend of

mine raised a female raccoon and released her from his weekend cabin. She returned frequently and would take food from
his hand. He missed her one spring. Some weeks later she re-
appeared, bringing two young coons along to be introduced.

If the question is whether a species can successfully be reintroduced to its native habitat after a number of generations
in captivity, the answer is almost certainly "yes." In some
cases, there should be no difficulty whatever. The animals
could be released with confidence that most of them would
do well. This would not be the case with gorillas or orangutans, for the captive-reared young would not have learned
their lessons. A period of introduction would be required.
It might even be necessary to establish a halfway house where
the captive-raised animals would live, though free to roam,
until they or their offspring chose freedom.

Complications could arise, and prudent men would take
precautions. Reintroductions, especially of the larger mammals, should not be made as hastily as dumping trout into a
stream. The captive years might have lowered resistance to a
disease endemic to the habitat. The ecology might have
changed subtly because the species in question had been absent for so long. The managers of the operation would experiment and observe. To most such difficulties they could
find answers.

Is it conceivable that a habitat from which a species is
eliminated could ever become hospitable again? Not in every
case, of course, but in many one can reasonably hope for such
an outcome. The wildlife of the Congo, including the gorilla,
was seriously imperiled during the hostilities there, but recent reports are encouraging.

The kind of warfare that has affected the Congo, Indonesia, Viet Nam, Laos, Cambodia, Korea, and other nations
takes a frightful toll of animal life. Bombing, fire, and de-

foliation have the most direct impact, but not necessarily the most extensive. Men with guns are all too likely to kill animals for target practice. Hungry people kill them for food, even species not usually considered prime eating. Displaced people disrupt previously quiet areas. In the absence of an effective civil government, squatters move into wildlife preserves from which they had been excluded. Conditions such as these can, one must hope, come to an end, and in peacetime some of the wounds will heal. In such places, restocking is a definite possibility.

A new government, or one coping with an economic crisis, may have to assign all of its limited resources to such immediate needs as food and transportation. Even schools may have a low priority, and the management of parks and wildlife preserves may be a luxury beyond reach. A number of governments have passed through such periods and now have time to devote to husbanding their natural resources. In this setting, too, reintroduction of vanished species may be possible. Israel now hopes to restore species eliminated from the Negev many years ago. The native ostrich is one that no longer exists. A related ostrich will be introduced instead.

But where will the animals come from? In some cases today there is no captive breeding stock. The kouprey, for example, was unknown to science until 1937, when it was discovered in northern Cambodia. At the time there were only a few thousand of them. The kouprey is a species of wild cattle, and there is no doubt that many have since been killed for food. Unfortunately, none were captured at a time when this might have been possible. Now we can only hope that some kouprey will survive until that part of the world is peaceful again.

Another form of wild cattle, the tamarau of the Philippines, is also seriously endangered. A few remain on the island of Mindoro, supposedly protected by game laws, but the laws appear to have loopholes, and enforcement is minimal, especially on privately owned land. In 1966 the Survival Service Commission recommended that tamaraus be captured, and the San Diego Zoo agreed to care for a herd if one could be assembled. Shortly thereafter, an animal dealer offered three for sale at $50,000 f.o.b. Manila!

He was merely an agent, he explained, and he could not divulge the name of the owner or the whereabouts of the animals. The price was exceptionally high, he admitted, but perhaps the owner would negotiate. To the price would have to be added the cost of moving the animals to an approved quarantine station, probably in Germany, holding them there for sixty days, shipping them to New York for another quarantine period, then to San Diego. If, in the course of all this handling, the solitary male should die, the hopes of propagation would die also. Even had the price been more reasonable, no responsible zoo or conservation group would have accepted the offer. Why all the mystery? If these three were sold, would this induce the capture of others?

The mountain tapir of South America is an endangered species, and none have been in zoo collections, nor had any been offered by animal dealers in recent years. Last year a pair appeared on the market, offered at $15,000. There was no evidence that they had been captured unlawfully, and no conservation group had asked zoos not to buy them. The pair was sold; I do not know at what price. Shortly thereafter other mountain tapirs were imported and sold, and more have been offered. Now the Survival Service Commission is concerned, and inquiries have been made. Is the sudden increase in trapping a threat to the wild population? Should zoos be asked to make no further purchases? Or is it in the best interest of the species that zoos acquire breeding stocks so that a captive population is maintained?

A number of other species endangered in the wild are present in captive collections. One of the best-known examples is that of Pere David's deer, extinct as a free species for several centuries. A herd had been maintained in the imperial game park near Peking, and in the nineteenth century a few were moved from China to Europe, then to the English estate of the Duke of Bedford. Shortly thereafter, the Chinese herd was wiped out during the Boxer Rebellion, and the fate of the species depended on the few in England. They multiplied, withstanding the effects of two world wars. In 1967 they were again threatened, this time by a fast-spreading epidemic of foot-and-mouth disease. The estate was closed, for a single case of the disease among the deer might have condemned the entire herd, which then numbered about three hundred. By then, however, about two hundred others were scattered among the world's zoos, all descended from the English stock. Had the main herd been lost, another might have been assembled. Our zoo had three males and two females then, and a fawn has since been born. If we succeed in establishing a breeding farm, the Pere Davids will be one of the first species moved there.

From United States zoos alone, today, breeding herds of a number of endangered species could be assembled: Przewalski's horses, onagers, Nubian wild asses, Hartmann's mountain zebras, Baird's tapirs, barasinghas, Formosan sikas, anoas, wisents, scimitar-horned oryxes, addaxes, and others. As yet, however, there is no place to assemble them under proper conditions. There is needed, for each species, a survival center comparable to the Chinese and English deer parks which, between them, maintained Pere David's deer for almost a thousand years.

Are survival centers suitable only for hoofed species? The endangered list extends from whales to tiny hummingbirds. Yet emphasis has, thus far, been on the ungulates. This is, in part, because of their special perils: they are rather large; they are hunted for meat as well as hides, horns, and trophies; their territorial requirements are substantial; and many of them require the kinds of habitats man requires for grazing cattle and growing crops. There are practical reasons as well. Most of the ungulates propagate well in captivity, and they are easily confined by fences. Yet because of their size, and because most of them are herd animals, they tax the capacities of zoos.

At his Catskill Game Farm, a private, profitable, and excellently managed establishment, Roland Lindemann has demonstrated what can be done. He specializes in hoofed animals, though he also keeps enough birds and carnivores to please his crowds of paying visitors. Unlike the game ranchers of Texas, Lindemann has collected breeding groups of endangered species. His latest count (1968) reports 21 Przewalski horses, 13 onagers, 7 Nubian wild asses, 6 Somali wild asses, and 10 Hartmann's mountain zebras, more than half of all these born at Catskill. He also had 13 vicugnas, 21 barasinghas, 12 Formosan sikas, 3 scimitar-horned oryxes, and 21 addaxes, most of which were born there.

Lindemann provides the expert care and meticulous attention rare animals need, and in this setting they propagate admirably. He owns additional land and is building larger paddocks for larger numbers. Still, this is an intermediate stage, between a zoo and a true survival center. Such excellent methods are too costly to apply to herds of a hundred head or more. Once basic security has been provided, the need is for a ranch or deer park on which animals can live with less attention.

That point is now being approached by several of the endangered species, thanks to successful zoo breeding. Surplus onagers, for example, are no longer in great demand. The Arabian oryx count, in the United States, now exceeds twenty. Before it doubles, a ranch experiment will be in order.

But where are the needed survival centers? Several zoos, including our own, have plans for them, but the plans have not come to fruition. The problem of course is money.

The San Diego Zoo has a splendid site, and its plans were developed with care and imagination. Expert planners and economists advised that the enterprise could be self-supporting if it were developed as a major tourist attraction, offering a full range of services and entertainments. Our own plans are more modest, based on several hundred acres of farmland owned by our parent Smithsonian Institution. There we could maintain adequate herds of six species of hoofed animals, in a setting propitious for research as well as propagation. It would not be designed for paying visitors, however, and the cost of preparing the site and operating the farm is beyond our means today, although it would be only a tenth of our present budget.

The San Diego region is singularly favored in its climate. We in the National Zoo would have to confine our efforts to hardy species. Both San Diego's plans and our own call for more intensive management than would be required if the climate and vegetation were such that the animals could subsist without daily care. Such a survival center would have to be spacious, with thousands of acres instead of hundreds. It would resemble a game preserve more than a farm.

Could a survival center become self-supporting through sales of animals? One might think so, since cattle ranching is profitable and zoo animals bring higher prices than steers.

But the market for beef is large, the zoo market small. Greater kudus can be sold for $10,000 a trio if only a few are available each year. If a survival center offered twenty, the price would tumble. Selling surplus animals to zoos and private ranchers would bring in a significant amount of revenue. Perhaps, as wild-caught animals vanish from the market, a well-run survival center could break even, but this is too speculative to put in an honest prospectus.

The Fish and Wildlife Service of the Department of the Interior operates refuges for native species, and it has undertaken efforts to save such threatened natives as the whooping crane, Everglades kite, Texas red wolf, black-footed ferret, and other species. Several years ago, when I was president of the Friends of the National Zoo, we proposed to Interior Secretary Udall that his department also operate survival centers for exotic species which could not be made secure in their homelands. He was receptive, a task force was organized, and I served for a time as its consultant. Sites were found, plans made, budgets calculated. Congressional authorization would be needed, as well as an appropriation. Several congressmen were sympathetic to the plan but advised Udall not to submit it. The time wasn't right.

But conservationists are persistent. Zoos have not yet found it possible to finance survival centers; the government has not chosen to do so; ranchers have thus far held back; and foundation support has not been forthcoming. Those who are persuaded of the need will keep trying, and it would be surprising if at least a few survival centers were not established in the next decade.

Designing a center for antelopes or wild asses is relatively simple. An eight-foot game fence is enough for confinement, and this can be built for a few thousand dollars per mile.

Such a fence would be no barrier to a gorilla or a tiger, however, and it would not hold a rhinoceros.

A leading primatologist has suggested that an uninhabited Caribbean island could become a sanctuary for orangutans. They would not find sufficient food there, presumably, and supplements would have to be provided. Yet the cost might not be prohibitive.

An island would probably be the only feasible sanctuary for tigers or other large predators. The cost of fencing or moating an extensive mainland preserve would be unacceptably high, as would be the risk of an accidental breach. There are many uninhabited islands in the tropics, and it would be an interesting challenge to attempt construction of a predator-prey balance. A number of such islands have feral populations of pigs and goats which ruin vegetation. They would be a natural food supply for big cats. The prey species might require periodic replenishment, but this would be less costly and more satisfactory than daily provision of slab meat.

Ecosystems are multidimensional, and an island refuge might well be used for several endangered species which occupy different niches and which are not threatening to each other. Crops might be planted to augment natural food supplies. Management would be required, and local supplies would probably need supplementation. Still, such an island operation would be more economical than a mainland survival center requiring secure fencing and full feed.

The San Diego concept may well prove to be more practical than centers in isolated places. When I first worked on such plans, I was convinced that a survival center should not be open to the public. It seemed to me then that the need to make provision for visitors would so increase development costs that the main purpose would be compromised, and that the need to please visitors would subvert the project's aims.

I may also have had a romantic bias, imagining myself riding across thousands of acres, delighting in the herds of oryxes and gazelles with no crowds of people to spoil the view.

Yet visitors become supporters, and a project open to the public may be more attractive to those called on for capital funds. Conservation efforts need constituents, people who see for themselves what can be achieved. We are, after all, seeking patterns of coexistence. Survival centers can be designed as preserves, offering visitors not the sight of wild animals in cages, but wild animals living much as they did in their homelands, running free, perpetuating their kind.

13

Strategies of Survival

A decade ago, loud alarms warned that Africa's larger mammals were doomed. With the end of colonialism, said the pessimists, wildlife protection would cease. The game preserves were known to natives as "white men's playgrounds" and would be abolished as symbols of colonial rule. In some native tongues, the same word served for "animal" and "meat." Natives would kill a zebra to sell its tail for a fly whisk. Rhinoceroses were slaughtered for their horns. To make matters worse, more and more cattle were being introduced, and successive years of drought had dried up water holes and reduced food supplies.

I wrote one of the pessimistic articles that appeared then. Were we wrong? The gloomiest predictions have not been fulfilled. Africa today has more parks and preserves than before. Wildlife protection laws are more stringent, and they are better enforced. Far more important, wildlife management is rapidly replacing simple protection. Young Africans have been trained in the techniques of management, and increasing numbers of them are obtaining university degrees in zoology, ecology, range management, and other specialties. Teams of scientists, some from the United States, have been making pioneer field studies. Realistic conservation plans have been shaped which hold the promise of permanent security.

It was not wrong to sound the alarm. The warnings aroused people who could help, so that financial and technical assistance was forthcoming. Nor has the danger passed. Many species are still insecure. Africa is a large continent whose nations differ in their attitudes toward wildlife and in their administrative resources and effectiveness. Kenya and Uganda are among the leaders in wildlife conservation. Most of the Arab nations lag far behind, both in policy and in practice, though there are some hopeful signs. The root problem, however, is one Africa shares with other continents. A "developing" nation is one that is developing its resources. Almost inevitably, this means the conversion of wild lands: construction of highways, construction of power dams with consequent flooding of bottomlands, drainage of wetlands, deforestation, increased grazing by domestic cattle, more extensive cultivation. All such changes reduce wild animal habitats. "Conservation" has a hollow ring if it is equated with "preservation" and restriction of sorely needed economic growth.

In the United States, the Sierra Club, the National Parks Association, the Audubon Society, the Wilderness Society, and other groups have often campaigned on what are, essentially, issues of preservation: saving the Grand Canyon, the California redwoods, the Allagash canoe country, Padre Island, the Indiana dunes. In such cases, preservation may conflict with local or special economic interests, such as those of certain lumber companies or steel mills. Neither individually nor in sum are the issues significant in our total national economy. Were the preservationists to win every case, the people as a whole would suffer no hardship. Had we preserved the Great Plains, however, to maintain a population of millions of bison, our economic history would have been quite different. We would not be producing food for two hundred million people.

In the course of America's development, we have suffered losses. Among the mammals, the sea mink, plains wolf, eastern cougar, eastern elk, Merriam elk, and Badlands bighorn became extinct. Among the birds, we lost the Labrador duck, great auk, passenger pigeon, Carolina parakeet, and heath hen. These losses were not necessary. Species could have been saved, though not original populations.

Some species that came close to extinction were saved, notably the American bison, the snowy egret, and the least tern. Unless effective measures had been applied in time, we would have lost a number of species of migratory waterfowl; and the elk, beaver, black bear, and bighorn sheep would be in far worse condition than they are. The positions of the whooping crane, masked bobwhite, and black-footed ferret are still precarious.

Good intentions, even when backed by persuasive public crusades, are not sufficient to save threatened species. In our complex modern world, conservation requires expert knowledge and scientific skill, as well as managerial resourcefulness and money. To save a species, one must understand it and the habitat to which it is native, as well as the events that have put it in jeopardy.

The bighorn sheep is not now in grave danger, though two subspecies are on the critical list. Adapted to mountain life, the bighorn might seem safely removed from civilization. Probably because of its rugged habitat, however, the bighorn restricts its wanderings, so that herds live as island populations. If hunters eliminate a group from one mountain area, the herd may not be replaced from neighboring groups.

Further, as domestic sheep graze farther and farther up the mountainsides, they often occupy, in summer, areas the wild sheep use in winter. Scabies, a disease of domestic sheep, is thus transmitted to the bighorns, who are highly susceptible. Hunting and disease can eliminate herds, one by one.

Hunting is now regulated. The California subspecies is fully protected. Now the need is to reintroduce bighorns to mountains from which they were eliminated, for it seems unlikely that they will find their own way back.

The technician's guide to the endangered wildlife species of the world is a pair of thick, red, looseleaf binders. These are the *Red Data Books* of the Survival Service Commission, published by the International Union for Conservation of Nature and Natural Resources, IUCN.

IUCN's Ninth General Assembly, held in 1966 at Lucerne, Switzerland, attracted several hundred delegates from forty-six nations. Only twenty years old, IUCN has become the chief international planning and coordinating body for conservation efforts. A number of national governments are affiliates. Private conservation groups may also join, a fact which has, thus far, prevented the United States from becoming a full national member. Our Department of the Interior has affiliated, however, as have the National Zoological Park and its parent, the Smithsonian Institution.

Between assemblies, much useful work is performed by IUCN's several commissions. The Survival Service Commission (SSC) is an international strategy group, largely concerned with saving threatened animal species. It meets somewhere in the world several times a year, and while it is seldom that a majority of its members appear, the minutes of meetings show remarkable continuity. Several members are likely to be absent, not because they can't leave home but because they are engaged in field work in such out-of-the-way places as Aldabra Island or Udjung Kulong.

The SSC, which I joined by invitation in 1967, has about sixty members from twenty countries. Little could be accomplished if we were bound by formalities and procedures, acting only in the presence of quorums and by majority vote. While disagreements can happen, decisions are rarely made by counting noses. If a project in Malaysia is up for consideration, the members who know the circumstances are expected to set the course. If my Smithsonian colleague, Dr. Lee Talbot, on a mission in Africa or the Orient, has an opportunity to supply helpful advice, I'm sure he does so, informing Chairman Peter Scott and Secretary Colin Holloway. Whenever any of us travels abroad, we seek new information for the *Red Data Book* sheets.

No one pretends the *Red Data Books* are complete even for the birds and mammals. A page is not inserted until the staff at Morges, Switzerland, has sufficient data to indicate that a species is in some peril, and such data are not readily come by. Some zoologists believe the chimpanzee is endangered, for example, but this species has an extensive range, only a part of which has been covered by recent field studies. Certainly the chimpanzee population has been much reduced, but there is not yet sufficient evidence for a *Red Data Book* page.

The page for the Brazilian giant otter was printed on red paper, signifying critical danger. In keeping with the standard format, there is a brief description of the species and statements of its former and present distribution. Footnotes cite the sources of facts, and in this case the sources were recent.

Next is "Status": In certain areas, extinction of the otter appears imminent. In others, populations have markedly declined. "The decline is due solely to commercial hunting for the skin, which is equal in value to that of the jaguar. . . ." Peruvian export statistics are quoted. Despite high prices and ready buyers, only 210 skins were exported in 1966, less than one tenth the number shipped in 1955.

"Protective measures taken": Essentially none—at the time of the last revision. The otter had been included in protective legislation proposed in Peru, but not yet enacted. Within a few months following this revision, however, two significant steps had been taken. Brazil declared all wildlife to be national property and listed the giant otter among the species to be given special protection. Peru proclaimed a new national park within whose boundaries an SSC member, Ian Grimwood, had found one of the last relatively undisturbed otter populations.

Further sections consider such possibilities as captive breeding. Fourteen otters were then in captivity, in eight zoos. A few young had been born, but none were successfully raised. What should be done to save the otter? The Survival Service Commission believes the chief need is to stop the traffic in skins, by persuading European and American countries to prohibit importation and transshipment.

About three hundred species and subspecies of mammals are currently included in the *Red Data Books*. Among them are some little-known animals, such as tiny voles of species that were always restricted to small habitats. Some of the species listed were always rare. The eastern barred-bandicoot of New South Wales has not been seen for many years and is probably extinct. Some of the listings are eloquent evidence that habitat destruction damages wildlife: Fifteen species and subspecies of lemurs are called endangered, all native to Madagascar.

Many of the species are familiar: the orangutan, mountain

gorilla, blue whale, polar bear, giant panda, Siberian tiger, Florida manatee, black rhinoceros, Key deer, and European bison. Others are little known, even to zoologists: the hispid hare, for example, and Fea's muntjac. When I make a speech to a general audience, I can count on their sympathetic response when I mention orangutans, but they look puzzled if I talk about the Haitian solenodon. What is it? Is it worth saving?

This is a troublesome question for conservationists, since most of their projects must be supported by popular contributions. Should exclusive or special emphasis be given to saving those species which are large and showy, the ones people like to see? Even conservationists have their favorites. Some endangered species get far more of their attention than others.

The scientist, if he can suppress the preferences he shares with other mortals, makes no such distinctions. Little-known species have special interest because of their uniqueness. How were they confined by nature to such small habitats? How do they differ from wider-ranging species? How has isolation affected their evolution? Since many of the rarities inhabit islands, population surpluses cannot be relieved by dispersal, and thus there are exceptional opportunities for studies of population dynamics.

The *Red Data Books* include endangered subspecies, and this causes some controversy. Our North American pronghorn, for example, has the scientific name *Antilocapra americana,* and its population is divided into a number of subspecies, regional populations with distinctive characteristics. The species as a whole is not endangered, but two of the subspecies are, the Lower California pronghorn (*Antilocapra americana peninsularis*) and the Sonoran pronghorn (*Antilocapra americana sonoriensis*). Both have pages in the *Red Data Books.*

Some scientists disdain subspecies classifications, and some conservationists think it impractical to consider them. Resources are too limited to assure preservation of important species, they say. We can't afford the luxury of undertaking to save subspecies. And, to a layman, the differences among subspecies often seem minor if, indeed, they can be distinguished. One pronghorn looks much like another. If I were to show a taxonomist a living pronghorn and ask him to assign it to a subspecies, his first question would be: "Where was it collected?" Only if I told him it came from Lower California would he confidently assign it to the subspecies *peninsularis*.

On the other hand, Florida's Key deer is much smaller than the commoner subspecies of white-tailed deer, and its habits differ from those of the others. Should the subspecies be wiped out, it is far from certain that deer from other parts of the United States could be established on the Florida Keys. The Key deer have attracted much popular attention, while another subspecies, the Columbia white-tailed deer, has received little, although it is no more secure.

Quite apart from scientific considerations, subspecies have political importance. If the people of Formosa, for example, understand that their native deer are of a special kind, which only they possess, national pride may prompt conservation efforts which would not otherwise be made. Even on a local basis, citizens may act to save animals that are uniquely theirs, especially if they could not be replaced.

Thus it is well, I believe, to include subspecies in the *Red Data Books*. It does not follow, however, that such alternatives as zoo breeding are justified for all subspecies if preservation in their habitats seem about to fail. The resources for such undertakings are far too limited.

Several subspecies of the tiger are endangered, among them the Siberian, a magnificent creature considerably larger than the Bengal, paler and with a longer coat. Bengal tigers are relatively common in zoos. About 160 Siberians are reported, but some are undoubtedly crossbreeds. There are enough purebloods for sustained breeding, however, and in this case it would be inexcusable to let the identity of the subspecies be lost. For the Siberian tiger—and for a number of other species and subspecies—zoos around the world cooperate in maintaining stud books, similar to dog pedigrees. Only a thoughtless zoo director would knowingly cross a Siberian with some other tiger.

The *Red Data Books* try to explain why each threatened species is in danger. In the case of the Brazilian otter, the cause is hunting for furs. Madagascar's lemurs are chiefly threatened by destruction of their forest habitats. The douc langur of southeast Asia is hunted for food. Mexico's rare volcano rabbit has suffered from the growing popularity of plinking, target practice with living targets. The disappearance of the Caspian tiger is attributed, in part, to effective control of malaria along the Caspian coast, which has led to a larger and more active human population.

Hunting alone has been the primary cause in relatively few cases. When forests are cut down or grasslands are plowed, however, a common effect is both reduction of natural habitat and the division of what had been a single, extensive population of a species into a number of isolated populations. These isolated groups are highly vulnerable. Should one be wiped out by a disease epidemic, for example, it would not be naturally replaced.

The golden marmoset of Brazil is endangered chiefly because it is now confined to a small area. It has been a popular zoo exhibit because of its rich, glowing color and its liveliness, and for a time it was also sold in the pet trade. The methods of capturing marmosets were exceedingly wasteful, and the wild population was reduced to an estimated four hundred. Various control measures have now reduced the rate of capture, and Brazilian conservationists are attempting to establish a golden marmoset preserve.

The closer a species comes to extinction, the more difficult it becomes to save it. A familiar case is our own whooping crane, a five-foot-tall bird whose wintering grounds once extended from Florida to California, though it may never have been numerous. These great white cranes are so big, and fly so slowly, that irresponsible hunters knock them down with ease. By the winter of 1938, only eighteen of them remained. They are fully protected now at both ends of their 2,000-mile migration route, and protectors keep as close a watch as possible when they are in flight. The wild population has increased slowly, with some dismaying setbacks, until it has now reached fifty.

Conservationists have argued long and at times bitterly about what should be done. Some urged that the remaining cranes be captured and held for breeding in a safe place, before hunters and hurricanes wiped out the remnant. Others were horrified by this idea, contending that the feasibility of captive breeding had not been proven. A few injured birds were placed in zoos, but arguments flared over their management. Two eggs were laid at the San Antonio Zoo. One was lost, but one chick was raised. Zoo director Fred Stark, who had lavished care on the precious birds, had the satisfaction of delivering the chick to the Patuxent Wildlife Research Center in Maryland a few months before his untimely death. At Patuxent the scientists hit upon a plan that has, thus far, worked astonishingly well. Twice now, eggs have been carefully removed from the Canadian breeding grounds and rushed to Patuxent. This, according to the experts, does not reduce the breeding potential of the wild cranes, since the females lay replacement eggs. All but one or two of the eggs brought to Patuxent have hatched, and, for the first time, the whooping crane situation has taken a positive turn.

No expert now believes that monkey-eating eagles can be raised in captivity. At least, the possibilities are not bright enough to justify interfering with the few wild eagles remaining in the Philippines. Perhaps this species is doomed, since protection of them is far from adequate. But zoos will not hasten their demise. Our American zoos, and zoos in several other countries, have bound themselves not to buy, accept as a gift, or seek to capture any of them. A similar self-imposed ban has been placed on Sumatran and Javan rhinoceroses, only a few of which remain.

Critics have accused the *Red Data Books* of "brinkmanship." Why wait until a species is one step from oblivion before listing it? By that time it may be too late for any but the most difficult and costly measures, and even these may not avail. In addition to "endangered species" should there not also be identification of "declining species"?

IUCN's tiny staff shrugs or winces at these thrusts. Compiling the *Red Data Books* has been a prodigious chore. Rather than sitting in judgment, they struggle to gather facts.

The Chilean pudu is a tiny deer. How widely does it range? Noel Simon, compiler of the *Red Data Book* on mammals, pieced together information from four published sources. Each, however, contributes only fragments. There has been no comprehensive field study. Indeed, such a study would be extraordinarily difficult, since the pudu occurs in rugged and inaccessible places. One way to determine where a species is found is to go look for it, noting tracks and droppings if the animals themselves are elusive. Often far more information can be gathered by talking with local farmers and hunters and others who travel the backcountry. A man who has hunted in a region all his life knows far more about its wildlife than a visiting scientist could learn in weeks of field work. I talked with such people in South America and gathered information, about pudus and other species. How reliable was it? Some of their statements conflicted. Some were based not on their own observations but what they had heard from others. A scientist gathering information in this way may publish it in a paper, and publication makes it seem reliable. It may not be wholly accurate, but even crude data, if sifted by a capable man, are better than none.

As to the number of pudus that remain, the *Red Data Book* is silent. No one has ventured an educated guess. Why, then, is it considered endangered? Here, too, local sources may be best. If a farmer or hunter says that no pudus have been seen in his region for a year or two, whereas they were common a decade ago, this is significant. If similar reports are gathered over a major portion of the pudu's range, it is reasonable to conclude that the species is in trouble. If a species is valued for its meat or fur, the record of hunters' kills may be a more reliable index of population than infrequent field surveys.

It would be splendid if IUCN could sponsor its own field surveys, even if these were limited to systematic collection of local reports. The truth is that IUCN's prestige and influence are far greater than its resources. What makes the organization effective is a small but dedicated staff and the voluntary efforts of a far larger group.

Ian Grimwood, for example, is a Survival Service Commission member who served for years in African game protection work. Responding to a request from Peru, the British government sent him there for extensive studies of Peruvian wildlife and its conservation. When I saw him last, he was on his way to another assignment in Nepal. Lee Talbot, another SSC member, is on the staff of the Smithsonian Institution.

His work in Africa, Indonesia, the Philippines, and elsewhere is sponsored by the Smithsonian, but much of it contributes directly to the Survival Service Commission. Some
SSC members are government employees. Others are on the
staffs of museums, universities, and private associations. Almost all of them travel extensively, and a map of their col-
lective expeditions in the course of a year would show few
corners of the earth untouched.

In 1961, SSC heard that the last wild herd of Arabian
oryxes in the Aden Protectorate had been wiped out by hunting parties. Hunters had sought the oryxes for years, but of
late it had become sporting to organize mass hunts, using
automatic weapons from skirmish lines of moving vehicles.
There was little hope of protecting the few scattered individuals that might remain. One slender chance remained: capturing a few which might live and breed in some sanctuary.

The Fauna Preservation Society organized Operation
Oryx. Added financial support came from the World Wildlife Fund, the Shikar Safari Club, and other groups. Ian
Grimwood led the party that went in search of the rare desert
antelope, a needle-in-haystack quest. Even were oryxes found,
capturing them and bringing them out alive would be immensely difficult. Yet it was done, and three oryxes were air-
lifted out. The London zoo contributed a fourth. The sponsors had chosen the Phoenix, Arizona, zoo as the site for the
new "world herd," in part because of its desert climate. Other
oryxes came later from Saudi Arabia and Bahrain. By 1968
zoo births had doubled the size of the herd. Through private
channels, the Los Angeles zoo acquired a trio, and two have
since been born there.

By 1966, it was known that the wild Arabian oryx population was not quite so small as had been feared. More had
been seen, and there might be as many as four hundred of

them, but there was no reason for complacency. They were still hunted, still endangered. Survival still, in all likelihood, depended on the captive herd. Phoenix, of course, cannot keep fifty or a hundred oryxes, and the risks of keeping most of the breeding stock together could not be ignored. The probable next steps are to establish other zoo herds, then seek a ranch where they could be well managed, where a herd of considerable size might be built. Eventually, it is hoped, some part of the native habitat can be protected well enough to warrant restocking it.

While the Survival Service Commission often acts as an international flying squad, responding to emergencies, its members must observe diplomatic niceties. Each government has the unqualified right to do as it pleases with its native fauna and flora. In only a few cases, such as that of the whales, are there international conventions. Further, leaders of young nations are sensitive to anything that smacks of colonialism. Much of SSC's work is therefore unobtrusive. A few months ago, for example, a high official of an Asian government met privately with three SSC members to seek advice on new wildlife regulations. One of the members knew this country and its problems well. The other two knew how such things are done. When the official returned home, he had a draft of new regulations in his briefcase. They were promulgated a few weeks later. SSC's part in their authorship will remain unpublicized.

Last week I received a letter from a zoo man who has often visited a certain nation. He is well acquainted there and speaks the language. He was disturbed by evidence that one of the wildlife officials of this country is corrupt, accepting bribes from animal dealers and sharing in the profits of illegal transactions. He urged me to forward this evidence to

IUCN headquarters so that IUCN could expose the male-factor.

The information was forwarded, but I am sure IUCN will make no exposure, at least not publicly. Whether anything will be done depends on close knowledge of the situation. Is the bribe-taking official acting in a manner that his superiors would condemn if they knew of it? Would they welcome the evidence of his misbehavior? Quite possibly they would not.

It is both easy and offensive to assume that our own code of ethics and morals is either universally accepted or divinely right. In some countries it is almost impossible to have an official document issued or stamped without paying what we call a bribe. This is no secret to anyone, certainly not to higher officials, nor is it any secret that the salaries paid minor civil servants are often less than a subsistence wage. At higher levels, where officials issue contracts, the bribes are often larger. We call it "conflict of interest" if a government official approves a contract with a company in which he holds a financial interest, but in some nations this is not an offense.

This does not mean that anything goes, that minor or major officials will do anything for a fee. The prevailing code may not match ours, but it may be even more rigid, and the penalties for violating it may be swifter and more severe. While the complexities of a local code may be difficult for a foreign mind to grasp, two general principles are reasonably reliable: a lower-ranking official puts himself in peril if, for money or other inducements, he sabotages a policy his superiors support; and he cannot safely deceive his superiors.

The important objective for IUCN is that policy-making officials give their support to wildlife conservation. Denouncing a minor officeholder might offend higher-ups and cause them to lose face. On the other hand, an SSC member who knows a high official personally may, with delicacy, feel out the situation. The evidence in the hands of IUCN might be just what he needs to bring a troublesome situation under control, if it is given to him privately. It is also possible that the bribe-taking officeholder is, on balance, a useful person, doing the best job possible under the circumstances.

IUCN and its several commissions link together a worldwide array of conservationists. Despite the lack of formal procedures, or perhaps because there are so few, the network responds quickly to crises. A Malayan member reported that a plan was afoot to capture a Javan rhinoceros. The sponsors of the plan meant well, but in the opinion of most experts they were misguided. Very few of the species remain. Any capture attempt presents risk of mortality. In this case, darting with an immobilizing drug was planned, and there had been no previous experience to fix the safe dosage. The intention was to capture only one, so captive breeding was not envisaged.

No special meeting was needed to trigger action. Within hours, cables were flashing around the world to key people who promptly called others by telephone. By next day, cables were deluging the sponsors of the planned capture. Had they been malefactors, they might have shrugged off the protests, but they were people of good will who were doubtless shocked to find themselves under fire and who may well have been convinced the protesters were wrong. Nevertheless, their plan was shelved.

Pleas and protests are necessary in conservation efforts, but IUCN is also influential in less direct ways. Conservationists were lonely people in the United States until the early twentieth century, and they are even lonelier in some other countries today. I know one man, for example, who heads his government's department of resources conservation, but most of his efforts have been frustrated for lack of support at higher levels, even within his own ministry. Another acquaintance heads a private conservation association which, until recently, has had little influence on his government's policies. Both men, in their own countries, have been ignored, if not ridiculed, as advocates of unpopular causes.

Both were representatives at the last IUCN General Assembly, and both take part in IUCN's work. Thus they are involved in an international fellowship, and they enjoy special recognition in IUCN circles because so few others in their countries are committed. This, in turn, has given them greater status and influence at home. They speak now not just for themselves but as members of a worldwide organization whose policies have been shaped by many governments and private organizations. The resolutions adopted by IUCN's General Assemblies are not binding on governments, even on those affiliated, but they have had influence on every continent.

IUCN and its commissions are not chiefly engaged in pleas and protests, however. Most of the work is highly technical. It achieves constructive changes not so much by arguing for them as by diagnosing problems and devising solutions. The Survival Service Commission is a group of experts who design strategies. The strategies of survival require intimate knowledge of a species and its habitat, understanding of the conditions threatening to survival, and a coldly realistic set of attainable objectives. While some undertakings seem formidable and fraught with difficulties, others require surprisingly modest interventions.

Before me is a list of projects financed by the World Wildlife Fund, an organization that serves as a fund-raising companion body to IUCN. Many of the grants made by the Fund to benefit wildlife species have first been reviewed by the Survival Service Commission. For example, the greater flamingos of the Camargue, on the southern coast of France, habitually nested in a certain lagoon, but erosion had progressively reduced their favorite island. It cost only $2,085 to repair the damage. The Swiss National Appeal of the World Wildlife Fund contributed most of it.

In Botswana, the members of a hunting tribe, the Batawana, were persuaded to set aside seven hundred square miles of their territory as a wildlife preserve. The British National Appeal of the Fund provided the first installment of $42,000 needed to make the new preserve operational.

The white-bearded spider monkey of Costa Rica was thought to be extinct, unless some remained on the tip of Nicoya Peninsula. A modest grant was needed to send a scientist there, find the monkeys if they still existed, assess their situation, and determine what might make them more secure.

Aircraft have been supplied to game departments to help in surveys, censuses, and enforcement. Provision of a small boat and motor established game patrols on a previously unpatrolled river. It would not be difficult for the Fund to spend its entire annual budget, which is raised by public contributions, on a single project. When many small projects are scattered around the world, however, each becomes a demonstration of what can be done, a little splash with spreading ripples.

I could not attend the most recent SSC meeting, because our Director, Ted Reed, was off on a trapping expedition in Africa. The minutes have just arrived. Thus I learn that the Duke of Bedford, whose estate houses the only large herd of Pere David's deer, plans to use four hundred acres of it for other purposes. The deer herd must be reduced. SSC will intervene, seeking other parks where herds might be established.

Dr. George Shaller, best known for his studies of gorillas,

reported on his visit to the Dachigam Sanctuary in Kashmir. He estimates that only 150 Kashmir stags remain, the summer range is overgrazed, and poaching continues. The Indian Wildlife Preservation Society will be approached in hopes that an alternate site can be found for establishment of another herd.

A British corporation is about to develop a jet airport and tourist center on Anegada, a previously undisturbed small island in the Caribbean. The Caribbean Research Institute asked SSC's advice, since the project cannot be stopped and Anegada has several unique species, including an endemic iguana. The Institute will make an ecological survey. Perhaps an adequate sanctuary can be kept on the island. If not, the iguanas might be colonized elsewhere.

The government of Ethiopia is considering a plan to restock certain of its game refuges with Somali wild asses, an endangered species. Asked for advice, SSC endorsed the plan, making several suggestions. This led to a more general discussion, and I see that I have been named to an ad hoc committee assigned to prepare a general policy statement on the capture, translocation, and breeding of rare species.

Dr. Curry-Lindahl reported that the most imminent threat to the mountain gorillas in the Congo had been eliminated. We hear such good news now and then. For example, the *Red Book* has a green page for the southern square-lipped rhinoceros, native to southern Africa. Its status: "Today, as a result of sound conservation measures, a subspecies once on the brink of extinction has been restored to abundance."

14

The Smuggled Orangutans

It was the evening of February 25, 1967, my birthday.
The telephone rang while we were at dinner. This was the
call I had been hoping for. The cake could wait.

Several days earlier, officials of the Fish and Wildlife Service of the Department of the Interior had received advice
that an orangutan might be shipped from Bangkok to the
United States, in apparent violation of federal law. Our information network had been on the alert ever since. Bulletins
arrived. The animal had left Bangkok. The shipment had
been rerouted. Now it was expected to land at Dulles Airport, outside Washington. Customs agents and agents of the
Fish and Wildlife Service were waiting.

"It's here!" said my caller. "We've taken the crate off the
plane. Now we need someone to identify it."

Identification is a problem for customs agents, who have
many responsibilities. They cannot be expected to know the
difference between a golden marmoset and a cotton top, or
between a macaque and a mangabey. Something was in that
crate at Dulles, and it was obviously some kind of monkey or
ape. No customs agent was likely to open the crate for a closer
look!

Don Dietlein, then our Animal Manager, was on standby. He left for Dulles at once with his secretary, Billie Hamlet. At Dulles, he found a group of men gathered in a cold and cavernous shed, contemplating a rickety crate marked "One Head Monkey." He opened it and lifted the animal out. It was, indeed, an orangutan, a young male, scrawny and pot-bellied, almost hairless, hungry and cold. Now there were certain formalities. The federal agents made their seizure. Don signed a receipt. National Zoo had agreed to care for the animal until its fate was decided. Billie took the young ape under her fur coat. It clung to her for warmth and fell asleep.

A dozen of us were at the zoo hospital when they arrived. Director Ted Reed, a veterinarian, made a careful examination and administered medication. Head Keeper Bert Barker brought food from the commissary, no doubt the best meal the youngster had had since he was taken from his dead mother in an Indonesian forest. He was obviously accustomed to people. He was also resourceful, we learned shortly. On the following night, he discovered how to unlock his cage in the hospital quarantine room. Veterinarian Clint Gray and his staff cleaned up the wreckage the next morning and named their guest "Dennis."

The orangutan—which means "man of the forest"—is a large ape with reddish hair and a soberly comical broad face. Once wide-ranging, it now lives only in Borneo and Sumatra, where it is making its last stand. The territorial requirement of the species has been estimated to be one square mile of forest per individual. Deforestation has reduced its habitat, and an unknown number are killed for food. About five thousand are believed still in residence. Like all small populations, the orangutans are now vulnerable to man's predations.

Dutch law protected the orangutans in colonial times.

The Republic of Indonesia adopted the Dutch game laws and strengthened them. Sarawak and Sabah, the only other nations with orangutans, protected them by law, and these laws remained in effect when the Malaysian Federation was formed. Poachers and smugglers could evade the laws with little risk, however, and the common method of capture is appallingly wasteful.

The collector is a man with a gun who happens to see a female orangutan with young. He shoots her. The baby may not survive the fall. If it does, it may be too young to survive without nursing. If it lives through the first few days after capture, it is likely to succumb to malnutrition, disease, or mishandling as it travels the long route to market.

We do not know how Dennis came to Bangkok, but the general pattern of such cases is familiar. The collector carried the infant orangutan to the seacoast, where he sold it, probably for less than five dollars, to the operator of a small boat. The boatman's next stop was Singapore, just across the Straits of Malacca. Almost anything can happen in this crowded, bustling harbor, where commerce is lively and uninhibited. Dennis was probably sold for less than twenty-five dollars to another sailor, who took him up the Gulf of Siam to Bangkok.

The next guess is confirmed by Dennis's physical condition and behavior on arrival. The signs of nutritional deficiency were consistent with a rice diet. He had obviously been a house pet. Orangutans are often kept as house pets in this part of the world. Dennis might have been kept in this way for a year or more. Like most wild-animal pets, orangutans become more difficult to manage as they mature. Dennis had become strong enough to be destructive, too strong and dextrous to be confined in a frail cage. So, like many before him, Dennis was sold to an animal dealer for, perhaps, $150.

Bangkok, Singapore, and Hong Kong are centers of the wild animal trade. Here dealers collect birds, mammals, and reptiles from many parts of Asia and Africa, for sale to buyers in Europe and America. A primate research center in Georgia buys directly from a Bangkok dealer. A zoo in California scans the Hong Kong price lists for offerings of rare birds. A German pharmaceutical laboratory obtains many of its laboratory animals from Singapore. The Singapore dealer obtains his stocks from as far away as Nepal and the Congo.

Until a few years ago, orangutans illegally captured and illegally removed from Sumatra and Borneo were openly advertised and sold by dealers in these centers, as well as by others in Japan and Holland. Conservationists were bitter about this trade, in part because each one sold could mean as many as eight dead ones left behind, but also because most of the buyers were "respectable."

Most of them, in fact, were zoos. While the largest collection of orangutans in the world is at the Yerkes Regional Primate Center at Emory University in Georgia, the species is not generally used in research, nor is it considered a pet in the Western world. Zoos consider all of the great apes prestige exhibits, however. A majority of the world's principal zoos have orangutans.

Zoo directors defended themselves against occasional criticism of these purchases. They bought orangutans openly, from established dealers. No laws were violated in their transactions. They could not possibly trace the origins of the orangutans. Perhaps it was true that Indonesia, Sabah, and Sarawak prohibited capture, but it was obvious that the laws were not being enforced—and who had ever seen the laws? But the criticisms continued.

At about the time IUCN published its first list of endangered species, the orangutan trade became a major issue.

Why this species was singled out for a crusade is not entirely clear. No doubt the reasons included both sentiment and strategy. It was a good choice, however, and the crusade has changed laws, policies, and precedents around the world. It began when IUCN asked the world's zoos to stop buying contraband orangutans.

The International Union of Directors of Zoological Gardens agreed, and passed an appropirate resolution, but IUDZG has a limited membership. In 1962 the American Association of Zoological Parks and Aquariums (AAZPA) adopted a comparable resolution. It had some moral effect, but no teeth. A few members, both dealers and zoo directors, denounced the admonition not to buy.

"I just came back from Hong Kong," one said. "I saw twenty young orangutans being kept under the worst possible conditions. They can't be returned to the forest. If we don't buy them, they'll die."

Perhaps so, others agreed. But if the twenty were sold at fancy prices, more would soon come to the market place. Dealers were asking $3,000 to $5,000 for an orangutan, and such prices were a strong inducement.

In 1966, the AAZPA took a stronger stand. From now on, any member who violated the resolution risked expulsion. A special subcommittee was named to review orangutan transactions. I was named chairman. Members were now required to consult this committee before buying any orangutan. Further, it was the Association's policy to cooperate with federal authorities, who had a new weapon, the Lacey Act, which forbids importation of any bird or mammal illegally removed from its country of origin.

The Lacey Act was not really new, but it had not been enforced. The legal difficulties were substantial. If an orangutan came to the United States from Singapore or Hong Kong, who could say where it originated or prove that a law had been violated? Dealers continued to offer the species, confident that no one would interfere.

IUCN's emissaries were hard at work, however, persuading governments of Hong Kong, Japan, Singapore, and Thailand to outlaw transshipments of contraband animals. Results were useful but not decisive. Singapore, for example, made it unlawful to import or export undocumented orangutans, but it was still legal to possess them. Unless a smuggler was caught in the act, he was still safe.

Bit by bit, the pressure went on. A Hong Kong dealer responded to it ingeniously, though he was not discreet in his choice of correspondents. We were sent a copy of one of the letters, which said, roughly:

We have orangutans for sale. It's against the law, so don't mention "orangutan" in your order. We'll call them "baboons" on our invoice. You must send us an irrevocable letter of credit. We won't ship the orangutans ourselves. We have connections. Each will be in a special crate behind a secret panel. We'll put a python up front so nobody will investigate. Add five dollars for the python.

Several zoos, offered orangutans, asked dealers to produce documents proving legal origin, then refused to buy when the documents were not forthcoming. This shook the trade. Overseas dealers were further shaken when they began receiving letters from our Endangered Species Subcommittee inquiring about the orangutans they had offered for sale, declaring that no zoo would buy them without legal documents.

One zoo, rather credulously, imported orangutans from Japan on the strength of certificates attesting that they had been zoo-born. We soon had a list showing every orangutan ever born in a Japanese zoo. All were accounted for. The certificates were false. Japanese zoo leaders, stimulated by this incident, had their zoo association adopt a resolution matching AAZPA's. Later, they persuaded the Japanese government to outlaw transshipment of illegal animals.

One Monday morning, a Fish and Wildlife Service official called on us for aid. A tipster had reported that two orangutans had slipped through a West Coast port over the weekend. If we could trace them, some action might be possible. A committee member in the area picked up their trail. They had gone to a pet shop, then to a privately operated zoo. Federal agents moved in, asked questions, inspected documents. The case was referred to the U.S. Attorney. For technical reasons, no legal action was taken. This defeat was compounded when AAZPA's attorneys advised the Board that a defect in its resolution precluded disciplinary action against the offending zoo.

The news from overseas was better. Trade in orangutans had been stopped in Japan and Hong Kong. Dr. Reed, representing the AAZPA, visited officials in Singapore and was assured of their cooperation. Only Bangkok still seemed open.

Now and then we had a flurry of activity, for our international information network was not infallible. One day a German contact reported that a Dutch ship had left Borneo with a consignment of more than thirty orangutans. The destination was said to be Singapore. We put out an alert, though we were skeptical and could find no such ship in Lloyd's Registry. Next came word that the ship had been diverted to Bangkok, but now the ship had another name! The report was never confirmed. No such ship ever appeared, nor did any such number of orangutans ever enter the market.

Several flurries were caused by the trade practices of animal dealers. A Central American dealer advertised a pair of orangutans for sale. We made inquiries. The dealer had received a Bangkok price list. It cost him nothing to add the Bangkok offerings to his own advertising, with a suitable markup. Had a customer appeared, he would have negotiated with the Bangkok supplier. The pair was one we already had under observation.

In the second half of 1966, no undocumented orangutans came to the United States, though several were sold in Europe. Except for one firm in Bangkok, international dealers had ceased offering the species—at least publicly. Then came the case of Dennis. This one seemed critical. Legally, it is more difficult to take action once an animal has entered the United States. Now we would see how the law worked if brought to bear at the time of entry.

For months we had been pursuing animals we never saw— orangutans moving through obscure and secret trade channels, orangutans hidden away in private homes, orangutans we knew only as specimens on foreign price lists. Then came Dennis, a cold and hungry waif, all the way from Bangkok into the temporary safekeeping of our zoo.

I stopped by to see him one evening. Turning on the lights, I saw only a heap of blanket at the rear of his cage. Then a corner of the blanket moved, and large brown eyes regarded me with interest. I spoke, and the young ape rolled over, clear of the blanket, and waddled forward. He had gained a few pounds, and his reddish hair was growing nicely.

Long arms reached through the bars and embraced me. Then, slowly and gently, he began exploring with strong but delicate fingers, untying my bow tie, grasping my holstered pipe. I opened the cage door and he came into my arms for a moment, then wanted to play. His eyes gleamed when I produced an ice cream cone. He took it and licked it like a child.

Dennis was not ours. He was only with us for safekeeping until the courts decided what should be done with him. The importer, pleading innocence, was urging that Dennis be released. Meetings with government attorneys were inconclusive. The law had not been tested before. Like most legal cases, this one had complications. I suspected that certain of the attorneys thought it ridiculous to involve so much highly paid talent on behalf of one small ape.

Then, one day, we won. A federal judge signed an order declaring Dennis forfeit, and now the property of the United States. The order approved a plan turning Dennis over to the National Zoo, not to keep but to deposit elsewhere.

So the second chapter began. It seemed unlikely that any other dealers would risk confiscation of valuable property. Bangkok adopted new regulations, closing the market there. Indonesia tightened its controls. Eighteen months earlier, pessimists had declared that orangutan smuggling could never be halted. Now it had been, substantially. We are sure that occasional orangutans are still captured illegally, and we hear reports of orangutans being sold. In South America I saw two pairs that had been shipped from Japan. One pair, we knew, had passed through Kennedy Airport en route, but our authorities cannot intercept such international shipments. The Japanese have tightened their controls since, however. Piecing scraps of more or less reliable information together, we believe that at least seventy-five orangutans are in private hands in southeast Asia. As they mature, their owners will probably wish to dispose of them. In at least three nations, they will not go into black-market channels if existing regulations prove effective.

The second chapter will decide the fate of the species in

captivity. Until a few years ago orangutan births in zoos were rare, and losses were replaced by wild-caught animals. This was attributable in part to an undesirably high death rate. Too many of the animals died before reaching sexual maturity. But mature orangutans often failed to mate.

The outlook has brightened dramatically within the past five years. Of about four hundred orangutans in the world's zoos, one in eight was captive-born. In the United States, better than one in six was born in a zoo. The birth rate has risen rapidly, and a statistician might conclude that the captive population would soon be self-sustaining.

Zoo men are hopeful but aware of an open question. Thus far, almost all of the captive births have been to wild-caught orangutans. No one yet knows whether zoo-born specimens will reproduce as well. There are some negative indications, chiefly that many orangutan mothers have declined to nurse their zoo-born infants, and it has been necessary to take these infants for hand-raising. They are then doubly handicapped. They have been deprived of maternal care. Further, when they are raised by humans, some degree of imprinting occurs, and they may have difficulties in relating to their own species.

We were fortunate with Jennie, one of our two females, who proved to be a splendid mother. For many months her new son, Atjeh, was never out of her arms. He was held affectionately throughout his early development. As he gained strength and initiative, her devotion became even more impressive. Rarely was Atjeh restrained. If he attempted to climb, she allowed it, but always within her reach, so she could catch him should he fall. As his second birthday neared, Atjeh was physically competent, but Jennie was still protective. I came into the house one night with guests, turned on the lights, and found the two asleep on their high shelf. Both awoke and looked down at me. Curious and friendly,

Atjeh was all for climbing down alone, but this Jennie would not allow. Strangers were present. Since Atjeh wanted to visit, she would also. Down they both came, Atjeh eager to play games, Jennie ready to carry him away if she sensed danger.

If we had an infant female to add to this group, we would have greater confidence in our future with the species. Now that the illegal trade has been suppressed, of course, orangutans are not readily obtained. The Orangutan Committee of the Wild Animal Propagation Trust keeps watch over the captive population, recommending exchanges and transfers between zoos and keeping a waiting-list of zoos that need additional breeding stock. We are on the list—but so are others.

To hear zoo directors talk about themselves, one might think they were incorrigible individualists, jealous of each other, sometimes feuding, with a gypsy flavor in their animal trading. The compelling need to conserve threatened species has unified them, however, and the Wild Animal Propagation Trust succeeds because of voluntary self-discipline. An example was the case of the orangutan from Singapore.

When he visited Singapore, Dr. Reed talked with officials there about the problem of confiscation. What if they seized a contraband animal? They had no holding facilities. The orangutan could not be sent back to the forest. Could he propose some orderly method of disposition? Months later we received word that the government of Singapore wished to present a young male orangutan to the government of the United States.

The National Zoo has been the beneficiary of many gifts from other governments. In this case, our natural acquisitiveness was subordinated to the welfare of the species. Another young male would add nothing to our breeding potential.

WAPT's Orangutan Committee should make the decision. Where should the animal be placed on deposit?

At the time, no zoo had a single juvenile female as a potential mate. Several requests for females were pending, as well as requests for pairs from zoos that had no orangutans. From among the latter, the Committee chose Seneca Park at Rochester, a small zoo but one that could provide good facilities and care.

Arranging safe transport for such an animal is quite an operation. Cables went back and forth. The American Embassy at Singapore had a crate built to our specifications. Pan American Airways arranged the schedule as if a VIP were traveling. Ambassador Galbraith himself accompanied "Gambar" to the Singapore airport. Agents of the Public Health Service, Fish and Wildlife Service, and Customs were ready to receive the orangutan and speed the formalities when it entered the United States at Los Angeles. The veterinarian of the Los Angeles Zoo was there to check on Gambar's condition and care for him should the connecting flight be delayed. He telephoned to report all was well. At Kennedy Airport, in New York, Louis di Sabato, then Rochester's zoo director, was waiting with his veterinarian and Fred Zeehandelaar, a leading animal dealer who had volunteered assistance. One of the government men stationed at the airport, a bit awed by all the fuss, told me: "Gambar came off the plane with a stewardess on his arm and a big cigar in his hand!"

Several weeks later I went to Rochester with an official of the Embassy of Singapore to accept this gift for the United States. The night before, as I was talking with Clayton Freiheit, Buffalo's director, who would represent WAPT at the ceremonies, the telephone rang. Fred Zeehandelaar was calling. A juvenile female orangutan was available for sale in Holland. I happened to know that this was a legal animal, exported from Indonesia under license. It was the only legal female that had been available for months. The WAPT waiting list included Rochester, Buffalo, and the National Zoo. But Rochester had priority.

At the ceremonies next day, attended by many city and county officials and members of the zoological society, I pointed out that Gambar was not a gift to Rochester. He would remain government property, under WAPT management, and his future home would depend on where he could best be used for propagation. Unless Rochester could pair him with a suitable female, he might be transferred elsewhere someday. Gambar, in a cage beside the podium, watched the proceedings with interest. I'm sure it was an optical illusion that his eyes brightened when I mentioned the availability of a potential mate. The price was $3,500. I knew that the zoo had no such amount in its animal purchase fund. But a member of the zoological society stood up.

"Buy it, Louis," she said. "We'll get you the money."

A happy zoo director dashed for the telephone.

The WAPT Orangutan Committee also considered the case of Dennis. This time the choice was Omaha, where the zoo had one male and three females. We were sorry to see him go. Dennis had become a favorite with visitors and staff. The ceremonies attending the transfer were impressive. Zoo director Dr. Warren Thomas flew in from Omaha. The presidents of AAZPA and WAPT were there, as well as Don Davis, Director of the Cheyenne Mountain Zoo at Colorado Springs, Chairman of WAPT's Orangutan Committee. Officials of the Fish and Wildlife Service and the Bureau of Customs came, too. Television and newspaper crews crowded the meeting place.

There have been times when we wondered if so much time and energy were justified. The orangutan is but one of many endangered species. Yet it has been a popular symbol, a good test case. The issues were clear, and it was a case we could win. As the second chapter unfolds, the orangutan will present us with another challenge, another kind of test case.

If breeding results continue good, zoos will soon have an embarrassment of orangutans, zoo-born. Further, as controls tighten overseas, more confiscated or surrendered orangutans will need homes. Zoos now have about all the orangutans they can house. Indeed, I suspect facilities are not yet available, in some cases, to house the many young animals as they reach adult size.

What should be done if such a surplus develops? What should be done with the seventy-five or more illegally captured animals now in private hands overseas, which will almost certainly be sold or surrendered as they mature? It was once assumed that wild-caught young orangutans could not be returned to the wild. Lacking the training wild apes receive from the time of birth, they could not survive at large.

Barbara Harrisson hoped she could find a way. Mrs. Harrisson and her husband, both archaeologists, have devoted years to study of orangutans. Mrs. Harrisson was one of the first to attack the smuggling trade. She organized the Orangutan Recovery Service, which rescued many forlorn animals from the hands of smugglers.

In 1962, with financial aid from the World Wildlife Fund, Mrs. Harrisson began her experiments in the Bako National Park of Sarawak. Later the undertaking was transferred to the Sepilok Center in Sabah, where it is managed and supported by the Sabah Forest Department. A number of young orangutans were brought to the center for "rehabilitation." They are kept in pens but released for several hours each day, with unlimited freedom to roam. Not surprisingly, the young apes have shown no eagerness to leave their comfortable quarters, their assured food supply, and the association with affectionate keepers. Their wanderings have become somewhat more extensive as they mature, and individuals have occasionally remained out all night.

Does this mean failure? Certainly not. The center had a mature female who seemed more adventurous than the younger males. She vanished into the woods and did not return the next day. Search parties failed to find her. Eventually she did return—pregnant! She had mated with a wild male. Her infant was delivered at the center.

The Sepilok Center, under Stanley de Silva of the Forest Department, has done invaluable pioneering. But the center's capacity is limited, as is the protected forest area adjoining. In Washington, Dr. Lee Talbot and I talked with visiting Indonesian game officials about the possibility of a more ambitious project in Indonesia, where at least fifty orangutans are in captivity now, in zoos or in private hands. They were interested, and I discussed what might be done when Barbara Harrisson visited me a few weeks later.

The site would be an Indonesian preserve which has a wild orangutan population. A center would be built there with the intention of making it a permanent facility, for research as well as rehabilitation and propagation. The presence of the center would help deter poaching in the surrounding preserve, where there are no permanent game wardens now.

There would be no urgency in persuading captured or zoo-born orangutans to leave the center and take up the free life. The plan would be to have some apes resident at the center at all times, and to encourage a free association between them and those living wild. Indeed, the center would become an attraction to the wild apes, who would come to accept it as a sanctuary and a source of food.

Diffidently, since I am not a scientist and have never studied orangutans in the wild, I outlined some notions I had conceived through reading the available literature. It did not seem to me that this huge ape could have evolved in swamp forest habitat. Perhaps its present habitat, a small remnant of the territory it once occupied, is only marginally suitable, and its low density—less than one individual per square mile —is enforced by limitations of food supply. Perhaps in the past, I speculated, orangutans could live more closely together, and under such circumstances were more social in their habits.

What would happen, I asked Mrs. Harrisson, if, once an Indonesian center was established, the area surrounding the center were cultivated and heavily planted with food crops suitable for orangutans?

Having had years of experience in that part of the world, Mrs. Harrisson recognized the immense difficulties that would have to be overcome to establish and maintain such a center. Even if financial support could be found, she said, the project would fail unless skillful and dedicated people could be found who would commit themselves to it. Not many people who have the necessary training are willing to live in such complete isolation for long periods of time. Yet she was encouraging, seeing no fatal flaw in the concept.

A few years ago, support might have been found more readily. There was then a boom in primate research, but funds are now harder to come by, especially for long-term projects. What matters most, at the moment, is having confidence that even this relatively difficult species can be returned to the wild. Until that becomes a practical possibility, we must still seek some way to accommodate zoo-born orangutans when their number exceeds what zoos can house.

15

The Animal Trade

The Smithsonian-Chrysler Expedition sailed from New York in March 1926. Dr. William Mann, then Director of the National Zoo, headed the party, which included scientists, newsreel cameramen, and aides. Field gear was provided by the Marine Corps, medicines by a Washington hospital. Their supplies included crates for the animals they hoped to capture.

Arriving in Africa, the party set up headquarters at Dodoma, in Tanganyika Territory, and hired local hunters, interpreters, and hands. In October, after four months of collecting, they returned triumphantly with more than a thousand birds, mammals, and reptiles. Back to the zoo came giraffes, gnus, impalas, reed bucks, kudus, elands, wart hogs, leopards, hyenas, foxes, ratels, porcupines, hedgehogs, and jackals.

Such expeditions were high adventure, but there will be no more of them. The world has changed, and so has the animal business. One measure of the change is the embarrassment of our librarian who ordered a copy of a new magazine, *East African Management,* expecting something about wildlife. We received a magazine for African businessmen, featuring advertisements for electronic data-processing equipment, microfilm apparatus, electric typewriters, and industrial production machinery.

Zoo men still travel the world, more often than in the past, but the modern "expedition" is likely to be one man aboard a jet, reaching his destination in a few hours rather than weeks. East Africa is the zoo man's Mecca. If he is a good customer, he may be invited to join a team going out to capture zebras or giraffes. He'll use his camera, though, rather than a noose. Catching is a business for professionals. If a visiting zoo man wanted to try it independently, he would probably be denied a license.

Zoo men still do some collecting. Kerry Muller, our Bird Division Manager, traps ducks on Chesapeake Bay each year, and he flew to Alaska last year for ten days of trapping. Scientist John Eisenberg sent several unusual mammals back from Madagascar as a by-product of his field research. Four of our keepers, on their own, recently collected reptiles in Florida, and another collected reptiles while vacationing in Guatemala.

But we buy most of our animals from dealers, the majority of whom are middlemen who do no collecting themselves. Price lists come in the mail almost every day offering birds, mammals, and reptiles from every corner of the globe.

In the old days, wild cargo crossed the seas on slow freighters. The animals had to be fed and watered, and they were more likely to survive with expert care. So it was best to ship them in lots and send a good man along. If there were enough for a charter, the voyage could be made shorter.

Animals are still shipped by sea if they are too large for the available aircraft or if a sufficient number are being dispatched at one time. When a German quarantine station is unsealed after the required sixty days, a batch of ruminants may be moving next to United States quarantine. Shipping by sea is less costly than by air, and the route is direct.

Most animal shipments are made by air, however, and airlines are accustomed to wild cargo. Last week the director of the Smithsonian Tropical Research Institute telephoned from Panama asking if we could obtain two male red uakaris for him. The species is found in the upper Amazon Basin, but we made our inquiries in Florida. Within an hour we found a dealer who could supply the monkeys. One of them arrived at National Airport that same afternoon!

In some of the older types of aircraft, the belly compartments where freight is stowed were neither pressurized nor heated. Even now we sometimes hear of animals dying en route because a careless dealer allowed them to be loaded on an old-style plane. In modern, smooth-flying jets, wild animals travel in comfort, with a minimum of stress. Many journeys are so swift the animals need not be fed on the way.

The chief hazards in air shipping are what can happen on the ground. Things are most likely to go wrong when a shipment must be transferred to a connecting flight. Crates are off-loaded. Unless someone is vigilant, the crated animals may be left to stand in the broiling sun, or in rain or snow. If the connecting flight is delayed, or if there is no room for the animals, they may be held for hours without food or water. Humane societies operate animal shelters at a few of the largest international airports, but the longest delays occur at smaller airports where missing a flight could mean a two- or three-day wait.

When we shipped a young Nile hippo to Chile, two keepers drove it to New York in one of our trucks, learned the flight was delayed, and stayed with the crate all night to make sure it was kept in warm shelter. People who ship animals to us are asked to let us know the flight numbers and arrival times, so we can meet the planes. Once we were not informed until a shipment had arrived in New York, too late to meet a connecting flight. The Bronx Zoo generously sent a man to Kennedy Airport to care for the animals.

Even with close attention, things can go wrong. Recently a group of animals was shipped to us from Australia. We had word of their arrival in San Francisco and subsequent departure for New York. Then they vanished. San Francisco insisted the animals had been put on the correct flight. Kennedy insisted they hadn't arrived—and it was a nonstop flight! Hours were passing, and the animals needed attention. We called San Francisco again, asking for the exact language of the waybill. It said: "FAUNA."

"Oh, sure, that's here!" said Kennedy. " 'Fauna' means 'plants.' That's over in the plant quarantine section waiting for the inspectors."

Airline officials would like to be cooperative. Their communications networks operate swiftly and efficiently. On many occasions, a special shipment has been given such extraordinary handling that the operating cost could be justified only by favorable publicity. If animal shipments were rare, they might all be given such attention, but the airlines haul live cargo daily: chicks from hatcheries, mice for laboratories, birds for the pet trade, show dogs, racehorses, and house cats, as well as zoo animals.

A keeper and I took three kangaroos to the airport one day, in a cold rain. Most flights were off schedule. Other cargo was moved about routinely in the freight hangar. We stood guard over the kangaroo crates. At loading time, the plane was assigned to a position some distance away. We refused to let them put the 'roos on an open baggage cart for the transfer. Someone had to find a closed cart, pick it up with a tractor, then make a special trip to planeside. We stood in the rain until the three crates were loaded.

It would be splendid to have animal shelters at every airport, and many animal lives would be saved by such care. But who would provide the needed funds? The airlines cannot be expected to do so. Shelters would be required not only at the international airports but at the far larger number handling domestic traffic. Perhaps some kind of tax could be levied on animal shipments, but it would be difficult to apportion this equitably among the shippers of laboratory mice, pet dogs and cats, prize bulls, racehorses, canaries, goldfish, bees, mealworms, venomous snakes, ants, homing pigeons, and zoo animals.

At the time of the Smithsonian-Chrysler expedition, animal collecting was no threat to wild populations. Collecting for zoos and museums is still an insignificant drain, except in a few special cases. But the animal trade as a whole has boomed, reaching such an enormous volume that some parts of the world are being stripped of their wildlife. Birds and primates are most seriously affected because of the demands of the pet trade and the laboratories.

Birds are offered for sale not only in pet shops but in drug stores, department stores, discount houses, and hardware stores. A recent price list sent by a Belgian dealer to wholesalers in the United States offered birds from around the world. Cordon bleus from Africa were $1.10 a pair, silverbills only 70 cents a pair. Pairs of gray Java sparrows were $1.20, Mexican nonpareil buntings were $4.50. Some species were more expensive: red-and-yellow macaws at $56.00.

One day we were called to the airport and asked to pick up a shipment of birds the consignee had refused. More than four hundred birds were in the lot. Almost two hundred were dead and others were dying. We managed to save about a hundred. Not long afterward, we heard of a shipment that arrived in London: seven hundred birds, all dead. Since then we have learned of more cases. Losses of 40 percent were termed "not unusual" by one bird importer.

Some of the birds offered by the European wholesalers come from South America. A typical supplier is a small businessman, untrained, who has acquired some skill in catching birds. Once or twice a month he makes the rounds of native villages, in each of which he has a chosen man who does the collecting for him on piece rates. The supplier has provided these men with nets, often the almost-invisible mist nets, explained which kinds of birds he will buy, and taught them how to capture and hold the birds. On his rounds, he picks up whatever they have caught, pays them—perhaps less than one cent per bird—and tells them what he wants next time.

Kerry Muller visited a South American supplier's aviary. The stench was overpowering. Birds were crowded together in row after row of small cages. Dead birds, some in advanced stages of decay, littered the cage floors, which seemed never to have been cleaned. It was cheaper for the supplier to buy more birds than to pay someone to care for them.

This supplier had neither the skill nor the resources to develop an international customer list. Instead, he sold birds by the thousands to a European wholesaler. To keep shipping costs to a minimum, birds were packed together in shipping containers, some of them diseased and dying before they left.

Buyers are not penalized for losses in transit. They pay for live birds only. Indeed, it has been the practice to collect customs duty only on live arrivals. The harsh economic fact is that birds are too inexpensive to warrant better care. Better containers, better handling, and health certification would drastically reduce losses but increase prices.

In 1968, bird importations to the United States alone exceeded 490,000; well over 90 percent of these go to the pet trade. A Colombian conservationist, Dr. Carlos F. Lehmann, has estimated that of the more delicate species, as many as fifty die because of poor handling for every one reaching a pet shop alive. Some species have been almost eliminated from his country, he told me.

The best that can be said of this disgusting trade is that its rapaciousness will be its undoing. As birds become scarce and more difficult to collect, prices will rise, and this may tip the balance in favor of the commercial breeders of cage birds, who are now at some disadvantage except in their production of canaries and parrakeets. There is little chance that the trade can be outlawed, unless by the nations where birds are collected.

Zoo purchases are a relatively minor factor in the total bird market, although zoos are the chief buyers of costlier species such as penguins, storks, cranes, ostriches, owls, humming-birds, tinamous, and kookaburras. Zoos tend to be discriminating in their choices of suppliers. If we buy quetzals, we want prime specimens, not birds that arrive sick or dying. A zoo will give preference to a dealer known to be careful in his collecting and handling, who will ship only healthy birds and ship them properly.

The United States has a law to penalize anyone who ships live animals under inhumane conditions. Thus far it has not been enforced, in part because a foreign shipper cannot be prosecuted here, but also because there has been no precise definition of "humane conditions." A code of shipping standards has recently been compiled in England, through the joint efforts of many organizations, including conservationists and the International Air Transport Association. If the code proves workable, regulations to enforce it could be issued under existing law. The chief result would be that co-operating airlines would refuse noncomplying shipments, and the code might well become an international standard.

Birds are not the largest part of the animal trade. In 1968, the United States imported sixty-seven million living animals! About sixty-four million were fishes, most of them cultivated in hatcheries, most of them for the pet trade. About two million were crocodilians, turtles, lizards, and snakes, almost all of them for the pet trade.

A generation ago, "baby alligators" came from Florida. My parents brought me two from Miami, as souvenirs, the year I was twelve. We had no idea how to care for them. At times they were too hot, at others too cold, and they were not properly fed. They soon died, as most "pet" reptiles do. Today our American alligators have been so depleted that the pet trade imports South American caimans instead. Driving through Florida a few days ago, Jane and I saw dozens of roadside establishments offering "baby alligators" for sale. A few had added, in small type: "caimans." Almost every souvenir shop had a supply of stuffed caimans, on sale for as little as seventy-five cents. Under this heavy pressure, the caiman population is fast collapsing.

The Florida roadside stands offer baby monkeys, too, and the people who camped beside us one night had bought one, a little capuchin, for their ten-year-old daughter. It clung to her, resisting attempts to pry it loose. Like most of these babies, it had been forcibly taken from its mother, far too soon. I told our temporary neighbors what I could about caring for it, but with the unhappy knowledge that it could not live long.

The chief demand for monkeys, however, comes from medical and pharmaceutical laboratories. This demand soared in the late 1950's and early 1960's when rhesus monkeys were used in polio vaccine production. In the peak year, 1958, the United States alone consumed a quarter-million monkeys. Consumption then declined to about seventy thousand in 1967. This was somewhat reassuring to conservationists, although they were alarmed by the increasing demand for species far less numerous in the wild than the rhesus. No one expected the demand to decline further, because monkeys were being used in more and more kinds of research, notably in testing cosmetics. Then, in 1968, imports suddenly rose well above one hundred thousand again. At least some part of the increase is attributable to the pet trade, but how large a part is not yet known.

The 1958 rate of consumption could not have been sustained for very long. Field studies leave little doubt that the rhesus population was depleted by the heavy drain. The quarter-million imported were only a fraction of the number taken. The monkey trade was poorly organized then. Collectors assembled their catches in native villages, exposing the monkeys to diseases carried from different parts of their own habitat as well as to human diseases. They were inadequately fed and poorly cared for, and kept in close quarters. One expert estimates that eight died for every one reaching a laboratory alive. Some estimates were higher.

Conservationists were alarmed and horrified. There was no possibility of stopping the use of monkeys, but this was not the chief issue, for only a fraction of those captured were ever used. The largest part of the drain would be relieved if capture and handling were properly organized. It was difficult for conservationists and medical researchers to find common ground, however, and many harsh words were exchanged. The medical men had their missions, and they needed monkeys. They bought them from dealers. They had neither the time nor the knowledge to concern themselves with how the dealers acquired their stocks.

Some of the better dealers complained that they could not sell their monkeys to the medical laboratories because of price competition. The laboratories bought the cheapest monkeys they could get, or bought on competitive bid, and this gave the advantage to dealers who bought at the lowest prices overseas and spent the least on care.

The friction between medical men and conservationists was most unfortunate in that it made practical improvements almost unattainable. Medical men felt they were being attacked by people who would like to stop their work altogether. On the defensive, they were reluctant to listen to experts who understood the animal business and could suggest ways of saving animal lives. Organized efforts to establish a dialogue were largely abortive. Patient men on both sides have continued to seek common ground, and they seem to have found it. Leaders of the medical and pharmaceutical groups are now convinced that the supply of primates is not inexhaustible, and they are alarmed by the prospect that some species may disappear.

While the number of primates imported has declined, research interest has shifted to rarer species such as the chimpanzee. Chimps have been used as human analogs in many experiments. "Ham," now a resident of the National Zoo, was the first primate to travel down the Atlantic Range in a space vehicle. Others have since orbited the earth, and many more have been used in ground-based experiments to test conditions to which human astronauts are exposed. Chimpanzees are currently being used in automobile crash experiments. Organ transplants from chimpanzees to men have been proposed.

The first human-to-human heart transplants were made in

late 1967 and early 1968. In these cases, surgery could not proceed until a donor was available, a suitable human just pronounced medically dead. If chimpanzee organ transplants should become feasible, this deterrent would be removed. What if chimpanzee kidney transplants were to become predictably successful? Assuming that only chimpanzees with blood type O could be used, the total number of these now alive in the world is less than the number of people who die each year from kidney deterioration in the United States alone!

With changing emphasis in research, demand swings from species to species. There have been runs on green vervets, cottontop marmosets, squirrel monkeys, baboons, macaques, langurs, and others. Of late I have received letters from troubled wildlife management officials of several foreign governments who believe they must apply export controls and restrict capturing before their native species vanish altogether. Typical regulations prohibit capture, possession, or exportation of certain animal species without specific permits or licenses, and these are issued only for "scientific, educational, or zoological purposes." Such regulations seek to eliminate commercial traffic but permit museums, zoos, and research laboratories to obtain animals. When the research demand is the only one of consequence, however, the only possible control, short of outright embargo, is a quota system. If the quota is only a fraction of the demand, who gets the animals?

An official of one government was troubled by the size of a new demand for monkeys. A local trapper had asked him for collecting permits, exhibiting orders from American institutions in support of his request. The official consulted our embassy. Were these institutions reputable? The embassy relayed the inquiry to Washington, fortunately including

photostats of the research institution orders. Washington officials checked the orders.

They had been faked. In one case, a legitimate order had
been doctored by the trapper in such a way as to multiply the
desired quantity by twelve. Another order was an outright
forgery.

An African wildlife department asked the United States
government for help in screening requests from scientific institutions. The requests were all in order, and the institutions
were legitimate. The Africans feared that such large demands
could not be met for very long. Could the United States help
by ranking such requests in priority order?

No government official was likely to take such responsibility, advising that University X should get its monkeys and
Institution Y should not. Yet if all demands cannot be satisfied, who is to say which are given preference? There is good
reason for research men to be alarmed. Prices have gone up.
Some orders have not been filled. Foreign nations are putting
export quotas on some species, and primates are likely to
come under such restrictions.

Why not raise primates commercially? Scientists have long
used commercially bred rats, mice, and other rodents. For
most research purposes, they are preferable to wild-caught
specimens, since they can be raised under controlled conditions. Some colonies have been kept pathogen-free for generations, so they lack the immunities acquired by free-living
animals, and are thus more suitable for research in infectious
diseases. Primate farming was proposed at a 1965 conference
of conservationists and research scientists. Prior to that time,
rhesus monkeys had been introduced on three small Caribbean islands, and they were multiplying satisfactorily. With
improvements based on experience, it might be possible to
produce rhesus monkeys in some such way at acceptable costs.

It might be possible, but this has not been demonstrated. Mice and rats are prolific, often raising several litters per year. Primates are several years old before they reach sexual maturity, and their reproduction rate is much lower. They require more space, more food, and more attention than rodents. Some research projects call for superior monkeys, with known health histories, in some cases monkeys that are known to be free of specific pathogens. Such monkeys bring premium prices, five to ten times the general market price. But the bulk of the demand is still for monkeys that are alive and in apparent health, at the lowest available cost.

Rhesus monkeys propagate well in zoos, but zoo maintenance costs are too high to compete with the price of wild-caught monkeys. Some research centers have experimented with captive breeding, but their overhead costs are higher than ours. If a pilot primate farm were established, with the aim of producing healthy animals at the lowest possible cost, it would be at least ten years before propagation rates and operating experience permitted reliable cost projections. A primate farm would not attract venture capital today. At least ten years of subsidized experimentation will be needed, and thus far no such subsidies have been proferred.

As a member of the Survival Service Commission, I am much concerned with endangered species. I scan dealer price lists daily to see who, if anyone, is offering golden marmosets, Zanzibar red colobuses, Aldabra tortoises, and Baird's tapirs. In most cases I see no such offerings. Few of the red-listed species are used in research, and few are sold in the pet trade. Neither the rhesus monkey nor the squirrel monkey yet rate *Red Data Book* entries.

It would be absurd to ignore unlisted species, however. They may exist still in considerable numbers, but we should be concerned if these numbers are declining. If the *Red Data*

Books were to include declining species, they would have several thousand pages, not a few hundred.

The traffic in wildlife cannot be stopped, nor should it be. Much medical and pharmaceutical research is valid and important, and I am not one of those who would prohibit experiments with animals. While I despise the brutal wastefulness one finds at all points in the pet trade, from the forest to the drug store, there are people in the trade who despise it as much as I do, and who manage the animals in their care intelligently and humanely. It should not be necessary to outlaw wild pets to outlaw abuses, and I doubt that efforts to outlaw wild pets could succeed.

The most sensible concept is "sustained yield," and this should attract the support of anyone who looks beyond tomorrow, whether he be a research physiologist, a pet dealer, or an official of some foreign government concerned with his country's export trade. A healthy wildlife population is not prejudiced by an annual harvest, if the harvest is not so large as to impair reproductive potential. Hunting seasons have the effect of limiting annual take and of scheduling the hunting at the season when it will be least disruptive to species life. In a regulated situation, hunting methods would also be brought under control, if only to reduce waste.

Each nation, of course, has the ultimate responsibility for its own resources, for protecting wildlife or allowing its extinction. As we learned in South America, however, enforcing wildlife laws can be next to impossible, unless a nation has outside help.

"How can we enforce our laws when you reward people for breaking them?" a Peruvian asked me when we visited Lima. "Suppose we put a game warden in one of our parks. In a month he'll be the worst poacher in the area. Why? He can make ten times as much money poaching.

"It's your money that pays him and the smugglers. Your country allows our hides and furs to enter, even though they were taken illegally. Once they get across our borders, they can be bought and sold openly."

At an IUCN conference in Bariloche, Argentina, delegates from other Latin American countries voiced the same complaint, directed chiefly against the United States as the largest importer of live animals and wild animal products, but also against Great Britain and the nations of Europe. By resolution, they asked for help, urging that all national borders be closed to unsanctioned animals and products. One speaker noted that all the game wardens in Florida have been unable to stop the nightly slaughter of alligators, and for the same reason: once across the border, their hides can be sold openly.

Such international meetings often have results not stemming from the formal agenda. At IUCN's Lucerne assembly in 1966, I attended an informal gathering one evening summoned by Colonel Leofric Boyle of Great Britain, who has campaigned vigorously against commercial exploitation of wildlife, especially of the spotted cats. Boyle told us how the recently adopted British regulations were helping and urged that every nation follow this example. Those of us who came from the United States met later. John Gottschalk, representing the U.S. Department of the Interior, told us that he would put his staff to work on a draft of new legislation.

Congressman John Dingell introduced a splendid bill in 1968, which other congressmen soon joined in sponsoring. It went far beyond the British legislation, in that its provisions applied to wild animal products such as hides and furs, as well as to living animals. It would authorize the Secretary of the Interior, after consultation with the proper foreign governments and the IUCN, to declare any wildlife species endangered. Thereafter it could not be imported to the United

States, although the Secretary, at his discretion, could sanction imports for scientific, educational, or zoological purposes. The bill also strengthened the ban against contraband animals and animal products and included specimens taken illegally within the United States. This struck at the shameful trade in alligator hides, where poachers became legitimate businessmen by crossing a state line.

Our American Association of Zoological Parks and Aquariums was one of the first organizations to endorse the bill, and I had the privilege of testifying for the AAZPA at both the Senate and the House hearings. The House of Representatives passed the bill without visible opposition. At the Senate hearings, no witnesses spoke against it. In the closing days of the session, however, many Senators received telegrams opposing the bill. The fur, leather, and tanning industries, their unions, and some leaders of the pet trade were alarmed. There was too little time to cope with this, and the legislation died.

As I write, in 1969, the legislation is moving through Congress again, and it may well have become law by the time this book is published. Conservationists have met with those who opposed the bill, and an accommodation appears possible. Assured that only endangered species would be affected, the industry people seem likely to withdraw or modify their stand, especially if clarifying amendments are included. Colonel Boyle's crusade has borne fruit, and it will be surprising if other nations fail to follow the British and American examples.

The animal trade has become a substantial business chiefly because of the huge volume of sales to the pet trade and research laboratories, which buy in quantities rather than by ones and twos. A zoo director can consult dealer price lists, pick up the telephone, and order a pair of giraffes, a small herd of gnus, wattled cranes, a baby elephant, or a batch of reptiles. Like other businesses, the animal trade has practitioners who are honest and ethical, and who genuinely care for the animals they buy and sell. It also has its share of rascals. It is not easy for an animal dealer or, for that matter, a zoo director, to be scrupulous. If we ask a dealer the source of a particular animal, he may be unable to tell us, since his supplier may be another dealer in Holland or Germany. We might prefer to be sure that every animal we buy was legally obtained, but it is often impossible to be certain.

A few days ago we were offered a rare species by a New York dealer we had not dealt with before. The species is protected by law in one country, but not in two others where it also occurs. Where had this shipment come from? The dealer admitted he didn't know, since he had bought in Europe. He might have assured us that it came from the unprotected territories. We couldn't have checked his statements.

Some zoo buyers don't ask questions. How can they be expected to know which of thousands of species are protected by law in more than a hundred nations? Some shrug and say, reasonably enough, that law enforcement is for the authorities to worry about.

There are exceptions. Every zoo man knows that orangutans, monkey-eating eagles, Galapagos tortoises, and a number of other species are under tight controls. Unless these animals are accompanied by unimpeachable documents, zoo men can safely assume they are contraband, and most will refuse to buy. Brazil has declared all of its wildlife to be national property, and exports are subject to licensing. Zoo men and American dealers know this, and federal officials keep a close watch on imports from Brazil. The Indonesian regulations have been publicized in zoo circles. Kenya has imposed stricter controls. Australia has had export bans that many zoo men consider overly rigid, since they apply to common species as well as rarities.

But how can one be sure? Today I received a price list from a Bangkok animal dealer. I know this dealer has, in the past, dealt in smuggled animals. Of more than two hundred species he now offers, I am reasonably certain that four or five came through illicit channels. Others are questionable, but one cannot be sure. This dealer trades in species native to Africa and Asia. No one has compiled the immense jumble of laws and regulations of all the many countries in this vast area, nor can anyone know from which country a particular animal came.

Should one simply refuse to buy from a dealer who is careless about his sources? I might think so, but many zoo directors would disagree. They have responsibility for maintaining their collections, and this Bangkok dealer has one of the world's largest and most varied price lists. Suppose a zoo director has a single male palm civet. He can buy a female from this dealer, and it may be the only one currently on offer. Should he refuse to buy?

What is an appropriate code of ethics for dealers? A friend of mine worked for several years as an animal dealer overseas. He was young, possibly naïve, but honest and ethical. He was soon insolvent. In the part of the world where he was working, he told me, you live by the prevailing code or you fail.

The animal trade has many degrading aspects. In South America I visited a number of dealer establishments and came close to nausea. The typical dealer has no zoological knowledge and no training. He buys from many sources, among them gypsy truck drivers returning from trips to the interior. As a sideline, the drivers pick up animals from native villages. Those that are still alive are sold to dealers like the one I visited. His establishment stank. Many of his animals were sick and dying. It was difficult to see how any could live long amidst such filth. He had no understanding of what to feed them or how to cope with diseases. Yet at the time of my visit he was making up a shipment for a well-known animal dealer in Florida.

There is no quick or easy remedy for this wasteful drain on the world's wildlife. Yet changes are occurring, bit by bit. A few nations have outlawed such dealerships, and others have brought them under at least limited regulation.

All animal dealers cannot be outlawed, nor should they be. Competent dealers perform an essential function. No one else can master the complex intricacies of international shipments, making sure that the proper stamps are on each document, that airport health officers make their inspections before loading time, that customs declarations are properly filed. Good dealers abhor waste. They carry insurance on their animals, and high losses are quickly reflected in premium increases. We have a high regard for those dealers who can deliver what they promise: good animals in good health.

The clock cannot be turned back to the romantic days when zoos sent out their own collecting expeditions. No zoo man making an occasional trip can have the competence of the professional trapper. In nations with effective game laws, trappers are licensed and regulated. Amateurs would be far more destructive. Waste of wildlife is reduced to a minimum when a capable trapper, who conditions his animals carefully before shipment, sells his stock through a capable and conscientious dealer.

16

Alligators in the Bathtub

"I have a monkey I'd like to give to the zoo," said a man's voice on the telephone.

"That's very generous of you, sir," I replied, with practiced caution. "What kind of monkey is it?"

"I don't really know," he admitted. "It's mostly brown, I guess."

"Our monkey house is quite full," I told him. "We couldn't accept your monkey unless it fitted into a group. Why not bring it in and let us see it? We can at least tell you what species it is."

"I can't bring it in!" the caller declared, and now there was a note of strain. "You'll have to come get it."

"Why? What seems to be the problem?"

"It's loose in the house!" he shouted. "It got loose, and it bit my wife, and she won't come home until I get rid of it! And I can't catch it!"

This one was not for us, but I told him whom to call. Years ago our zoo, and many others, cheerfully accepted any and all gifts of animals. The zoo's annual report for 1928 acknowledged presentations of a horned toad, a screech owl, baby alligators, numerous box tortoises, an opossum, a raccoon, three skunks, a white Pekin duck, two finches, and several parrakeets, as well as rarer and more valuable species. When Junior's pet became a nuisance, someone persuaded him to take it to the zoo, where it would have a good home.

Eventually the open-door policy had to go. Zoo directors plan their collections, and cage space is limited. No one wants valuable space taken up by a motley array of castoff pets. Some zoo directors, not wanting to seem uncooperative, continued to accept all gifts, quietly disposing of those they didn't wish to display, but this policy has perils. Junior wants to be shown his former pet when he visits the zoo.

The passion for wild pets has grown with the years, although most of the stories have unhappy endings. Visiting a pet shop recently, I saw on sale a chimpanzee, several ocelots, a margay, a jaguarundi, two kinkajous, numerous monkeys, and many exotic birds. In New York City, I saw a full-grown ocelot sharing the front seat of an MG with the driver. A Texan converted his convertible so he could carry a young elephant round the town.

"Where can I buy a chimpanzee?" a lady asked me. I didn't refer her to the pet shop that had one for sale. A few questions brought out that she had seen chimps only on television. I doubt that she believed me when I said that adult chimpanzees are immensely strong, that they often become unmanageable, and that they can inflict deep, mangling bites. The chimp on "Daktari" isn't like that at all, she assured me. She was sure one would give trouble only if the owner was unkind.

Lion cubs are cute and cuddly, and Elsa of *Born Free* seemed gentle as a tabby. Lion cubs are not expensive, and a surprising number of people buy them to take home. I have known two or three owners who came close to panic when they couldn't find a zoo willing to accept a maturing lion as a gift. They had become frightened of their pets, had no cage strong enough to hold them, and were staggered by the mounting meat bills.

I was riding my scooter through the zoo one morning when I saw one of our welders sitting on a pigeon trap inside a waterfowl enclosure. This was such an improbable sight that I stopped to learn what was happening. A few minutes earlier, he told me, the Director had driven by with a visitor. An automobile had stopped just ahead and the driver had stepped out clutching an animal, which he had tossed over the railing into the waterfowl exhibit. He then drove off hastily. Dr. Reed saw that the animal was a coatimundi, hardly a good companion for our precious birds. He leaped over the fence, grabbed the coatimundi by the tail, and thrust it into the pigeon trap for safekeeping. The active little animal could escape, however, unless the trap were firmly held to the ground, and Dr. Reed couldn't wait. So the welder, working nearby, was drafted for sitting duty until a keeper could arrive with a cage.

The telephone rang in the Animal Department office a few minutes later.

"I just left a coatimundi down by the duck pond," a voice said.

"Why in the world would you do something like that?" our man asked.

"Well, I called the zoo, and you wouldn't take him, and I just had to get rid of him. Good-bye!"

Wild pets in the house can generate all manner of problems. The havoc one small chipmunk can cause in a single day must be seen to be believed. We had a delightful cockatiel who pleased most of our guests by perching amiably on their heads, shoulders, or knees, but he systematically shredded the leaves of our potted plants and had great fun shredding draperies. One zoo man, Joe Davis, is an authority on otters and has kept them in his house, uncaged. Not much was left of the wallpaper when I saw it. The bookcases were guarded by electric fence, since the otters had repeatedly toppled them. Joe's bed was high above the floor on otter-proof stilts.

Some pet-lovers are undauntable. I was taken to visit a house in California shared by an elderly woman and over a thousand parrakeets. Her share, from which the birds were more or less excluded, was the kitchen and a small bedroom. The birds had all the rest, and she had long since given up any thought of housecleaning.

Several times each day, the telephone rings in our information office and someone asks for advice on the care of a wild pet. Our staff tries to be helpful. They have prepared leaflets describing how best to manage turtles, squirrels, and other common pets. If a zoo man is asked for advice before the pet is acquired, he is likely to be discouraging. Once I advised a woman caller against acquiring a raccoon. She was indignant.

"I'm ashamed of you!" she cried. "You just don't like animals!"

But I do, and I can be as emotional and sentimental about them as a lonesome old maid. Jane and I have a swimming pool in our patio, and there is a recently born sea lion in the zoo nursery. What could be more delightful than raising it at home and teaching it how to swim? The patio is secure, with shade and basking space, and the relationship between the sea lion and our Labrador would be fabulous.

As a zoo man, however, I have some familiarity with such technicalities as water filtration. Sea lions defecate in the water. The filtering system attached to a home swimming pool isn't designed to cope with this. Putting the sea lion into our pool would keep us out of it. One resident of the Washington area did put a sea lion into his pool—but soon changed his mind and gave it to the zoo.

Most owners of exotic pets lose their enthusiasm more gradually. The young pup or cub is delightful. Young boys and girls are happy with the responsibilities of care. But daily cage cleaning is maintained for only a brief time. A day is skipped, and then several days; and after a time the cleaning is performed only when parents become insistent because of the pervasive stench. Even feeding may be neglected.

Then the youngsters are off for summer camp and parents become the caretakers, feeding time now taking precedence over social engagements. They are invited to spend a weekend at the beach—and wonder what they can do about the dependent skunk or monkey. Even tolerant friends may not include an ocelot or a boa constrictor in their invitation. Who will take care of the raccoon when the parents go vacationing?

A pet that must be caged is seldom satisfying, for the average owner can provide only a small cage, and in such confinement the animal can exhibit little of the behavior that makes it attractive. Periods of freedom and play are rewarding to the owner and often to the pet as well. With sexual maturity the animal's playfulness may wane, however, and now may come incidents that cause owners to complain their pets have "turned against them." Monkeys bite, and so do raccoons.

Play periods give rise to all kinds of unexpected incidents, some of which make good stories. One of Gale's hamsters vanished mysteriously. We found him, after a time, in the fireplace ashpit. A parrakeet vanished even more mysteriously. We could hear him but not see him. He was at last located inside the stairway newel-post, from which the cap had been removed for repairs. We could not reach him, nor could he climb out. Finally I lowered a belt, and he rode up on the buckle. One of Gale's mice escaped. We set a live trap —and caught the wrong mouse! Trapping, caging, and releasing now became a game, until she was catching mice that were obvious crosses between her original white strain and the household variety.

Escapes during play periods and moments of carelessness often terminate ownership abruptly. Free-living parrakeets appear regularly at the feeding station beside my mother's home in Florida. We have captured several escaped parrakeets in Washington, where they would not have survived the winter. Humane societies are called to attempt recapture of escaped monkeys. Many escaped small birds and mammals are never seen again; they die or are killed by predators. Pet lions have escaped on occasion, and in such cases the police take over the hunt, with guns.

The most common end to pet-owning is untimely death. Most wild animals kept as pets die young, killed by ignorance, neglect, or misdirected affection. This is almost invariably the case with alligators, caimans, turtles, tortoises, snakes, lizards, and toads. Some birds and mammals, such as common parrots and squirrels, are relatively hardy. Others, such as the woolly monkey, rarely live long in private hands.

Zoos keep their animals alive by providing a kind of care the private owner cannot supply. Even a small zoo cage may represent a capital outlay of $5,000 or more. It is designed for the animal's comfort, with regulation of heat and, in some cases, humidity. The designers have given thought to requirements for ultraviolet light, provided naturally or artificially, and to such fittings as sleeping shelves, scratching posts, trees for climbing, and privacy areas. Cages are cleaned daily with detergents and other chemicals. Diets are scientifically calculated. The veterinarian makes daily rounds. Periodic fecal examinations warn of parasite buildups. Skilled keepers are alert for any change in an animal's appearance or behavior; and any change, such as refusal of food or unaccustomed indolence, calls into consultation men with experience and knowledge. In the zoo, animal care is a full-time occupation, not a part-time hobby.

There are exceptions, some of them notable. Ocelot owners are so numerous they have formed a club which publishes a magazine. Some of the owners are devoted and skillful in managing their wild cats. Some excellent books have been written by people who acquired wild pets, often by chance, and became fascinated by them. An intelligent person who gives time and energy to the care and study of a single species may well, if he is sensitive and observant, learn more about it than a zoo-keeper responsible for half a hundred species.

The private breeders of waterfowl and upland game birds have done outstanding work. More rare pheasants are hatched and raised by these private breeders than by zoos. Perhaps a Manchurian pheasant does not qualify as a "pet," but it would be difficult to write a definition that excluded pheasants but included quetzals and blacksnakes.

Some people say there ought to be a law, and I, too, am outraged by what I see in many pet shops. Some of the privately owned and personally operated pet stores are excellent, holding to high standards of care. Generally, the worst of the lot are the pet departments of drug stores, novelty shops, and department stores, which are often manned by clerks with little more skill than is needed to ring up sales. Far too many animals in these debased establishments are half-dead before they are sold.

But what kind of law? Conservationists are most concerned by the immense and growing drain on wild populations caused by the depredations of the pet trade. The most logical points of control are the protected habitats, the commercial suppliers in countries of origin, and the customs stations of importing nations. Some controls exist and they are becoming tougher. A humane shipping code would help, too, and this seems attainable.

Policing the pet trade is not a task for the FBI, however. State and local humane societies have lobbied for local ordinances with considerable success, and they have done much to bring pressure on pet shop operators who neglect their live commodities. Indeed, some devoted members of humane societies are so persistent and formidable that ordinances become superfluous. A shopkeeper would rather be served with a summons than confront one of these zealots!

Anyone who proposed a total ban on the keeping of wild pets would arouse a storm of angry protests. Yet there are now substantial legal restrictions, federal and local. No one, not even a zoo, may have a bald eagle in his possession without the government's permission, which no private individual would be likely to get. Even eagle feathers are under regulation. One must have a license to trap migratory waterfowl, and a good reason for seeking the license. Many states prohibit the taking or possession of native wild animals by private individuals. Most cities have ordinances prohibiting the keeping of farm animals within the city limits, and most of these ordinances also ban the keeping of wild animals which may be dangerous or annoying to other residents.

What do zoo men do? We advise amateurs against trying to keep wild pets, but do we keep them ourselves? In my own case, household livestock is presently limited to Tor and two cats. This is all we can manage, with the children away, since we both work long hours and travel frequently.

Yet I must admit that working in a zoo has increased rather

than satisfied my impulse to keep some wild creatures. At the zoo, I have too little time to spend with any one species. My personal desires could not be satisfied, however, by mere ownership. I would want to provide the kind of environment and care which exceed present zoo standards.

In short, I would have to be living in the country, where the animals could have ample space and a seminatural setting. I would want more than one, the number depending on the species' normal social behavior. I would most enjoy management of a "contact" relationship, where the animals were not confined but were attracted by the setting and the food provided.

One member of our staff keeps a two-toed sloth at home, to their mutual satisfaction. Another has kept genets, which behave much like house cats, but he is a scientist who was studying this genus. A number of our keepers who live on farms often pick up abandoned young raccoons, opossums, blue jays, crows, and other local animals, rear them, and release them. A majority of the staff members keep only dogs and cats, or no pets.

I have convictions about the pet trade, but on pet ownership I am ambivalent. The boy with the boa constrictor in his pocket today is a likely candidate for the ranks of the conservationists tomorrow. There is no intellectual substitute for the experience of caring for a living creature, nor is there any better approach to understanding the interdependence of man and other animals.

The best biology teachers know this, and their students' contact with animals is not limited to squeamish sessions in which they dissect preserved frogs and cats. Their classroom windows are lined with vivariums, and biology is taught in terms of life processes, with living plants and animals as illustrations.

Some things must be outlawed if man and other animals are to coexist on this planet. But it would be a grave mistake, I believe, to lessen the already attenuated exposures of man to other animals. The city boy who owns a pet rabbit may learn less about rabbits than does a farm boy who lives among them, but he will learn far more than if he never saw one nose to nose. Perhaps conservationists should take a more positive view of pet ownership, encouraging and guiding rather than deploring it.

17

A Barrel of Giggles

In the most recently reported year, 174 live ocelots were shipped from Peru. In that same year, more than 11,000 ocelot furs were exported for the fashion salons of Europe and North America. This is one measure of the bloodiest and most ruthless assault on the survival of many handsome species.

Fashion is fickle. The masculine passion for beaver hats came close to exterminating our dam-building rodent in colonial times. Beaver pelts brought seven shillings each in 1620, and trappers were complaining about the scarcity of beavers only a generation later. About 1870 the millinery trade's demand for plumes and feathers threatened the egrets, spoonbills, and least terns with sudden extinction. They were saved only by a courageous and bitter battle against the poachers and their eager customers.

For a time, ranch-raised minks, chinchillas, and other farm-produced furbearers satisfied the fashion dictators, and synthetic furs were fast gaining popularity. Then some merchandising genius conceived the "fun fur" kick, and women loved it. Judging by their responsiveness, he had evoked a primitive urge in the half-civilized female breast: a desire to adorn the form divine with the skins of dead animals. The urge is now being satisfied by the indiscriminate slaughter of hundreds of thousands of ocelots, leopards, jaguars, cheetahs, tigers, and other cats, as well as zebras, giant otters, caimans, and seals. One leading furrier boasts he can make up coats from any of eighty-eight kinds of furs, including those of the rarest species.

To the fashionable woman, rarity adds distinction. She delights in knowing her fur coat is unique. Recently a leading furrier warned conservation groups that their public attacks on the spotted-cat trade were self-defeating. Since certain leopard species had been mentioned as threatened by the trade, more women had bought leopard coats!

Members of the fur industry have, understandably, been unhappy at the attacks on their trade. The industry is among the oldest. Men have worn furs since the Stone Age. Furs are bought and sold on the open market. Indeed, some nations control fur exports, and a few have made fur sales a government monopoly. While some furs are illegally collected and smuggled across national boundaries, a fur buyer in the United States is in the same position as a zoo director: He cannot always trace origins.

At a meeting with representatives of conservation groups, spokesmen for the fur industry put their case strongly. They were frank about the size of the trade, providing statistics the conservationists had not seen before. I, for one, was shocked to learn that the world catch of ocelots is about 200,000 per year, and that 20,000 leopard skins are marketed.

The United States is, by far, the largest importer of furs. But industry representatives told us something we had not known: Most of them are re-exported after processing. Two thirds of the ocelot furs are exported, and a slightly larger proportion of the leopard furs. Banning imports to the

United States would have little effect, they argued logically. Processing plants would be set up elsewhere, and the trade would continue. While their concern was understandable, Congress has considered a ban only on endangered species. The principal fur animals are not yet listed as endangered, though it is unlikely that the ocelot can withstand such a huge annual harvest.

Peru alone exports a quarter-million wild animal hides and skins in a year. Almost as many are shipped from a single Brazilian port. Prices of rare furs have risen steeply. Leopard coats have been sold for more than $15,000 each.

"A monkey-fur dress is a barrel of giggles," one fashion advertisement urged. A salesman explained how many furs were needed to make one dress, which no self-respecting lady would wear more than once in the same company. Is she oblivious to the way these skins were obtained, to the rifle shots, the thuds of twitching bodies falling from the trees, and the cries of the infants, too small to kill and too young to survive alone. Or does milady harbor a secret pleasure at her taste of barbarism?

No one knows what effect this sudden fad has had on the world's wildlife, but it is clear that some field studies made by scientists only two or three years ago are now invalid. In South America, I talked with men who had visited hunting regions recently, seeing almost no furbearers where they had once seen many. About two hundred giant otter skins once cleared through a Colombian port each month. Now only one or two are brought in, despite higher prices. Hunters complain they must go deeper and deeper into backcountry.

The boom couldn't have come at a worse time. Its impact hit many countries just when their efforts to protect native animals were taking shape, when laws were being sharpened and enforcement was beginning to have effect. Such promis-

ing beginnings collapsed in disorder when the fur buyers appeared, offering lush rewards. Officials were corrupted who
might have resisted smaller bribes. With even modest luck,
a hunter could now earn more with a few well-placed shots
than from a year's labor at legal occupations. Several nations
scrapped their wildlife protection efforts altogether, for the
immediate revenues from fur sales mattered more to their
shaky economies than conservation of a natural resource.
The fad might not last, and the time to reap the rewards was
now.

Most of the damage is being done in South America,
Africa, and Asia, but the United States is not immune. The
latest survey reports that Florida's alligators have been reduced to 10 percent of their former numbers, and large alligators are now rarely seen. Four of our zoo-keepers recently
returned from a reptile-collecting expedition in southern
Florida. In the areas they visited, they told us, most of the
local residents carry guns, or keep them ready in their cars,
and the custom is to shoot at anything that moves. Game
wardens make a few arrests, but the fines are too small to
worry anyone.

Jane and I met a state game warden in a remote section of
the Everglades, outside the national park. We were on an
old logging road which came to a dead end ten miles from
its beginning. We had completed our photography and were
driving out when he flagged us down, inspected our car, and
saw we had cameras rather than guns. We asked him about
his work.

"It's a big country," he said. "I try to get up here once a
day, but I can't always make it. This section is pretty good,
because a car can't get out but one way, and I can block the
road. But you only catch the amateurs. The pros are too slick.

"They all work together, and they always seem to know

where I am. Someone sees my car and passes the word. The
serious poaching is at night, and they set up their operation
pretty good. Along here, for example, they'll drop a man off
with a walkie-talkie. Once I show up, he lets the boys know.
By the time I get up there, they're just fishing. If they have
any skins, they're stashed back in the woods. If I try to wait
them out, the word gets passed to the rest of my district that
I'm out of the way."

So, almost every night, alligators are shot, skinned on the
spot, and the skins are moved north across the state line.
There are no border stations, nor would it be feasible to halt
every car and truck and require them to unload for inspec-
tion. Even if this were done, the poachers would not be
deterred. The Everglades and the coastline have an intricate
network of waterways where many a boatman has become
lost, as well as grassy marshes which can be traversed only by
airboats. Were the highways closed, smugglers could take to
the water with little risk.

Once out of Florida's jurisdiction, they are safe. Now they
can sell the alligator hides openly. One wonders how many
banks would be robbed if the robbers had only to cross a state
line to be safe from prosecution!

When Jane and I visited South America in 1968, the fur
market was still big, and we heard bitter comments about the
willingness of our government, and others, to allow illegally
taken animal products to enter without challenge. Peru, for
example, is making substantial efforts to save its remaining
vicugnas, which produce an exceptionally fine wool. A Peruvian conservationist is understandably indignant when he
sees vicugna coats advertised by the leading shops of New
York and London, knowing that the wool probably came
from his country, and that vicugnas were illegally slaughtered
before shearing.

Vicugnas are also found in Chile, Argentina, and Bolivia, though they are scarce.* The four countries have not yet harmonized their laws. Thus a Peruvian, knowing that poaching in his country occurs, may be morally certain that a given batch of wool came from his homeland, but a foreign customs inspector would find this difficult to prove if the wool had passed through another country on its way.

Many wild animal species, like the vicugna, are international, not endemic to single countries; and within their ranges they cross borders even more freely than smugglers. The trade in animal products is also international, furs and other commodities often traveling by devious routes. A single bale of furs may assemble specimens from two or three nations, and national identities are lost along the way.

What makes the boom in the fur market especially deadly is the unpopularity of predators among the people who live near them. Poultry farmers have a natural antipathy for weasels and skunks. When Chile wanted a symbol to use in its public campaign against forest fires, "Don Puma" was patterned after our "Smoky the Bear." "Smoky" is a popular figure, with a volume of fan mail that keeps an office staff busy. "Don Puma" is less warmly regarded, for the puma is hated and feared.

People living at the outposts of civilization have almost invariably warred on predatory animals. In India, a tiger near a village endangers human life. In our country, states and territories offered bounties to hasten the extermination of wolves, coyotes, cougars, and other species considered hostile to farming and ranching. Most of these bounty offers have now been withdrawn, but only after earnest campaigning by conservationists. Most of our larger predatory mammals were gone before conservation became a popular theme.

* Some sources state vicugnas are now extinct in Chile and Argentina.

This is too often forgotten by those who preach wildlife conservation to people in less developed nations. We did most of our developing first. Although individuals urged restraint in the exploitation of forests, grasslands, wetlands, and wildlife, even in colonial times, such words had little effect until the first decade of the twentieth century. Yellowstone National Park was established in 1872, but not until the administration of Theodore Roosevelt were large areas of public lands set aside as national forests.

Even then it was too late to preserve significant samples of all of the natural splendors of North America and too late to save some wildlife species. The eastern elk was gone by 1880, the eastern cougar by 1899. The sea mink, once seen on the New England coast, had been wiped out by 1890. The passenger pigeon, Carolina parrakeet, and heath hen lingered for only a few more years.

It is inconceivable that we should persuade the people of other countries to refrain from cultivating arable land, cutting merchantable timber, and using grasslands for production of edible meat. Nor, having set the example, are we likely to persuade them not to build hydroelectric dams. Indeed, it has been our national policy to foster accelerated development overseas, providing both technical and financial assistance.

The most we can hope for is that such people, profiting by our experience, may avoid some of the excesses, the wasteful and destructive practices, which have proven so costly to us. In the past thirty years we have spent hundreds of millions of dollars in efforts to repair some of the damage caused by needless abuse of cropland, grasslands, forests, and watersheds. We are spending millions more to bring back into public ownership bits of land which are now recognized as valuable and extraordinary because of their scenic beauty, historical significance, recreational value, or critical importance to particular wildlife species.

We are now making last-ditch efforts to save wildlife species that were once killed on sight. One of them is the Texas red wolf, whose extermination was once subsidized by bounty payments. Experts are not quite sure that any pure-strain red wolves remain alive. Environmental changes to which the wolves did not readily adapt encouraged the more competitive coyotes to invade their territory. Wolves and coyotes have interbred, and wolves may also have crossed with feral dogs. "Red wolf" specimens which have been shot and brought to taxonomists for study exhibit varying degrees of genetic mixing. Currently, the Endangered Species Office of the Fish and Wildlife Service is collecting pups from parents which show wolf characteristics. Three Texas and Oklahoma zoos will house and rear the pups, and their development will be closely observed. This is the first step in what may become a controlled breeding program to establish a line of red wolves which is as genetically pure as possible.

The last of the timber wolves in the conterminous United States now have some degree of protection. A few dozen remain in Michigan, three or four hundred in northern Minnesota, and both states have withdrawn their bounty offers. Minnesota has outlawed snares, and the few wolves on Isle Royale are fully protected by law. Wildlife officials are now considering restocking areas where the presence of wolves would not threaten the interests of farmers.

With the decline of our native predators has come a belated recognition that some of them were not as bad as most people believed. The coyote, for example, is now a welcome resident on some ranches where it was once killed by traps and cyanide guns. These ranchers are convinced the coyote is useful for rodent control, and that it is not a significant menace to cattle or sheep. They are in the minority; long-established ideas die hard.

Driving through farming country, we have often seen dead hawks nailed to fences and barns, downed by farmers' shot-guns. Most of them are broad-winged hawks. The faster-flying accipiters are less easy targets. Conclusive evidence has long shown that the broad-winged hawks are helpful to farm-ers, chiefly as rodent suppressors, and that they rarely kill barnyard fowl. Many farmers, told this, still kill hawks. Old hostilities are not easily put aside.

Thus it is a mistake to consider the hunter who collects the skins of jaguars and ocelots for the fur market as a skulking criminal, a lawless person motivated by greed. In many na-tions, people who live in thinly settled country keep their guns at hand, as our frontiersmen and settlers did, and kill predatory animals for the same reasons. No system of game wardenship can function in such a setting.

Had our fashion-fur industry not created the present ex-traordinary demand, events in South America and other fur-producing regions might have followed a course roughly parallel to our own. Spotted cats and other furred predators would have been killed by people living near them, and a modest quantity of furs would have been marketed. The predators would have been largely eliminated from areas ad-jacent to towns and cities, as well as from land which was cleared for agricultural purposes, but most species would persist in the more remote regions.

At the same time, however, the worldwide urbanization trend holds the possibility of providing sanctuaries for many of these species. While crowding together in cities may prove to be a disadvantage for humans, it can lead to changes bene-ficial to wild animals. Wherever urbanization occurs, there is greater public demand for outdoor recreation, and greater public support for establishment of public parks, forests, and wildlife preserves. Attitudes toward predators change. City-dwellers want to see wild animals when they visit the forests and jungles.

The situation of the handsome furbearers is thus by no means hopeless. Their numbers have been reduced, and under the best of circumstances they will be reduced farther. It should be possible, however, to achieve a level of stability, chiefly by means of parks and preserves wherein both predators and prey live in relative security. While a number of races of lions are now extinct and the Asiatic lion is endangered, the lions of West Africa seem to be safe. Lion skins are not in style.

It is even possible that the fur industry and conservation groups can work together. Basically, their interests are not opposed. Here I must put aside what are admittedly personal prejudices and approach the problem realistically. Personally, I dislike the killing of wild animals to supply luxury goods to a relatively few people. As a conservationist, however, my concern is with survival. Hunting as such does not threaten survival. It becomes threatening only if the annual kill exceeds the replacement potential of a population. Hunting does not threaten the white-tailed deer, for example, or the commoner species of waterfowl.

Surely the furriers are not so shortsighted that they want to put themselves out of business by exterminating the species in which they trade. The alternative is not to stop using these species altogether but to accept the principle of sustained yield, limiting the annual harvest to the kill that can be sustained permanently. In our meeting, it seemed to me the industry leaders were quite receptive to such a scheme. They pointed out that international agreements would be required, but they are organized internationally, and they suggested that an IUCN representative attend their next international meeting.

No one today could establish the sustained-yield numbers for ocelots, or for most other furbearers, but such quotas could be developed, as they have been for whales. Indeed, in some cases the information available to the fur industry may be superior to IUCN's. A coordinated effort to regulate production, leading, perhaps, to a system of export quotas, could achieve far more than prolonged and unresolved battles between industry and conservationists.

I am even prepared to take a more charitable view of fur-bearing women. Perhaps their motives are neither vain nor bloodthirsty. By wearing furs, they may be expressing a subconscious wish to recapture the closer relationship that once existed between man and other animals, to see and touch symbols of this earlier life.

18

Tomorrow's Zoo

Someone had said there was a zoo "like Whipsnade" somewhere in Uruguay. When we arrived in Montevideo, we tried to find it.

Whipsnade is the zoo-in-the-country operated by the Zoological Society of London. The Society's city zoo in Regents Park has one of the world's largest animal collections crowded into 36 acres. Whipsade, with 566 acres, has fewer animals. Jane and I saw Whipsnade just after visiting several of the best traditional zoos in Europe. It was a startling contrast: open country instead of rows of barred cages. Whipsnade's designers made no attempt to counterfeit the African veldt or the Amazonian jungle. The woods and pastures are those of the English countryside. Dry moats keep animals and spectators apart. Some startling effects are achieved by using "ha-has," fences hidden in moats to make it appear that incompatible species are confined together.

Finding Uruguay's "Whipsnade" proved difficult. It was Holy Week, and almost everyone seemed to have gone vacationing. We found a pleasant city zoo in Montevideo, but an elderly keeper was the only employee present, and he had difficulty with our halting Spanish. He might have heard about the rural zoo but dismissed it with a disparaging gesture. We should not go there.

A tourist leaflet vaguely mentioned a zoo in a national park. This sounded promising. We found it at Minas, eighty miles to the northeast, but it was only a small collection of animals in the smallest cages we had ever seen, yet quite well kept and surrounded by charming gardens. On the trip we did see wild rheas and great flocks of parrots.

Next day we found a young lady in a travel bureau who had heard of the rural zoo and even knew its name, Parque le Coq, though she had never been there. By the next morning she had found a driver who guaranteed to take us there. He drove confidently toward Colonia, where the hydrofoil ferry crosses to Buenos Aires. We almost missed the zoo. Less than an hour from town, Jane spotted a small, weathered wooden sign hanging crookedly from a post. The driver stopped, backed up. This was it? We turned onto a blacktop road in need of repair, passed through unmanned gates, and stopped in a grove of trees. Yes, there were some animals.

We had to leave Uruguay the next morning, and I have not yet discovered the true story of Parque le Coq. Letters of inquiry have not been answered. We could only interpret what we saw. Someone had had a bold and brilliant idea. A promising beginning was made. Something went wrong. Even the initial projects had not been completed. Much of what had been is now rusting and eroding.

But what a splendid concept! Never have I seen a better site for the zoo of tomorrow. The park seemed to have no boundaries and no visible limits to its extension. It overlooks a river, tributary to the Plata, and broad expanses of marshland well populated with birds. We saw countless acres of forest, brush, and pasture. The land is gently rolling. The climate is mild, never so cold that heated shelter would be required.

Several paddocks had been enclosed with simple barriers of low fence and shallow moat, so unobtrusive as to be unnoticed a few yards away. They held a motley and undistinguished assortment of various deer, zebras, and ponies. But the paddocks were huge, large enough for substantial herds, retaining most of their natural vegetation. A steep hill had been built, presumably for wild goats, but the soft earth was heavily eroded. Two very large flight cages had been built, and one had been completed by construction of a rocky mound and shallow pool inside. The other held several condors, but the only perch was a short dead tree with one broken branch, large enough for only one bird.

The most elaborate exhibit held lions, and it may well be the world's largest moated lion enclosure. How many lions it held we cannot say, because the lion house was badly placed. Standing on tiptoe, we could glimpse a pair of ears here, a bit of tawny mane there. Unless a lion stood, it was almost invisible.

The wire of the flight cages was fast rusting away. The wooden fence around the lion moat had broken sections. Someone had fed the animals before we arrived, but no employees appeared during our visit. A dozen carloads of visitors arrived.

What went wrong? Zoos are popular in Uruguay. We saw long lines of people outside the city zoo, waiting to pay their admission fee. Parque le Coq is out of town, but it is closer to Montevideo than many of the popular beaches. The physical evidence points to lack of money, a not uncommon problem for zoos anywhere. I gathered that the city zoo and Parque le Coq have the same management. The city zoo is being refurbished, and that may well consume whatever funds are available. The city zoo is also understaffed.

Perhaps the zoo director was overenthusiastic and tried to achieve more than his resources permitted. I can understand why he would have. To have such a site available would be an irresistible challenge. He may have been ahead of his time, but he foresaw a trend. Parque le Coq may still become one of tomorrow's zoos.

Elsewhere in South America, a zoo director introduced me to his city's new park commissioner, a vigorous man who had quickly recognized that the zoo was in sad disrepair. He posed the right question: rebuild on the same site or choose another? We inspected possible locations and talked about what might be done. Before I left, he asked me to write a report suggesting how an all-new zoo should be planned.

It was easy to talk in general terms. Tomorrow's zoos will be spacious. Large herds and groups of animals will live in settings that promote natural activity, including propagation. It was instructive to try relating such general ideas to the needs and resources of this one city. The plan would be worthless unless it could be brought to fruition. The condition of the old zoo showed that resources were limited. Could new kinds of resources be tapped?

The city has no botanical garden and no museum of natural history. No nearby university offers degrees in zoology, and few courses in the natural sciences are available. This has retarded the teaching of natural sciences in public schools. The nation has a few national parks, but none have yet been developed for tourism. There are no popular guidebooks to the nation's fauna and flora. In this setting, it seemed to me that a zoo exhibiting animals from foreign lands would be out of place, and that "zoo" was an inadequate concept. Why not create a unified presentation of nature?

The delightful botanical garden at Santa Barbara, California, has a number of sections, each exhibiting one of the typical plant communities of California: the desert, the coastal range, and so on. Why not, in this South American country, adopt this same theme, but incorporate native wild-life?

The Arizona-Sonora Desert Museum, near Tucson, has done this. It is in and of the desert, and even a short visit makes one more aware of deserts, their causes, and their qualities. It is a zoo, a botanical garden, a museum, a research and experiment station, a survival center, and an educational facility. Some of its living animals are confined. Others have been attracted. We sat in the museum's photographic blind one night as deer and peccaries came to the waterhole.

When the first zoos were built in the Western Hemisphere, our native animals were familiar to most people. Exotic species were curiosities. Since then, millions of people have left the land and congregated in cities. Now, on their television screens, they can see herds of elephants, tigers stalking and killing prey, giraffes browsing on tree tops. The city-dweller's exposure to live animals is so limited, however, that several entrepreneurs in the United States are making money by exhibiting cows, pigs, sheep, and goats.

In the United States, the trend to urbanize is matched by a rising demand for outdoor recreation. Some of our national parks are now so overcrowded in season that many people avoid them. The same trend is gathering momentum in South America. In Brazil, we were caught in an immense traffic jam as weekenders drove from São Paulo to Santos. In Chile, thousands drive from Santiago to such seaside resorts as Viña del Mar. Shops selling camping goods are opening in more and more cities.

As yet, however, only a few of the South American national parks have been developed for tourists. In many of North America's national parks, one of the attractions is seeing wild animals. South American parks do not have such large animals as bison and bears. In visits to nine parks, we saw many birds but no mammals other than a small group of marmosets.

A nature center such as I suggested in my report would be a kind of national park in miniature. Like the Arizona-Sonora Desert Museum, it could exhibit native species, some confined, some attracted by skillful manipulation of the environment.

Was it realistic, however, to propose a project that would be larger and more diverse than the run-down city zoo? Paradoxically, a large rural zoo can be built for less money than a smaller traditional zoo in the city. A city site must accommodate many people in a small space. City zoos are almost inevitably committed to elaborate buildings. A rural zoo can look more like a farm. Gravel paths can take the place of thirty-foot sidewalks. When animals are closely confined, enclosures must be stoutly built. Much simpler arrangements are possible when enclosures are spacious.

If local conditions are favorable, much of the construction work can be done with bulldozers. As demonstrated at Parque le Coq, most hoofed animals can be confined by inexpensive dry moats. Many species are safely confined on islands surrounded by water, if the climate is such that the water does not freeze in winter. Even those animals that swim well may be confined by water if pipe rails are placed just above and below the surface or if a strand of electric fencing is stretched a few inches above the water. If enclosures are large enough to permit keeping several species together, costs are further reduced. Small enclosures must be cleaned daily. In large enclosures, droppings are more widely scattered, sunlight reduces the disease hazard, and natural decomposition occurs.

I suggested to my South American friends that they seek a site with good natural qualities. Ideally, it would have ponds and streams, perhaps a marsh, acres of grass, shrubs, and trees, and it would combine expanses of gently rolling land with a hillside or some rocky mounds. If possible, it should adjoin a much larger area of publicly owned land which would be protected from development for years to come. In such a setting, they could hope to attract a variety of native birds and mammals. Such a site would not require the costly landscaping and grounds maintenance of a city zoo.

The site should be accessible to visitors, but people are now sufficiently mobile so that twenty miles is not prohibitive for a day's outing. City zoos are unduly burdened by casual visitors who come to stroll or picnic but have little interest in the animals.

The old city zoo, I had noticed, displays a large variety of animals in aisle after aisle of cages. Watching visitors, I saw them pass many cages without a glance. A few exhibits, such as the chimpanzees, polar bears, sea lions, and elephants, collected crowds.

Why keep several hundred animals that almost no one notices? Museums keep specimens for study and reference. These zoo animals were serving no such research function. Yet they occupied cage space, and they were costing the zoo as much for food and keeper care as animals which attracted interest.

No species should be included in the new nature-center zoo without a reason, whether it be research, education, propagation, or public entertainment. Entertainment should have a high priority, since public support would be essential, but an entertaining exhibit may serve other purposes.

What does entertain zoo visitors? Not individual animals lying listlessly in small cages. They want action, animals behaving as they do in nature or, if not that, animals demonstrating their physical and mental capabilities. If the South

American zoo chose to give chief emphasis to native species, or to exhibit them exclusively, their behavior should be considered and exhibits planned accordingly. The continent has a great variety of monkeys, canines, large and small cats, and marsupials, as well as tapirs, cavys, llamas, guanacos, pacaranas, capybaras, sloths, armadillos, and anteaters, in addition to a spectacular array of birds, reptiles, and amphibians.

One way to heighten public interest, and to build economically, would be to design the park around a few "spectaculars," exhibits which would attract crowds. These would focus attention. Other exhibits could be quieter in tone.

Visitors like the illusion of naturalness. In this case, the illusion could come closer to reality, since native plants and animals would be used. At Parque le Coq, I photographed a deer standing among the tall white plumes of pampas grass, and the picture cannot be distinguished from one taken in open country.

If ponds or paddocks are large, can they be good exhibits? Some zoo men believe visitors want to be close to every animal. There is excitement when only a sheet of glass stands between a visitor and a leopard, so they can be only inches apart. But a spacious exhibit offers another kind of excitement, the kind I felt in Mexico when I first saw the giraffes at a distance. Interest is heightened by variety. For example, a viewing area might be located atop a low hill or elevated platform, from which visitors could look out in all directions, seeing animals of many species. The view might include both wetlands and pastures. As was true of our vantage point overlooking Blacktail Pond in Wyoming, one could sit or stand for hours, finding ever greater variety. If closer views are desired, this can be arranged. In some open zoos, visitors drive through the animal enclosures in their own cars or in special vehicles. At Busch Gardens in Tampa, Florida, visitors see the animals at close range from an overhead monorail. At less expense, overhead walkways could be built.

The new Parque de las Leyendas at Lima, Peru, offers a delightful sample of such a nature park. The region is arid, but artesian wells provide ample water. Thus it has been possible to create an Amazonian River scene, which one approaches over a jungle trail. Coming to the artfully created "river," one crosses a footbridge to an island. A seaplane is moored at the shore. Indians were brought here to build their typical huts on stilts. The plants are typical of the river shores. On the island, many animals are unconfined, including tapirs, monkeys, and toucanets. A heron had built its nest on a wing of the flying boat.

Such a nature park could offer far more than entertainment, especially in a region where people have little opportunity to learn much about natural history. It could serve as a rallying point and an experimental facility for the relatively few natural scientists and conservationists of the area and a place where teachers could come to learn as well as teach. Local conservationists are indifferent or hostile toward the present zoo. A nature park would have their support as well as the support of the scientific community.

This is not a plan I would advocate for Washington, D.C., or for Rochester, New York, where a new zoo is in the making. What I have called the zoo of tomorrow is not a standard formula to be copied over and over, but a concept, a theme which can have infinite variations. The animals included may be native or exotic. What matters is that they be managed not as specimens or as curiosities but as unique life forms with unique characteristics, managed in such a way that they can develop and express these characteristics with a minimum of constraints.

At a meeting of our national zoological association, Wil-

liam G. Conway, General Director of the New York Zoological Society, chose a provocative way of discussing zoo ex--
hibition. For his theme, he selected not some rare beast, such
as the platypus or giant panda, but the common bullfrog.
How does one display bullfrogs? If a zoo keeps such an ordi-
nary creature, it is likely to be in a small aquarium tank. Mr.
Conway's imaginary bullfrog show occupied an entire building and some of the surrounding grounds! With singular in-
genuity he developed the many ways in which the life history,
habits, and relationships of the bullfrog could be shown. Exhibits would feature its natural habitat, reproduction and
development, ways of feeding, and physiology. It would be
shown with species that prey upon it. Live exhibits would be
supplemented by models and dioramas.

No one is likely to build such a bullfrog display, which
might cost a quarter-million dollars, as Mr. Conway depicted
it. His point, of course, is that every species, however ordi-
nary, offers just such limitless display possibilities, and that
a bare cage with a label on its front is the irreducible minimum. How much more than this minimum is possible, however, when a zoo displays five hundred or a thousand species?

Such a zoo could, of course, reduce the number of species
it keeps, providing more space for each, with benefit to its
exhibit quality as well as to reproduction. With half the
number of species, each could be given twice the attention.
Many zoo directors have hesitated to take such drastic action,
for several reasons. First is the tradition that great variety
means excellence and prestige. It is difficult to see why, under present-day conditions. Scientific management, propagation, educational programming, and exhibition quality
would all be better if fewer species were shown. Certainly
the public cares nothing for large numbers. Visitors ignore
all but the most interesting exhibits.

The visiting public has responded enthusiastically to specialized collections when they have been handsomely designed or imaginatively conceived. Marineland of the Pacific, Sea World, and a dozen similar marine zoos are popular, despite their admission fees. Each has at least one "specetacular," usually a porpoise show. Busch Gardens, in Tampa, has two specializations: psittacine birds and hoofed stock. The bird collection, which also includes waterfowl, flamingos, and some birds of prey, is set amidst lush gardens. The hoofed animals wander over extensive paddocks. Visitors see them from the monorail cars. Attendance numbers in the millions. Roland Lindemann's Catskill Game Farm demonstrates that distance from a city is not a handicap. The farm, a hundred miles from New York City, is in a resort area, and open only from spring to fall, but it has been profitable, more than self-supporting. It specializes in rare hoofed animals.

One reason zoos have so many species is that zoo men, like museum curators, are enthusiastic collectors. If a zoo director has never had kiwis, lesser pandas, colobus monkeys, Chinese alligators, marbled cats, or Komodo monitors, he wants them. A curator of reptiles wants almost any species he has never had before, the rarer the better. In zoo circles, it is a mark of distinction to have what no one else has. A collection of common species may please the public, but it is the rare items that make for status in the zoo community.

This is changing, at least by compromise. While no bullfrog buildings are likely to be built, many new facilities in existing zoos are bigger and better than older ones, and more specialization is developing within large collections. Our new hoofed-stock paddocks are large enough for herds of ten to fifteen. We have assigned three cages to golden marmosets and will assign more as breeding succeeds.

I believe some downtown city zoos will move to the country, while others will establish rural annexes. Not all of to-morrow's zoos need have hundreds of acres, however. Space is required only for the large animals, such as rhinoceroses, and for herd animals, such as Pere David's deer. Even the smallest city zoo could achieve excellence through specialization by de-emphasizing elephants and giraffes and concentrating its efforts on birds and small mammals. What could be more exciting, and more pleasing to the public, than a small zoo which put all of its resources into monkeys?

Indeed, the small zoo could specialize in a number of ways. One might be designed as a teaching zoo, for example. All zoos do some teaching, and most hope to do more. Almost all are handicapped, however, by their physical arrangements, which make sequential presentation difficult. In a teaching zoo, the educational concepts would come first, and design would follow. Many themes are possible: comparative physiology, genetics, evolution, psychology, ecology. Living animals would be used as illustrations, along with inanimate exhibits. The teaching zoo would not have an elephant just because all zoos have elephants or because some well-wisher offered to supply one.

Each year we are visited by people from other cities who are planning new zoos or remodeling older ones. They include architects, city officials, zoological society leaders, zoo directors, and would-be zoo directors. Some of them are me-tooers, visiting other zoos so they can imitate what has been done in the past. With no little dismay I have gone over sets of plans for costly new zoos which have simply wrapped old traditions in modern packages. Even these were better than one set of plans which had been prepared by an architect whose imagination had been unrestrained by knowledge, and whose glamorous-looking structures would be unfit for man or beast.

These plans dismayed me because they were likely to be built. It was too late for effective consultation. I had more sympathy for the enthusiast who brought plans for a gigantic rural zoo, overwhelming in its scope and utterly unattainable. Even had he found the many millions of dollars his scheme would have required, he could never have assembled the hundreds of rare animals he hoped to have in this paradise.

Happily, these are the exceptions. Most of my colleagues in the zoo world know what needs to be done, and they are stimulated by the challenges. Many of the younger men, now subordinates in big zoos or leaders of small ones, are dreaming bold dreams, and they have years ahead in which to make them real.

19

Why Bother About the Animals?

"Why bother about the animals?" someone asks.

Why, indeed. The world is troubled by poverty, hunger, violence, and war. Our human troubles multiply. What serious person can give heed to the plight of the aye-aye and the Kauai thrush? Is it not racial treason to set aside wildlife refuges when every inch of arable land is needed to grow crops for people? Anyway, however we may feel about it, is it not inevitable that man will exploit the entire earth and other animals must go?

I have heard many people respond to such questions, each in his own way. The aye-ayes should be saved, according to some biologists, so scientists can study them. A certain South Seas island, as yet undisturbed, should be preserved exclusively for scientific study, they say. Indeed, only qualified scientists should be allowed to go ashore!

Other pleas for wildlife are sentimental, esthetic, or mystical, and these seem especially infuriating to highway planners, real estate developers, and dam builders. They have joined "nature lover" to "bird watcher" as a term of ridicule. Recently a group of suburban housewives joined hands to form a human barrier to the bulldozers about to invade a public park. Their protest was symbolic and futile. A new commuter highway had to be built, and the easy way lay through the quiet parkland. The only alternative route was through a neighborhood of expensive homes, some of which would have been razed and others devalued.

Some conservationists disdain such arguments. Why should every bird, fish, and tree be required to justify its existence? Has man become so arrogant in his lordship that nothing may live that does not serve him?

Still others try to play the game by the prevailing rules. They tot up the dollars spent on gasoline, sleeping bags, hunting licenses, fishing rods, taxidermy, and motel rooms. In the United States alone this exceeds a billion dollars a year. Therefore conservation is good business.

In circles where great issues are debated, however, the state of our natural resources is often simply ignored. For example, a magazine published for the intelligentsia recently brought out a special issue wherein some of the world's leading thinkers gave their views of the future. As might have been expected, an industrialist promised electronic miracles, a physician predicted victory over cancer, and an urban planner pictured bigger and better cities. I searched for something about nature and found it under "Man's Environment." The author of this forecast had reduced the earth's fauna and flora to elements of decor, which landscape planners might use for incidental relief, green spaces to break the urban monotony!

Then I think of the elephants in Africa's Tsavo Park. A mature elephant consumes about five hundred pounds of forage daily. When too many elephants crowd a habitat, foraging becomes destructive. Years ago, the density of the elephant population was relieved by dispersal. Now, however, only the park is a sanctuary, and the elephants are wise enough to know they court death outside the boundaries.

Within them they are safe, and their population has multiplied to more than Tsavo can support. Hungry elephants uproot whole trees, and marginal forest disappears. Each year of overconsumption reduces the next year's food supply, and the outcome is disaster, for the rate of destruction rises more and more steeply.

The human condition is similar. Our numbers have multiplied, and our food supply is insufficient. In the past decade alone, five hundred million people have been added to the world total, and four hundred million more people are now ill fed. If, as is now predicted, still another billion people are added in the next fifteen years, a crash seems inevitable. Many experts predict mass famines in the 1970's.

Since World War II, world food production has increased substantially. So has population, but there has been a modest gain in per capita food supply. Not everywhere, however. The largest gain has been in eastern Europe and the Soviet Union, followed by western Europe. Per capita food production has declined in the Far East and Latin America.

Reassuring things can be said. We are not elephants. We can apply science and technology to food production. Wherever we have done so, production per acre has increased. On the recent twenty-fifth anniversary of the Rockefeller Foundation's entry into agricultural assistance, good news was pouring in. After two years of severe drought, both India and Pakistan were anticipating record-breaking crops. If all Pakistan's wheat could be harvested without spoilage, there might even be a small export surplus. Using new methods, Indian farmers were harvesting double to quadruple their former yields. Mexico was a heavy importer of foodstuffs when the first Rockefeller scientists arrived there. In 1944, Mexico imported 431,000 tons of wheat. Twenty years later,

Mexico exported 684,000 tons! The Philippines once imported rice, now export a little.

Still, many people go hungry, even in India, Mexico, and the Philippines. Secure among our agricultural riches, it is all too easy for us to assume that the hungry people have not done enough to help themselves. We have given dollars, technical assistance, and tools, but the underdeveloped countries have failed to develop as they should have. So, rather resentfully, we are backing away. Our foreign aid programs have been slashed.

We have had, I am afraid, grave misconceptions, one of them being that if the people we sought to help would only bestir themselves their fields would burgeon like those of Iowa. A glance at a world soils map should be enough to shatter this notion. "Underdeveloped" is a grossly misleading term when applied to agriculture. Huge areas of the earth's land surface are hopeless for food production, being too cold, too arid, too steep, or too lacking in soil to permit cultivation or to support grazing. In the vast arid areas, a scattering of nomadic herders represents the production capability.

The equatorial jungles have fascinated and misled many people, myself included. Seen from the air, from a riverboat, or from a hacked-out trail they seem lush. And why not, with ample sun and rain? I was puzzled chiefly by the apparent paucity of wildlife amidst such dense vegetation. Then I spent a day in an equatorial rain forest with a well-known tropical biologist.

He reminded me that "standing crop" is no measure of productivity. In our own Northwest, a mature forest of Douglas firs represents a very large standing crop, but the annual growth is small. Measured in tons or cubic inches, the annual growth per acre of a young forest is far greater.

Despite the lush appearance, he said, the annual growth in

an equatorial jungle is slow. And, of course, it is annual production, not standing crop, that fixes the food supply of an animal population. Since animals come in many sizes, so that comparisons of numbers are meaningless, biologists use "biomass" as a measure. The biomass of a wildlife population is the total weight of the resident animals. Open grasslands, my friend told me, can support ten times or more the biomass of wildlife that can subsist in equatorial jungle.

There are several reasons why, but one of them quickly becomes apparent when men clear away the jungle to plant crops, as they have done repeatedly. Lateritic soils are characteristic of the tropics. Such soils are handy if one wishes to build a mud hut. Chop out a chunk, bake it in the sun, and it becomes a satisfactory brick. Something like this happens when jungle soils are exposed. The farmer may produce a few adequate harvests, but the soil in his field becomes progressively harder and less permeable. Soon he is forced to give up. Perhaps he then clears another portion of jungle and begins again. This, indeed, is one common pattern of tropical agriculture. The jungle slowly reclaims the abandoned farms and plantations.

I saw another pattern of defeat on the Brazilian savannahs. The region I visited is covered, for the most part, with dense scrub and stunted trees. Several farmers had laboriously cleared away this vegetation, either to plant crops or to establish pastures. Their failure was conspicuous. The clearings had been abandoned and the scrub was reappearing.

It is no coincidence that the richest soils are found in the richest nations. There are no undeveloped Iowas awaiting the magic of gang plows. To be sure, it is technically possible to make further increases in yields per acre by better cultivation methods, improved seeds, manipulation of soil chemistry, control of pests, and irrigation. Two decades of frustrating experience have shown that "technically possible" does not mean "attainable." Modern farm technology can exist only in the context of a technological society. It must be supported by the manufacture of tractors, trucks, fuel, fertilizer, fencing, binder twine, pipe, water pumps, and hundreds of other items, all of which must be available to the farmer at prices he can pay. Modern farming requires crop loans and crop insurance. Colleges must turn out numbers of scientists and engineers, and they must be able to find employment. The farmer must have ready access to laboratories which make soil tests and diagnose crop diseases. Finally, unless the crops produced can be marketed, they will rot in the fields, and marketing is a complex system of storage, transportation, processing, and distribution dependent on the buying power of consumers.

People can argue endlessly and inconclusively about the race between population and food production. Such arguments ignore a more fundamental condition, which published statistics do not report: the condition of the soil, the basic resource. Tsavo's elephants are gradually reducing the food-producing potential of their refuge. Man has, over the centuries, so abused the soil that vast areas which were once cropland are now deserts, unfit for further use. The destruction continues. The earth has less cropland this year than it had last.

P. V. Cardon once wrote: *

Perhaps no farmer has yet developed a permanent agriculture even within his own fences. It is still a goal to be achieved by communities, districts, or regions. No nation has it; no group of nations has done more than to recognize hazily the need for permanency in agriculture. . . .

* Introduction to *Grass; The Yearbook of Agriculture, 1948,* U.S. Department of Agriculture.

Traveling in the United States, Jane and I have seen far too much ruined land: man-made deserts, eroded hillsides, deeply gullied fields. We once came to a green valley amidst dry hills and were impressed by the results of irrigation—until we learned that the irrigation wells must be driven deeper every year, and that the desert will reclaim the valley soon. Talking with farmers, we found a number who understood the principles of soil conservation and were well aware that their own practices fell short.

"It doesn't pay," one said. "It takes more work and more money. Sure, it may make a difference fifty years from now, but I have to make my living today."

Many increases in food production are achieved at the expense of long-term productivity. Especially in underdeveloped countries, today's food needs are met by bringing into cultivation marginal lands not suitable for the purpose. Agricultural permanency is most attainable on the best soils, those that are rich and deep and least exposed to erosion. Cultivating marginal land may bring short-term benefits, but the outcome is negative. The same holds true when grasslands are overgrazed. People may have more meat today, but future generations will have less. Much of the world is living on capital, and the rate of drain increases with each increase in population and food demand.

Irrigation achieves what seem to be almost miraculous effects. Driving across a desert, one comes suddenly upon acres of green fields or orchards. Yet irrigation is usually a short-term enterprise. Progressive soil compaction, soil salinization, poor drainage, and siltation of reservoirs have already brought failure to many irrigation projects, and the lifetimes of others can be calculated.

We are not so different from Tsavo's elephants after all. Nations burdened by fast-growing populations appear to have little choice other than to feed people now, whatever the future consequences may be. We seem to have a blind faith that science will triumph over nature, that we can somehow escape the inexorable operation of natural laws.

One hears much talk about food from the sea, for example, the implication being that we can fall back on marine resources if we ruin those of the land. Yet marine resources have also been depleted, perhaps not on a world scale, but sufficiently to have reduced catches of some species. More lasting impairment has been caused by the pollution of rivers and estuaries, where many species of deep-water fish spend a critical portion of their lives.

Even if one take a more optimistic view of food production on land and sea, the most that can be gained is a little time. The rate of population increase is far greater than at any time in the past. No measures yet suggested, however fanciful, would double world food production—and then, in a few years more, double it again. The much more probable outcome is a reversal of the upward trend, that the measures taken to increase production will, before the year 2000, cause it to turn disastrously downward.

Our response to the portents of disaster is puzzling. Unlike other species, we can count our own numbers, measure our food supply, calculate deficits, and predict outcomes. Yet most people either ignore or refuse to believe the evidence. The consensus of the contributors to the magazine symposium I mentioned was that the future will bring hitherto unknown prosperity and leisure.

This is not the view of scientists such as those who attended the World Biosphere Conference at Paris. They put it bluntly: mankind is in mortal danger. Within the past few years a growing number of political leaders have recognized the danger and called for action to halt the population ex-

plosion. Yet we are generally complacent, perhaps because so
many of the people who have access to the data and the education to interpret it are themselves well-fed and living in
food-rich countries.

I have followed the statistics of food and population for
some years, and perhaps I understood them intellectually.
Yet they never seemed quite real until Jane and I traveled
through South America. We saw the reality first in Lima,
looking down from a bridge on the crude huts of the slums.
But we did not go down to them, talk with the residents,
share their food, and spend a night. We walked back to an
excellent dinner at our hotel.

Later we met a Peace Corps couple who had lived with the
slum-dwellers for months. They were despairing at the reali-
zation that their dedicated efforts really made little difference, that when they left, as they would soon, things would
be as they were before. When they come home, they will be
the victims of what some writers have called "cultural shock,"
a fancy term for readjustment. It is nothing of the kind, or
will not be in their case. Rather, it will be that they have experienced what we have not, learned what we have yet to
learn, and that we will listen to them politely but without
understanding.

We traveled on, and the view from the bridge was repeated
in other cities, in small towns, and in rural areas; and we
talked with others who, like the Peace Corps couple, had
come to grips with the situation. This was not a condition to
be remedied by urban renewal or vocational education.
These slums were not like those we had seen before.

We were in Brazil before their real meaning struck us.
These were not slums at all. They were waste-disposal areas
for a new kind of solid waste material, animate and human.
They were the dumping grounds for surplus people, people

the economy and the society could not absorb. They are growing rapidly.

There are various measures of poverty. One authority says that more than twenty million Latin Americans are seriously malnourished. Another says that a hundred million are poor and ill-housed. In Bolivia, Ecuador, Honduras, and Paraguay annual incomes average less than $200 per year, in Brazil less than $300, and these are averages, not minimums.

Such conditions would be bad enough if considered a base, a starting point for progress. But population is increasing more rapidly in Latin America than in any other part of the world. The rate of increase in Central America is more than four times the rate in Europe, and the rate for Latin America as a whole is half again as large as Asia's. Existing institutions and facilities, such as housing and hospitals and schools, already far from adequate, cannot possibly withstand the crushing burden the next few years will bring.

What will happen? The Malthusians predicted that population would come to exceed food supply, and people would starve. The world has experienced famines, and greater famines seem probable in the future. But life is not that simple, even for elephants. Starvation is not the only looming threat.

Atmospheric scientists tell us that fast-increasing air pollution may wipe us out, along with other species, in less than a century. Turbidity has screened out part of the solar radiation reaching the earth's surface, and some researchers report the long-term warming trend has been reversed, the climate is cooling, and another glacial period may be in the making. Water pollution has reached crisis proportions, and some large cities are close to water famines. Disposal of solid waste (the inanimate kind) is becoming an almost unsolvable problem for major cities. Despite clear warnings, larger and larger quantities of persistent pesticides are broadcast each year;

even Antarctic penguins are accumulating DDT in their livers, and a number of bird species are vanishing, probably because of these chemicals. Nuclear arsenals are still increasing, although they were quite large enough some time ago to obliterate civilization.

Is there a common denominator beneath this array of threats to human survival? When the population of a wildlife species increases beyond the carrying capacity of its habitat, the first manifestation of trouble is not starvation but stress. In some species it has been shown that stress is caused by population density alone. It will occur even if sufficient food is provided.

In the wild, stress tends to restore the balance. It may increase vulnerability to diseases, with consequent mortality, or lead to such sudden readjustments as the periodic and suicidal dispersal of lemmings. In some species it appears to reduce the birth rate by various means ranging from limited matings to resorption of ova.

Density-caused stress has other consequences, however, especially in a disturbed natural setting or in the artificial environment of a laboratory or zoo. Animals begin to behave in different ways. Fighting occurs, not the ritualistic fights seen in nature, but fights to the death. Behavior sometimes becomes frantic, self-injuring, and self-destructive.

In human society, the connection between population density and war was noted long ago. Many social scientists believe that much of the disturbed human behavior which arouses such concern today is a response to stress, and specifically a response to the worldwide trend to urbanize, the concentration of growing populations in cities.

We are not responding adaptively and appropriately to the real circumstances of our lives. The circumstances are reported in the press and debated in Congress, but we push them off as unrelated and remote phenomena. The food crisis is something happening in Asia or Africa. Air pollution is a technological aberration requiring some new legislation. Crime in the streets and riots in cities and on campuses are blamed on neglectful parents, black nationalists, and the Supreme Court.

Other species adapt to environments and circumstances. We try to alter environments to meet our needs, and we have let our technical capabilities outrun our scientific knowledge. We drastically alter vast areas of land or water without being able to predict the consequences. As one massive change gives rise to dangerous ill effects, we strive to overcome these by piling change on change, under- or over-compensating, until whole biomes are caught in the effect engineers call "oscillating," a destructive, out-of-control surging.

Our behavior is paradoxical. All of the visible threats to human survival are consequences of science and technology. The same knowledge and resources could be used to assure survival, at least for many generations. The fault lies not with science but with decision-making. Somehow our intelligence has given rise to a unique social structure, radically different from any found among other species and from that of early man. The interplay within this structure produces a pattern of decisions which almost consistently subvert survival values.

There is no mystery about the causes of air and water pollution, but we seem committed to an economy and society which cannot avoid outpourings of pollutants. We cannot consider abandoning our motorcars, our industries, our wealth, our way of life—even if it means the death of us. We are making faltering efforts to reduce the contamination, though the most optimistic calculations show that such half-measures will, at best, gain only a little time.

As a member of my species, I am confused. I am well in-doctrinated with the principles which underlie our decision-making. I have spent my life in advocacy and have strong convictions on many of the issues which divide men into hostile camps. Yet I cannot help but wonder: Does it greatly matter what one lemming says to another on their dash to the sea?

As a member of my species, and one now comfortably situ-ated, I am incorrigibly optimistic. I am writing these words in an air-conditioned study on a quiet, sunny afternoon, while our daughter romps with our Labrador retriever in the swimming pool outside. It is difficult to push away the thought that I have cast myself in the role of Chicken Little. Yet the cold statistics of acreages, yields, and population glare at me.

Perhaps we cannot envision racial disaster. Soldiers who have come home from the rice paddies of Viet Nam make the same bitter complaint as Peace Corps volunteers returning from Peru and India: that we at home cannot know what it was like. Perhaps we must experience great disasters before we can accept appropriate responses to their causes. Perhaps if our scientists lay the foundations for such responses, they can be effective.

Why bother about the animals? Because our remoteness from them and their lives is at the heart of our plight. Be-cause by studying their lives and their ecology, we may come to understand our own. Though we live in cities, the cities are not our habitat, for they furnish none of life's basic needs. We share with other living things a common dependence on the gas exchange that occurs in the leaves of green plants, a common dependence on rain and watersheds, on soils, on solar energy, and on the fruits of the soil. We, like they, must harmonize our lives with our environment, or perish.

It seems to me that the scientists and philosophers who best understand the human condition are those who have studied the lives of other species. Their laboratory-bound colleagues work in a world of sterile flasks wherein discoveries are precise and results are reproducible. In the sealed chamber of the physicist's domain, the collision of two nuclear particles can be observed. But the wilderness is a humbling and bewildering complex of materials and forces, processes and events, so intricately linked that descriptive equations cannot be constructed. Giant influences, such as the sun's radiation, blend with the chemistries of microorganisms and such random happenings as an acorn's bounce.

One spring day, Jane and I waded deep into the icy waters of an estuary, dragging a fine-mesh nylon net shaped like a long funnel, with a small bottle tied at its apex. Back on shore we set the bottle on a camp table beside our microscope, placed a drop of water from it on a slide, and looked to see what we had caught. A dozen weirdly shaped creatures were swimming and spinning in the flattened drop. Other drops added more specimens to our tiny zoo. We dragged again and found still more variety. We mounted the camera and photographed some of the living specimens as they continued feeding.

The scientist who "goes bush" may be on a vacation. His discipline may be solid-state physics, rather than botany or zoology. But he cannot leave behind his habit of observation or his curiosity, and his choice of vacation sites shows a predisposition to respond to what he sees. We are not scientists, except by persuasion, but our view of life and its events has been shaped by the forests and the sea.

The city is an artifact, a machine for living, albeit an inefficient and demanding one. No one writes rhapsodies about the chemically treated water flowing from a tap, nor do we drink it with the zest inspired by a hillside spring. Our organisms try to adapt, so we become accustomed to the constant background noises of furnace fans, air conditioners, sirens, aircraft overhead, the neighbor's television. We lose awareness of the fumes in the air and the vibrations underfoot. We learn not to see the shrieking clamor of neon signs.

Walk a few hundred yards into the deep woods and the hubbub is suddenly gone, as if an enormous machine had been switched off. As one walks farther, the defenses needed to withstand city life are gradually lowered, and one can hear, smell, and see again. The forest duff is soft and springy underfoot. The fluting song of a wood thrush fills a valley. The air smells of pine. A chipmunk scampers along a downed tree trunk.

At my desk I am a compulsive smoker. In a month of outdoor living I feel no urge to smoke. People call it "recreation," but this is more than rest and relaxation, which one can have in a hotel bedroom. It rains in the city, but one has little awareness of it, except dashing from the car to a doorway. Outdoors, rain and storms have many different qualities. On backpacking trips, we have been wakened gently by soft raindrops touching our faces, and roused just long enough to set the tent fly. We slept in our small boat one night, at anchor, with gale-force winds tossing us about and lightning flashing every few seconds, followed by great claps of thunder. Once we were seated comfortably in our big tent on an Adirondack island, watching a storm sweep down the lake. It was about to overtake a party of young girls in canoes, so we donned slickers, jerked loose our boat's mooring lines, and raced out to stand by until they were safely beached.

We have stalked herds of pronghorn, let our boat drift close to a ten-foot alligator, watched an ouzel fly into a cataract, photographed a nesting trumpeter swan. At night, as the campfire dies away and we contemplate the end of a trip, we ask ourselves why we return to the city. Biologically, we have made a poor choice. Yet we have made it, and we find satisfactions in city life.

Individually and collectively, we all make decisions which have negative survival value. My smoking is one of the minor ones, waging war considerably higher on the scale. In our society, an important part of the decision-making process is structured in legislative assemblies, where fact-finding and hearings precede voting. In recent years, many legislative decisions affecting natural resources have been guided by a disciplining of data in "cost-benefit ratios."

Typically, as in judging the merits of a large dam, the costs are set on one side of the equation: land acquisition, construction, operating expenses, and so on. The anticipated benefits are arranged on the other: the yield from sale of electric power, the value of irrigation water to be supplied, reductions of flood damage. The planners are aware that such a project has other effects, and they attempt to assign economic values to them: for example, the number of visitor-days of recreation provided. The logic is appealing. Since a dam costs money, should it not be justified economically?

The difficulty, of course, is that the qualities of human existence are not measurable in dollars, and thus tend to be ignored altogether. The existence of fish is "justified" by sales of fishing licenses, boats, and tackle, and the cost of maintaining migratory waterfowl is similarly balanced against the expenditures of gunners. Butterflies haven't a chance in a game played by these rules, nor does a hemlock glade in the path of a new highway. Nor, for that matter, have the economists ventured to set a dollar value on the survival of our species. To do so might be absurd—but far less absurd than carrying the value of survival at zero!

Have we decided that survival is a luxury we cannot afford? Human welfare seems to demand the progressive destruction of the landscape, the endless assults of bulldozers and drag-lines, the highways blasting through public parks, the forests turned into neatly geometric tree farms, more and more jets spewing tons of pollution across the skies, the chemicals that bring death to birds and fishes, the elimination of species after species of wildlife.

Why bother about the animals? Because our survival is bound up with theirs, and we will not survive if they perish. We have a common dependence on the woods and fields, the flowing streams, the fertility of soil, the purity of air. When an animal species succumbs because its habitat has been de-stroyed, man has lost a portion of his habitat, as well.

Why bother about the animals? Because they have a secret it is desperately important for us to learn. How do foxes and owls, trout and zebras, hummingbirds and giraffes, pythons and baboons regulate their numbers? What biological factors have cut our species off from such normal restraints and pro-pelled us into the wildest, most terrifying population boom ever known?

It is not because we have solved the food problem. Nor can it be explained by our conquest of diseases, because the prac-tice of preventive and clinical medicine is still primitive in many of the most populous regions. We simply do not know why national birth rates fluctuate, nor can we predict them. Population forecasts are stated cautiously, with high and low ranges.

This is the problem we must solve, for it is the common denominator of the others, of water and air pollution, of food scarcity, of land depletion, and of the tensions and pressures that lead to war. It is at the root of countless other problems we encounter daily. If the human population can be stabilized in time, perhaps even reduced somewhat, we could soon make this planet a decent place to live, for ourselves and our fellow creatures.

20

The World's a Zoo

For more than a year, Dr. Reed, our Director, has been working with architects on the design of a new building, a "multiclimate house." It will provide a range of special environmental conditions for species such as penguins and platypuses which are not easy to maintain in captivity. The sealed enclosures will be able to reproduce the climate of a tropical rain forest or an Arctic tundra. Water in the large swimming tanks will be filtered and recirculated, and heated or chilled as desired. Plants will grow under powerful artificial light. Animals can be exposed to measured amounts of ultraviolet radiation.

It will be one of the most complex zoo buildings ever constructed. The life-supporting environments require an intricate maze of pipes, valves, tanks, heat exchangers, pumps, compressors, filters, timers, lamps, circuit breakers, fans, and other hardware. To reduce the disease hazard, air exhausted from one enclosure will not be recirculated to another. The lives of the animals will depend on the reliability of all this apparatus, as the lives of astronauts do on the mechanisms of spacecraft.

I drove home one night after a long conference with the

architects, my head still buzzing with foot-candle intensities and filtration rates. Almost instinctively, I took the longer, slower rout through Rock Creek Park, avoiding city streets. The narrow road winds beside the creek through a forested ravine. Wild animals live there, without our help, without artificial heat and light. Once man lived that way.

Apollo 11 was a more complicated apparatus than our planned multiclimate house, yet far simpler than a modern city. Its life-support mechanisms provided for only three men. Those of a city, no less essential to life, must provide for millions. What would happen in any large city if there should be a power failure, an interruption of water supply, or a loss of fuel supply? Such failures have occurred, though they have soon been remedied. Were such a failure to last more than a few hours or days, life in the city could not continue. What would happen, once people knew their faucets would remain dry? Mass exodus? Where would the millions go? The city is no less dependent on the systems that bring food and that carry off sewage and other wastes.

No less vital to the city is the ability of its inhabitants to live together. In our zoo buildings, we know the limits of population density. If they are exceeded, we cannot expect to keep the animals alive. When young are born, we must soon arrange to remove the surplus. Most cities, however, are coping with more and more people, higher and higher population densities.

John Lindsay, Mayor of New York City, wondered publicly the other day whether so large a city could remain viable. He offered no answer to his question. In New York, as in Lima, Tokyo, and Nairobi, the urban apparatus is creaking ominously, and urban institutions are exhibiting alarming signs of breakdown. Traffic moves more and more slowly. Washington, D.C., has had ten bank robberies within ten days. In many cities, parks have become too dangerous for citizens to use them.

Two hundred years ago, the United States had 4.5 citizens per square mile of land area. We have more than 60 people per square mile now, but this is not a true measure of density. We were an agricultural nation in 1790. No city had as many as 50,000 people, and only 1 person in 20 lived in a town or city. Today 14 of every 20 live in urban places. Urbanization has been a worldwide phenomenon, and the population density of some cities exceeds 10,000 per square mile.

Some people—fewer now than yesterday—assert that the population boom is no reason for concern, that the riches of the earth and the resources of science can provide for the added numbers. No ecologist joins in this optimism, for ecologists are familiar with what they call a "J-curve," the graph that describes a population explosion. Numbers increase at an increasing rate. This year's increase exceeds last. The curve steepens.

One need not be an ecologist to predict the outcome. What assumptions could provide for infinitely increasing numbers within finite space? For that matter, what will be the consequences if, as demographers now predict, world population doubles within the next forty years?

Can we, within forty years, double the world's food production? Can we double the world's housing facilities, the supply of electric power, the production of mines, the output of every industry, the capacity of highways, the number of schools and teachers, of hospitals and doctors?

We cannot double the size of the earth, the supply of ores and minerals, the acreage of arable land, the flow of rivers, or the pollution-dispersing capability of the atmosphere. Even if the necessary life-support mechanisms were provided, each man's share of the quiet places would be smaller. And if the prodigious task were completed in forty years, would it then be possible to complete a task four times greater in less than another forty?

Not even the most optimistic assumptions escape eventual absurdity. One can assume that "science" enables men to become colonial animals housed in coffin-like cells, connected by tubes and wires to life-support centers. How high can the cells be stacked? A mile? A hundred miles?

The optimistic assumptions are fast fading. One of the clippings in my files provides this quotation: "Unless we begin now to wake up to the hazards of the population explosion, the future of civilization as we know it is in serious jeopardy." What makes the statement noteworthy is the source. The speaker, previously unknown to me, was Alan M. Resnick of Maryland's Seventh Congressional District. The quotation came from one of his campaign speeches. No candidate for office would have considered it politically safe to advocate worldwide birth control a few years ago. John F. Kennedy was the first President to discuss it publicly. Thanks to him, our government now supports birth-control research and public programs at home and abroad.

A few years ago, a publisher asked if I would be willing to substitute "family planning" for "birth control" in a book he was about to publish. He said it would remove an obstacle to selection by a book club. I agreed, more amused than irritated, since "family planning" seemed to be a euphemism that did not change my meaning.

I was wrong, but the distinction I failed to see then has not yet been widely recognized. The whole subject of contraception had been taboo. President Kennedy's boldness was one of the major events bringing it into the open. The advocates of birth control had long struggled for this, and their frustration had obscured the vital difference between the desire

of marital partners to plan their families and the need of the
human race to limit its numbers.

Contraceptive information and materials are now available
to any woman in the United States who wants them, whether
she be married or single. The United States has not, however,
embarked on a major effort to limit its population. A few
nations, notably Japan and India, have undertaken national
programs to reduce their birth rates. India set an objective:
to reduce births by 7,500,000 per year. Both countries have
made some progress, but India's goal has not been approached, nor does it seem likely to be. Awareness is growing
that the contraceptive methods which are suitable for family
planning are not effective for population control.

The pill, the coil, and other methods now in use are individually prescribed, and all require acts of volition by individual women, who must be instructed in their use. Even
were it true that all women, or a majority of women, want and
will use such means to limit their families—which is probably
not the case—the task of instructing and supplying them
would be prodigious, especially in a nation such as India.
How many doctors, nurses, and medical aides would be required?

Contraceptives are readily available in Japan, and women
are urged to use them. Abortions are legal there, and more
than a million a year are reported. But as has often been re-
marked, family-planning programs have their greatest effect
where they are least needed: among the upper- and middle-
class families. Those at the bottom of the scale, the poorest,
with the least education, are less likely to respond to family-
planning programs and less likely to use the available means
consistently if they are provided.

What limits the populations of other species? At one time
biologists thought the principal controls were hunger and

predation. Both are certainly influential, but together they fail to explain the regulatory mechanisms. Careful studies have identified other factors, for some species. Certain sea birds, for example, have established nesting grounds which, divided into territories, provide space for a limited number of nests. Surplus birds of the species, unable to find nesting room, alight on neighboring islands but do not nest. Among certain mammals, birth rates decline when their habitats become too crowded. In other words, populations of at least some species are balanced by reduced birth rates rather than by increased mortality alone. In ways not yet understood, the species respond to environmental conditions and fewer births occur.

We are far from understanding fully why the human population has multiplied so explosively. Various reasons are ascribed, such as the conquest of diseases, and certainly these have been important factors. But even before contraceptive methods were available, birth rates varied widely from region to region and from time to time, and the hypothetical explanations were not convincing. One popular theory is that wealthier people have more diversions than poor people, and therefore mate less frequently. A variation is that the advent of electric lights made a difference by widening the range of after-dark activities! Supporting evidence is not substantial.

Perhaps further study of the human and other species will, by explaining fluctuations in birth rates, identify factors which could be manipulated to bring the population boom under control. A more direct approach may also be possible, since physiologists are discovering more about the biochemical factors which influence fertility. It should not be impossible to hit upon some controllable environmental condition which would have a statistical rather than an individual effect on conceptions.

For example, scientists have identified chemical substances in the body which inhibit or increase fertility. Further research may lead to formulas which could be administered to people with predictable results. Conceivably, a chemical substance could be added to a public water supply, as fluorides are now, not to prevent all pregnancies but to reduce the fertility of the local population to a desirable degree. Carrying this hypothesis further, the individual's freedom of choice could be preserved. Couples that chose to plan their families would go to clinics for either of two purposes: to obtain contraceptives, or to obtain a countering drug which would make pregnancy more certain.

This is not offered as a pat solution, but as a suggestion of new approaches to population control. Some such biological control appears to be the only alternative to the lemming solution: readjustment by mass deaths. At the very least, the situation calls for substantial increases in research. With all of our knowledge and resources, it would be bitterly ironical if the human experiment failed because we could not keep our own numbers in check. Should we succeed in time, we could then address ourselves to designing a good life rather than struggling for marginal survival.

The concept of land-use planning has not had to contend with the massive opposition aroused by birth control. Since the 1930's, planning and consequent action have made great progress in the United States, Canada, and several other countries. Planning begins with an inventory of land and water assets. While the study discovers how each section of land is being used, it also determines its optimum use by analyzing soil characteristics, moisture supply, and terrain. A farmer in the United States can obtain from his Soil Conservation District a plan for scientific management of his land. Further, financial subsidies and technical assistance induce him to act on the recommendations. As a consequence of this national policy, millions of acres of land have been retired from cultivation and returned to grass or trees, and many physical changes, such as construction of ponds and check dams, have increased the land's productivity.

Underlying modern land-use planning is the concept of multiple use. The primary value of most forests, from the human viewpoint, is that they retain moisture and regulate stream-flow. The forest that maintains an urban watershed is also a wildlife habitat, however, as well as a recreation place and a source of timber. Other biomes, such as grasslands and estuaries, also have multiple uses.

A worldwide land-use study would provide massive evidence that man and wildlife can coexist. What has appeared to be competition between them is, in many cases, improvident land-use. When man cuts down a forest without providing for reforestation, he displaces wildlife but also depletes his own assets. In the United States, a highly developed nation, we have increased our forested acreage substantially since 1900. One third of our land area is now forested, and it is national policy to keep it that way. We need the forests, and by keeping them we also maintain a vigorous wildlife population.

A world survey would show that man has appropriated virtually all of the land that is suitable for cultivation. This is surprisingly little. In the United States, one of the richest farming nations, well under one fifth of our land is in crops. In many nations the proportion of land suitable for crops is even less.

We have almost twice as much pasture and grazing land. Most of it was grassy before man came along. Farmers and cattlemen have changed it by introducing new grasses, stopping wildfires, and killing most of the resident large predators and rodents, but overgrazing has caused even greater change. More rational use, conservative rather than exploitative, would foster multiple use of grassland ecosystems. Much can be done to increase the productivity of grazing lands and to reclaim abused land where the grasses have been replaced by cactus, mesquite, and brush. The primary competition for grass has been between domestic cattle and wild grazers. Many other wild species can coexist with grazing cattle. In some areas, such as East Africa, a mixture of wild grazers and browers will yield more edible meat than cattle, and it seems probable that species such as the water buffalo and eland will be introduced elsewhere as meat producers. Only in preserves can there still be wild herds of elephants, giraffes, and bison; but well-managed grasslands can support large populations of birds, small mammals, reptiles, and lesser creatures.

A world land-use survey would show, I believe, that less than one sixth of the earth's land surface is required by man for purposes which necessitate removal of the natural vegetative cover. It is in our self-interest to maintain trees, shrubs, and grasses on almost every acre where they now grow, and to return to natural plant cover millions of acres now under marginal and temporary cultivation.

Vast areas of despoiled land are available for reclamation. These are, for the most part, arid lands, but with sufficient precipitation to support vegetation. Present reclamation methods often use irrigation, the large investment being justified by the large payoff. Only a fraction of the damaged lands can be irrigated, however. There is need for plans based on more natural methods which would gradually restore a water-conserving plant cover. Without irrigation, these lands cannot be intensively cultivated, and they are highly vulnerable to grazing pressure. It should be possible, however, to rebuild the kind of plant-animal community that existed before the damage was done.

On these lands, as elsewhere, fast-growing population has impelled us into exploitation of the land, trying to meet today's needs without thought for tomorrow's. Too many of our manipulations of nature are violent, as if we were using a shotgun to kill a fly in a china closet. Some of our most extreme measures, such as broadcasting pesticides, are taken in efforts to compensate for the unwanted effects of earlier actions.

Were the human population stabilized, we would still have to manage the natural environment, but we could use more homeopathic means. With population fixed, it would take only a few years to make adequate provision for food supplies, and our land-use plans could be made within a stable framework.

For generations we have been wedded to a philosophy of growth. All trend lines must slant upward, the steeper the better. Communities boast about their growth rates. Industrial leaders make speeches: "The company that's not growing is dying." State and national tax policies often reward exploitation and penalize conservation of natural assets.

Now we are paying the price, and economists are calling attention to the fallacy of growth. Our cities have become monsters, consuming lives and energies just to keep their cumbersome machinery creaking along. Fast-growing suburbs are unable to keep pace with the need for roads, schools, and fire protection. Some of the world's poorest nations which have not responded to infusions of foreign aid would be on the verge of relative prosperity today had their populations remained stable after World War II.

Wildlife species in the path of this juggernaut society are wiped out or threatened with extinction. We have called them "endangered" and attributed their plight to human progress. Now it is all too evident that we who ride the juggernaut are in no less danger.

Life has a different flavor when Jane and I hike up Cascade Canyon, in the Tetons, where the spires of Engelmann spruces stand dark against the white of melting snowfields. A marmot looks at us curiously, only half alarmed, before taking cover under the talus rocks. For these few days we have reduced our living needs to the food, clothing, and shelter we carry on our backs. When the rain clouds roll over the mountains, as they do on most July afternoons, we slip ponchos over ourselves and our packs, find comfortable seats, and let the rain pour down on us until the sun appears again.

We can no longer pitch a tent on the Atlantic dunes, as we once did. One of our favorite campgrounds in the Shenandoahs is usually too crowded for comfort now. Rivers we once cruised in peace are now abuzz with powerboats and hazardous because of their unskilled pilots—and too many afternoons have been spoiled by the chore of towing some hapless boat jockey to the nearest marina. We will never see Yosemite again, unless out of season. We fled from Rocky Mountain National Park after one night in an outdoor slum.

Those were good times, before the crowds came. We needed photographs of pronghorn and sought them in Montana, driving slowly along a seldom-used dirt road. There was a sudden blur of motion in front of our wheels, and Gale saw a small animal vanish in the tall grass. We stopped and walked back. Forest, our older daughter, saw a female pronghorn looking at us from a hill some distance away. We saw nothing in the grass at first, until the wind touched it. There was an infant pronghorn at our feet, utterly motionless, so well camouflaged that the color pictures we took at three-foot range show only an ear.

We were cruising along a river in southern New Jersey, looking for a night's anchorage, when a black skimmer took up station beside us, matching our propeller's thrust with graceful wingbeats, now and then dipping its long bill to cleave the water's surface. Next morning I woke at dawn, lifted my head above the coaming, and saw a deer swimming silently across the rosy water. In those days there were osprey nests on almost every pole-top and channel marker. Last year we cruised the river again and sighted one lonely osprey.

Yet we and many of the wild animals of the forest and the sea can still find quiet places. It means a few more hours on the road, and our big tent, too heavy to carry far, is seldom used now. We backpack, or launch our boat for a weekend cruise, or drive our truck camper to some isolated place, or we enjoy the privilege of camping on private land. We are still in retreat, however. Each year we drop well-loved places from our list, either because they have become crowded or because they no longer exist.

We should not complain because other people feel the same needs we do, to leave the city and renew the deep sense of belonging to the natural world. It is just that there are so many of us, so many more each year, that our sheer numbers degrade the very things we seek.

Someday there may be a race of men who never know the quiet places and the creatures who now live there, who only read about them as we read about the way our country was in the days of Audubon and Michaux, how it looked to Lewis and Clark, to John Colter and to John Muir. Someday there may be men who never see the sky clear blue by day and ablaze with stars at night, who never taste spring water or wild blackberries. They may breathe filtered air, eat food synthesized in factories, and wear disposable clothing. The beaches from Maine to Florida may be as crowded and cluttered as Coney Island is now, a dirty ribbon of trampled sand bordering what has become one continuous city.

There may be a race of men who never hear the sound of rain on canvas or the night cry of a loon, or the hush of the deep woods. Their world may be the kind of world we are creating for the animals that will inhabit our multiclimate house.

This seems a poor solution to our present perils: that we should create machines only to reduce ourselves to their components. It is not, I believe, a genuinely available solution. I do not believe that men or monkeys can be severed from the environments that shaped them and breed new generations under perpetual stress.

The world is our zoo, an infinitely complex, delicately integrated, ever changing collection of more than a million species, large and small, plant and animal, each occupying a distinct and special place. It is a zoo that must be well managed, its resources carefully husbanded, for these are the only resources it can ever have. We have appointed ourselves as the keepers of this zoo, but we cannot live outside its gates. We are of it. Our lives are inextricably intertwined with the lives of all that live within. Their fate will be ours.

Index

2/15/71

DATE DUE

FEB 2 8 1996	
MAR 2 0 1996	
APR 0 4 1997	
FEB 1 8 2013	